Sport and Policy

Books in the Sport Management Series

Sport Governance
Russell Hoye and Graham Cuskelly

Sport and the Media
Matthew Nicholson

Sport Funding and Finance
Bob Stewart

Managing People in Sport Organizations
Tracy Taylor, Alison J. Doherty and Peter McGraw

Introduction to Sport Marketing
Aaron Smith

Sports Economics
Paul Downward, Alistair Dawson and Trudo Dejonghe

Sport Management: Principles and Applications
Hoye, Smith, Nicholson, Stewart and Westerbeek

More information on the series can be found online by visiting
www.elsevierdirect.com

Sport Management Series
Series editor
Russell Hoye

Sport and Policy
Issues and Analysis

Russell Hoye

Matthew Nicholson

Barrie Houlihan

ELSEVIER

AMSTERDAM • BOSTON • HEIDELBERG • LONDON • NEW YORK • OXFORD
PARIS • SAN DIEGO • SAN FRANCISCO • SINGAPORE • SYDNEY • TOKYO
Butterworth-Heinemann is an imprint of Elsevier

Butterworth-Heinemann is an imprint of Elsevier
Linacre House, Jordan Hill, Oxford OX2 8DP, UK
30 Corporate Drive, Suite 400, Burlington, MA 01803, USA

First Edition, 2010

British Library Cataloguing in Publication Data

A catalogue record for this book is available from the British Library

Library of Congress Cataloging-in-Publication Data

A catalog record for this book is available from the Library of Congress

ISBN: 978-0-7506-8594-8

For information on all Butterworth-Heinemann publications
visit our website at elsevierdirect.com

Printed and bound in Great Britain
09 10 11 12 10 9 8 7 6 5 4 3 2 1

Contents

List of Tables

List of Figures

Acknowledgements

This book would not be possible without the contributions from the academics and researchers who have an interest in sport policy and the other areas of public policy that intersect with sport. We wish to especially acknowledge the support and initiative provided by Chris Auld in the formative stages of this project. We are indebted to Eleanor Blow, Editor at Elsevier Butterworth Heinemann, for her support for this book. Finally, we would like to acknowledge the wonderful support and understanding provided by our respective families while we worked to complete this project.

Russell Hoye
Matthew Nicholson
Barrie Houlihan

CHAPTER 1

Introduction:
Sport and Policy

Sport has become an important aspect of government policy intervention, as evidenced by the number of nations articulating a discrete 'sport policy' with concomitant funding and support for elite and community sport development initiatives. Bergsgard, Houlihan, Mangset, Nødland and Rommetvedt (2007) argued that national governments consider sport to be an important facet of economic and social activity for three reasons. First, sport is of strong cultural significance to most developed nations, which is demonstrated by the amount of media attention devoted to national team success and the support for the construction of major stadia and other sporting infrastructure with public funds. Second, sport is considered a resource that can be used to help deliver non-sport objectives, such as demonstrating political power, combating social exclusion, reducing childhood obesity, improving economic development and facilitating urban regeneration. Third, sport is multi-dimensional in that it is not only a public service, but also an important aspect of welfare provision and facet of economic activity. Thus, it can contribute in many ways to the achievement of government objectives outside of sport policy that is focussed on instrumental aspects of sport, such as improving the performance of elite athletes and increasing participation in sport.

The reasons that governments support elite sport through mechanisms such as the creation of elite sports institutes, hypothecation of lottery funds for sporting infrastructure and targeted operational funding have been well-documented (cf. Green & Houlihan, 2005). Similarly, government policies aimed at increasing participation levels and general sport development have also been the subject of scholarly debate (cf. Coalter, 2007; DaCosta & Miragaya, 2002; Houlihan & White, 2002; Hylton & Bramham, 2008; Hylton, Bramham, Jackson & Nesti, 2001). The intersection of the sport industry with government policy, however, is not limited to what is generally accepted to come under the purview of 'sport policy'. Governments also enact policies that seek to regulate the actions of sport organizations as well as utilize sport for the accomplishment of other government policy goals.

One of the earliest attempts to analyse the intersection of sport with public policy was the edited volume prepared by Johnson and Frey (1985:13) who argued that 'sports activities are affected in myriad ways by public policy decisions'. They reasoned that, even in the 1980s, the nature of sport becoming big business, coupled with 'a general change in the values and norms of society affecting public expectations of government [that the sport industry had] become a legitimate area of interest for government' (Johnson & Frey, 1985:13). While the focus of their book was primarily the US sports industry and the impact of public policy on the broad areas of athletes, sports administration and public interests, it was one of the first concerted efforts to explore the questions of what might be the role of government in sport: should government intervene in sport through the development of public policy, and if it did, were public policy interventions more or less successful than market forces. Some 20 years later, Houlihan noted that 'sport is a focus for a growing volume of state regulatory activity' (Houlihan, 2005:164) and that 'the increasingly prominent role of the state as variously promoter, regulator, resource provider, manipulator and exploiter of sport is beyond challenge' (Houlihan, 2005:182).

This book explores those areas of government policy that fall outside what can be described as 'sport policy'. These include policies that seek to regulate the organizational practices of sport organizations, policies aimed at regulating how individuals might participate in particular sporting activities, policies enacted that are meant to protect individuals involved in sport, policies to control gambling associated with sport, policies controlling how sport is broadcast by the media and how physical education is delivered. Aside from areas of government policy that focus on regulation, governments have also sought to use sport as a vehicle or conduit for the achievement of wider policy agendas, such as seeking to increase physical activity and health, assisting to facilitate urban regeneration and economic development and enhancing social inclusion and community development. All of these policy areas significantly impact sport, and in particular the community sport systems and organizations that deliver much of the sport participation and competition opportunities within countries such as Australia, Canada, New Zealand and the UK. These three broad areas of government policy intersections with sport are depicted in Table 1.1.

The focus of this book is an exploration of the impact and effect of the policies that are distinct from what can generally be considered as sport policy – namely the middle (regulatory intersections) and right-hand (wider policy goals) columns in Table 1.1. This chapter presents a brief analysis of the focus of sport policy studies, including the elements that comprise sport policy and the instruments used to achieve sport policy outcomes. This

Table 1.1	Broad Areas of Government Policy Intersections with Sport	
Sport Policy Foci	**Regulatory Intersections**	**Wider Policy Areas**
1. Elite sport development 2. Anti-doping or drug control 3. Increasing mass participation 4. Increasing capacity of the community sport system	1. Organizational practices adopted by sport 2. Sport activity 3. Protecting members of sport organizations 4. Wagering and betting associated with sport 5. Sport broadcasting 6. Physical education policy	1. Using sport to address poor physical activity levels and ameliorate community health issues 2. Using sport for urban regeneration and economic development 3. Using sport to improve social inclusion and facilitate community development

provides the background to our arguments for a wider analysis of government policy that influences the sport system. The chapter also identifies in more detail the areas of government policy that fall outside what is commonly understood to be sport policy and poses a number of questions worthy of investigation in order to understand the effects of government policy intersections with sport.

SPORT POLICY ISSUES AND RESEARCH

Houlihan (2005:163) suggested that while other policy areas have been the subject of extensive analysis, sport policy 'has remained on the margins'. This is in contrast to the recognition by many governments that sport is an important area of policy. Houlihan (2005:163) argued that although 'few governments in the 1960s gave any explicit budgetary or ministerial recognition to sport, by the mid-1990s sport was an established feature in the machinery of government in most economically developed countries'. These developments have gradually resulted in more academic interest in the area of public policy in sport, an interest that has intensified as governments more frequently view sport as a panacea for a diversity of social and economic concerns.

The focus of national sport policies of western countries is generally accepted as being the twin objectives of enhancing elite sport performance and increasing the proportion of people involved in formalized competitive sport or physical activity (Bergsgard et al., 2007; Green & Houlihan, 2005; Stewart, Nicholson, Smith & Westerbeek, 2004). It is also possible to identify two further policy objectives – ensuring a fair playing field and developing the capacity of the community sport system – that have achieved prominence within the sport policies of countries such as Australia, Canada, New Zealand and the UK. The 'fair play' policy agenda has been dominated by anti-doping and drug policies, which have sought to control (mainly) performance-enhancing drug use in sport. The capacity of the community sport system in Commonwealth countries has generally been conceptualized as management improvement in the sport sector, and has primarily focussed on national sport organizations and clubs. The increasing attention devoted to the issue of drugs in sport is undeniably linked to concerns about the integrity of elite sport (and thus one of the key and most highly visible policy vehicles for government). On the other hand, management improvement programs are often framed around generic issues related to governance and organizational performance. However, even in the area of management improvement, governments have been concerned to maximize the value of their investment in sport. The interest in management improvement that emerged in the 1980s and 1990s engendered more 'business-like' and commercial approaches to managing sport. The consequences of these developments included the dilution of traditional democratic approaches to representative governance processes and a shift to a model encouraging people with business, marketing and entrepreneurial experience be appointed to boards. Such developments served to reinforce the largely instrumental paradigm evident in government priorities and the subservience of other policy concerns to elite performance, rationality and professionalization.

Sport policies are therefore arguably focussed on the achievement of instrumental outcomes, such as delivering elite success, increasing the talent pool of participants to support elite sport, ensuring sport is drug free and supporting the actions of community sport organizations to recruit and retain volunteer coaches, officials and administrators. Sport policies are usually encapsulated in a central policy statement that is the responsibility of a central sport agency such as the Australian Sports Commission (ASC) or Sport Canada. A common element of many western sport policies is the delivery of elite support programs through an elite sport institute. The development and debate associated with the elements that comprise a nation's sport policy are also usually restricted to a specific sport policy community made up of national sport organizations, national sport leagues, central government agencies and specific interest groups.

Unsurprisingly, the majority of sport policy research has tended to mirror the issues that comprise sport policy and have been focussed on topics such as elite sport (Bergsgard et al., 2007; De Bosscher, De Knop, van Bottenburg & Shibli, 2006; Green, 2005; Green & Houlihan, 2005; Green & Oakley, 2001; Houlihan & Green, 2008), or on broader topics, such as economic development and urban regeneration (Gratton & Henry, 2001) and sport development (Coalter, 2007; DaCosta & Miragaya, 2002; Houlihan & White, 2002; Hylton & Bramham, 2008; Hylton et al., 2001). There have also been a number of country-specific studies (Green, 2004, 2006; Oakley & Green, 2001; Sam & Jackson, 2004; Stewart et al., 2004) and a number of studies that have explored different approaches to the analysis of sport policy itself (Chalip, 1996; Henry, Amara, Al-Tauqi & Lee, 2005; Houlihan, 1997, 2005). One of the key foci of these sport policy studies has been to examine the composition of sport policy networks in order to fully comprehend how sport policy is developed and how its implementation impacts various stakeholders. These are critical questions because the dominant voices in a policy network help shape the conceptualization of an issue, the discourse surrounding the issue and therefore any subsequent response from government. Policy communities and networks in sport vary according to the policy issue or problem, the level or levels of government involved and the degree of professionalization and commercialization of the sports involved. Policy communities and networks may be facilitated via formal linkages, such as inter-departmental committees or consultative bodies (e.g. task forces and advisory boards), but also operate in a less formal manner through a shared awareness among those organizations that are affected by a specific issue. They also operate with varying degrees of influence and success. Green (2004) argued that in the UK sport policy sector, actions were increasingly shaped by the requirements of elite sport, and this served to subdue alternative perspectives within the sporting community. Green and Houlihan (2005) concluded that one of the striking features of advocacy coalitions in Canada and the UK was the strong influence of central government in shaping their values, organization and activities. Furthermore, while the advocacy coalitions could be classified as effective, this judgement was only in the context of progress towards state-determined objectives.

The actions of sport policy communities and networks are further defined by the fragmented and sometimes conflicting structure of the industry sector. This concern was recognized by Roche (1993) who argued that the British post-war sport policy was dysfunctional and was characterized by division, confusion and conflict. In Australia, the more narrowly focussed sport (rather than recreation) policy network was eventually able to develop a cohesive and structured policy framework and therefore promise more targeted and measurable potential to government, especially through elite sport performance. The announcement of Sydney's winning bid for the 2000 Olympic Games, and the build up to and staging of the Sydney Games, acted to further consolidate the position of the sport policy community, which is centred around the key agencies of the ASC, Australian Institute of Sport, Australian Olympic Committee, Commonwealth Games Association, professional sports leagues and key business interests. Those lead agencies with responsibility for sport policy still tend to reflect a somewhat constrained view of most issues that surface on the 'whole of government' policy agenda and frequently respond from a somewhat traditional and normative position (e.g. 'micro' issues such as increasing control over National Sport Organizations, drugs in sport and an emphasis on elite performance). Maintaining a specific issue network approach also minimizes the potential for policy intersections, as the issue network may not even register other broader issues on its radar and is likely to conceptualize them from a narrow perspective if it does.

In summary, the sport policy studies completed to date have demonstrated a relatively high degree of convergence of both the content and objectives of sport policies amongst Commonwealth nations, a significant degree of policy learning between these nations and a set of common challenges facing each of their sport systems in delivering both elite sporting success and increased community-level participation. There is, however, a significant difference in the degree to which the sport policy network of each country is engaged in policy issues outside of 'sport policy'. The following section explores the areas where sport intersects with or is influenced by other aspects of government policy, as well as the important questions the remainder of the book seeks to answer in relation to these policy intersections.

POLICY INTERSECTIONS WITH SPORT

As communities continue to be pressured by economic, social and cultural changes, sport is frequently advocated as one means by which communities can respond to interdependent 'wicked' policy problems resulting from the continually evolving pressures of globalization. Sport is often seen as a mechanism or conduit for assisting communities in maintaining cohesion and building both social and economic capacity. While the potential for individual benefits from sport involvement is well documented, for many policymakers the more fundamental and important concern is the potential for positive externalities to be aggregated to the broader community or social level. Long and Sanderson (2001:187) argued there is a 'belief that benefits accrue beyond the individual in ways that support community development and regeneration', while Coalter (2007) suggested that sport has achieved a relatively high profile in recent years partly due to assumptions about its potential in areas such as social and economic regeneration, crime, health and education. Green (2007) argued that a number of governments increasingly utilize sport to realize an array of objectives in a range of different policy sectors. For example, Green (2004:374) indicated that the 2002 UK sport policy 'Game Plan' pointed to 'the symbiotic, and overtly instrumental, relationship between sport (and increased physical activity, in general), education and health policy'. Houlihan, Bloyce and Smith (2009:5) noted that 'governments tend to treat sport in an extremely instrumental manner, seeing it as highly malleable and visible, but relatively low-cost response, to a number of non-sport problems ranging from nation building to social welfare'.

These expectations of sport have been partly encouraged by the emergence over the past decade of 'third way', 'active citizenship', 'social coalition' and 'mutual obligation' policies, which have direct relevance to sport and have also incorporated elements of sport into broader policy initiatives. In essence, third-way policies represent a shift in the focus of delivery from direct government service provision to 'whole of government' partnerships with private and third-sector agencies. Sport seems well-positioned to have an impact on a range of policy outcomes given the extent of its broad popular appeal (especially in the sense of the 'imagined community'), levels and nature of individual involvement and the economic scope of the sport industry. Thus, there has been a growing fascination among many national governments with the role of sport in delivering a raft of 'non-sport' outcomes to communities. Such benefits are frequently conceptualized within terms such as 'social capital', 'social regeneration' and/or 'social inclusion'. But, because of sport's increasing business and commercial elements, government policy now intersects with areas beyond the community regeneration/social inclusion agenda, such as broadcasting, gambling and economic development.

The increasing demands being made on sport should be considered in relation to the argument from Parrish (2008:80) that sports have 'long contended that the special characteristics of sport place them outside the normal scope of state regulatory oversight'. So, while sports would like to continue to be self-determining, Parrish (2008:80) concludes that (in Europe at least):

> *The plea for self regulation has received conditional support from nation states and the EU. This is because whilst the specificity of sport justifies limitations on states' control over sport, it also encumbers the governing bodies with social responsibilities not generally shared by 'normal' industries. Sport therefore has a public function and the expansion of its social and economic significance and its growing organisational sophistication and internationalisation has attracted increased interest from public policy makers. Sport is used as a tool of nation building (particularly when sporting individuals and teams assume a representative function at European and World Championships), as a provision of a public good, as a tool for health promotion, as a means of combating social exclusion, as a tool for crime prevention, as a vehicle for economic development and as a tool of foreign policy.*

Houlihan (1997:109) argued that the 'trend over the past thirty years has clearly been for central governments to become more closely involved in sport and to seek to exploit sports in pursuit of a broad range of domestic and international policy objectives'. Chalip (1996:viii) suggested that, 'the study of sports policies can tell us a great deal about our most instrumental policy concerns', while Green and Houlihan (2005) concluded that governments viewed sport almost exclusively in instrumental terms. Green (2006) argued that sport programs in the UK had been linked to realising social welfare policy goals in sectors, such as education, health, social exclusion/inclusion, drug abuse and safety, and the family. Green (2004:374) also noted that regional sport organizations were being encouraged to contribute to issues such as 'health, education, crime reduction, community cohesion and social inclusion, neighbourhood and community regeneration, and economic growth and sustainability'.

While such politically salient functions for sport might be attractive because they appear to underpin the 'value' of sport, the inherent non-instrumental qualities of sport might conversely be perceived as less important. Another theme evident in a number of analyses of the evolution of sport policy development suggests that 'conspicuous by its absence is any sustained attempt to defend the promotion of sport for its intrinsic benefits, thus creating a situation where the advocates of sports development were frequently those with little direct involvement in sport, but with a view as to how it could contribute to their own policy objectives' (Houlihan, 1997:22). Similarly, Green (2006) suggested that the change in policy priorities accompanied by the expanding intersection of sport with other sectors meant that sport policy initiatives have shifted in emphasis from those designed 'for sport' to those seeking extraneous benefits 'from sport'. While it might also be the case that the formation of links between sport and other functions means that sport has the potential to influence these agendas, it appears that so far, sport has generally fulfilled a secondary role as governments (rather than pluralist policy networks or communities) seek to increase their control over policy. This view is summarized by Green (2006:228):

> In sum, on the one hand, 'sport' in general now enjoys a far higher political saliency than at any time over the past 40 years. On the other hand, this increased saliency has to be tempered by the realization that government is also now 'shaping' sport policy development with a far tighter hand than ever before.

As indicated by Houlihan (1997), the sport policy network has not always featured centrally in framing policy responses with the other areas that engage or intersect with sport policy. As a 'policy taker', the sport sector frequently plays a secondary role in framing policy interventions in some of the broader social and economic areas. Consequently, sport has little control over the directions in which it is pushed and the responsibilities and expectations placed upon it through both regulatory and enabling policy initiatives. As a result, lead central agencies, such as the ASC, Sport and Recreation New Zealand (SPARC), Sport Canada and Sport England, are in danger of losing touch with their grass-roots constituency if they miss the opportunity for relevance and influence as sport policy intersections continue to expand. For example, if these agencies conceptualize community capacity building only in the context of sport's elite-participation dichotomy, then they will have only a limited capacity to influence policy development in areas and issues of intersection. Green (2007:944) argued that objectives in other areas are either peripheral or exist only to support elite sport objectives and thus 'it is the commitment to the elite level that frames strategic thinking and specific policy objectives'. By not engaging fully in a comprehensive array of future challenges, it is likely, therefore, that sport policy might evolve primarily through other related areas. Without increased involvement from the broader sport policy community in solving systemic wicked policy problems, the future of sport may be delegated to other policy communities with limited knowledge and understanding of the sport sector.

ANALYTICAL FRAMEWORK

In addition to the specific imperatives for organizational focus and activity that sport policy creates for sport organizations, they are also subject to a range of regulatory policies from government. In areas such as fundamental business regulations, health and safety requirements, or employment law, these regulations are no different to those imposed on non-sport organizations. There are, however, a number of regulatory policies that are unique to sport in areas such as sport betting and wagering, and broadcast rights and media content on free to air television. Some sporting activities also present inherent risks for participants and spectators, such as boxing, combat sports and motor sport, which are subject to direct additional regulation by government. Governments also seek to regulate the way in which physical education is delivered and controlled.

In respect to exploring the impact of these regulatory policies on sport, we have sought to apply the often cited regulatory analysis framework of Baldwin and Cave (1999), specifically the identification of the rationales for regulatory intervention and the regulatory strategies employed by government. Baldwin and Cave (1999:9) identified a dozen rationales (see Table 1.2) for governments imposing regulations, but stressed the importance of understanding that 'motives for regulating can be distinguished

Table 1.2 Rationales for Regulating

Rationale	Main Aims of Regulation	Sport Example
Monopolies and natural monopolies	Counter tendency to raise process and lower output, harness benefits of scale economies, identify areas that are genuinely monopolistic	Grant single licence for sports betting in order to maximize product quality and probity
Windfall profits	Transfer benefits of windfalls from firms to consumers or tax payers	Transfer portion of gambling profit to fund sport development
Externalities	Compel producer or consumer to bear full costs of production rather than pass on to third parties or society	Compel stadium operators to invest in water recycling and other energy efficient practices
Information inadequacies	Inform consumers to allow market to operate	Inform the public of the benefits of physical exercise
Continuity and availability of service	Ensure socially desired (or protected minimal) level of 'essential' service	Subsidize the cost for disabled athletes to participate in sporting activities
Anti-competitive and behaviour predatory pricing	Prevent anti-competitive behaviour	Outlaw price fixing for sport events
Public goods and moral hazard	Share costs where benefits of activity are shared but free-rider problems exist	Impose tax on all tax payers for development of sport facilities and parkland
Unequal bargaining power	Protect vulnerable interests where market fails to do so	Create employment law that allows collective bargaining by athletes
Scarcity and rationing	Public interest allocation of scarce commodities	Require sport facilities to allocate portions of time to specific disadvantaged user groups
Distributive justice and social policy	Distribute according to public interest, prevent undesirable behaviour or results	Impose manufacturing standards for sporting equipment
Rationalization and coordination	Secure efficient production where transaction costs prevent market from obtaining network gains or efficiencies of scale, standardization	Develop school sport curriculum to standardize development amongst the population
Planning	Protect interests of future generations, coordinate altruistic intentions	Plan for long-term water use reduction by community sports facilities

Source: Adapted from Baldwin and Cave (1999:17).

from technical justifications for regulating'. Governments can regulate to appease those lobbying on behalf of specific interest groups or may take a political decision to regulate in order to be re-elected. In this book, we confine our analyses to the technical rationales for regulating, which, in the main, can be 'described as instances of market failure' (Baldwin & Cave, 1999:9). In other words, governments in these cases choose to regulate on the basis that 'the uncontrolled marketplace will, for some reason, fail to produce behaviour or results in accordance with the public interest' (Baldwin & Cave, 1999:9).

We have also adopted their framework for categorising the various options available to governments that they can use to influence industrial, economic or social activity. These include to command using legal authority, to distribute wealth, to harness markets, to inform consumers, to act directly and to confer protected rights. Based on these options, Baldwin and Cave (1999) identified eight basic regulatory strategies that they could employ (see Table 1.3), which we will explore further during the chapters focussing on regulatory policies and return to this framework in our concluding chapter.

Table 1.3 Regulatory Strategies of Government Relevant to Sport		
Strategy	**Public Policy Example**	**Sport Example**
Command and control	Health and safety at work	Prohibiting involvement in some sports such as fox hunting or other blood sports, or specifying how sports may conduct their activities
Mandating self-regulation	Insurance industry	Corporate governance standards for listed football clubs
Incentives	Tax rebates on solar hot water installation	Tax incentives for individuals to donate to sport organizations
Market-harnessing controls		
Competition laws	Airline industry protection	Allowing sport cartels to operate
Franchising	Limiting the number of television broadcast licenses	Prohibiting proprietary racing, thus protecting non-profit racing clubs
Contracting	Rubbish collection	Agencies to conduct drug testing for sport organizations
Tradable permits	Carbon emissions	Emissions trading scheme relevant to large stadiums
Disclosure	Mandatory disclosure of food ingredients	Reporting requirements imposed on National Sport Organizations in receipt of government funding
Direct action	State agency delivers service	Creation of elite sport institutes
Rights and liabilities laws	Rules of tort law such as right to clean water	Right to access local sport facilities for people with disabilities
Public compensation/ social insurance	Workplace safety insurance schemes	Mandating the creation of specialist insurance cover for high-risk sports people, i.e. jockeys

Source: Adapted from Baldwin and Cave (1999:58–62).

The book focuses on six discrete areas of regulatory policy: (1) the regulation of organizational practices adopted by sport, (2) the regulation of sport activity, (3) the regulation of safe environments for members of sport organizations, (4) the regulation of gambling associated with sport, (5) the regulation of sport broadcasting and (6) the regulation of physical education. For each of these areas of regulatory intervention, we have sought to answer a number of questions. Firstly, what rationales have government used to justify policies designed to increase the regulatory burden faced by sport? Secondly, is the sport sector and specifically are sport organizations central to the policy communities that devise these regulatory policies? Thirdly, what regulatory strategies have government employed to achieve their policy objectives? Finally, what existing (or likely) impact or influence have these regulatory policies had on sport organizations?

Governments also seek to use sport to assist in the achievement of non-sport policy objectives. We have chosen to focus on three of the most prominent public policy areas where sport is considered part of the process of enabling these wider policy objectives to be achieved, namely, (1) the use of sport to address poor physical activity levels and ameliorate health issues among the community, (2) the use of sport for urban regeneration and economic development and (3) the use of sport to improve social inclusion and facilitate community development. In each of these areas, we have also sought answers to a number of questions. Firstly, what rationales have government used to justify using sport as a vehicle for the achievement of non-sport policy objectives? Secondly, is the sport sector and specifically are sport organizations central to the policy communities for these non-sport policies? Allied to this, we have sought to explore the role central sport agencies play in either the development or implementation of these policies. Finally, what existing (or likely) impact or influence have these policies had on sport organizations?

This book contributes to expanding our understanding of the role of the state in sport beyond the analyses that have thus far been almost exclusively focussed on sport policy, specifically the issues of elite sport development, drug use in sport, increasing mass participation and building the capacity of nations' respective sport systems. By examining how governments impose regulatory burdens on sport and increasingly seek sport's assistance in tackling wider public policy issues, we seek to understand the effects of these broader government policy intersections with sport.

CHAPTER 2

Regulating Organizational Practice

As discussed in Chapter 1, sport organizations are subject to a range of regulatory policies from government. In some cases these regulations are no different to the requirements imposed on other non-sport organizations such as fundamental business regulations, health and safety requirements or employment law. There are, however, a number of regulatory policies unique to sport, such as the regulation of sport betting and wagering, physical education or the regulation of broadcast rights and media content on free to air television. In addition, some sporting activities that present inherent risks for participants and spectators, such as boxing, combat sports, motor sport and sport parachuting, are subject to direct regulation by government. The following five chapters are devoted to exploring the intersection of these regulatory policies with sport, namely, the regulation of sport activity, the regulation of efforts to protect members of sport organizations, the regulation of gambling associated with sport, the regulation of sport broadcasting and the regulation of physical education. The first chapter in this section, however, addresses the regulation of organizational structures and practices adopted by sport.

This chapter examines the organizational and institutional context in which sport organizations operate, specifically the impacts of a range of regulatory policies that affect the way sport organizations conduct their activities. These include policies designed to regulate the structures adopted by non-profit sport organizations, policies surrounding compliance obligations associated with the receipt of public monies to support their activities and corporate governance requirements. These policies present a number of challenges for sport organizations in complying with these regulations. Drawing on a range of regulations at the national and state/provincial level from Australia, Canada, New Zealand and the UK, the following sections outline the nature and extent of these policies and the associated impacts on sport organizations.

REGULATING ORGANIZATIONAL STRUCTURE

The vast majority of sport organizations that deliver sport participation and competition opportunities in Australia, Canada, New Zealand and the UK are non-profit, self-governing and voluntary run and have been established for social or community purposes. As a result, the most common legal structure adopted by these organizations is an incorporated association. Incorporation allows a group of people to form a legal entity that is able to acquire, hold and dispose of assets, enter into contracts and limit the liability of members. This last point is particularly important because 'without incorporation, it is the individual members of the organization, or a few people who have formed a trust to hold the assets of the organization, who are liable for debts incurred by the group' (State Services Authority, 2007:8). Thus, incorporation reduces the risk to individuals of becoming involved in running a non-profit organization such as a community sport club, an often essential requirement to encourage people to join and contribute to such organizations. In order to facilitate sport and other non-profit organizations enjoying the benefits of incorporation, governments impose a number of conditions and criteria that distinguish incorporated organizations from corporations or profit-seeking firms. Responsibility for regulating incorporation requirements falls largely on state and provincial governments in Australia and Canada, respectively, whereas it is predominantly a national government responsibility in New Zealand and the UK. In each of these jurisdictions, governments have recognized the need to improve the regulatory systems in place for non-profit organizations.

In the Australian State of Victoria, the Incorporations Act 1981 requires incorporated organizations to fulfil a number of statutory obligations including the following:

- Holding an annual general meeting

- Lodging an annual statement of financial and non-financial data

- Reporting any changes to key officers of the incorporation or the purpose for which the organization was established

- Having their accounts audited and retaining records for 7 years

- Providing certain information to members on request

- Communicating with government any resolutions that alter its name, purpose or legal status (State Services Authority, 2007)

Similar statutory obligations are imposed by other incorporation regulations in other jurisdictions. In Australia, most state and territory governments since 2000 have moved to review their respective regulatory systems for incorporation. In the State of Victoria, for example, the Department of Justice, through Consumer Affairs Victoria, initiated a review of the Incorporations Act 1981 which culminated in an Interim Report being published in 2005 (Department of Justice, 2005). This report highlighted a number of deficiencies in the effectiveness of the legislation and accompanying regulations that detracted from the initial purpose of government seeking to support the efforts of small, voluntary, non-profit organizations. These deficiencies included unnecessary administrative burdens and high compliance costs associated with data collection and reporting requirements, record keeping, registration and submission of documents imposed on organizations seeking to maintain their status as an incorporated body (Department of Justice, 2005).

In the same year, a wider study of regulation in the non-profit sector was commissioned by the Department of Victorian Communities (The Allen Consulting Group, 2005). The study noted that 'at present there are more than 20 different ways to incorporate a not-for-profit organization in Australia' (The Allen Consulting Group, 2005:16). The majority of non-profit organizations tend to incorporate as an association under state or territory incorporations law or as a company limited by guarantee under the Commonwealth Corporations Act 2001. Each of the eight states and territories of Australia have separate incorporation legislation that differ in eligibility requirements, accounting and financial reporting expectations, members' rights and distribution of assets. These differences do not affect organizations seeking to operate within a single jurisdiction, but organizations that seek to operate across the country need to register separately in each jurisdiction or as a company limited by guarantee under federal legislation. The study noted that this two-tiered regulatory arrangement did not meet the needs of the non-profit sector:

> ... there is a 'misfit' between the nature of not-for-profit organizations and the incorporation vehicles available to them. The Corporations Act can be costly, complex and inappropriate in parts, and there are few tools to assist organizations with the practicalities of establishing under it; the Association Incorporations Acts are insulated, inconsistent and not mutually recognised and, while there are ways of overcoming this for multi-state bodies, they involve additional fees and reporting requirements.
>
> (The Allen Consulting Group, 2005:20)

The study concluded that regulation of organizational practices in the non-profit sector was 'failing in three core areas, namely: accessibility, transparency and accountability; integration and consistency; and compliance burden ... as it currently stands, regulation achieves few of its objectives and imposes significant costs' (The Allen Consulting Group, 2005:41). Finally, the study also concluded that the 'complexities, inconsistencies and unsuitability of some regulation means that it represents more of a barrier between the not-for-profit sector and the community than a support to that relationship' (The Allen Consulting Group, 2005:34).

In 2007, two concurrent reviews of regulations affecting the Victorian non-profit sector were also completed. The first was a review conducted by the State Services Authority that sought to examine the 'impact of Victorian Government regulation and other contractual and accountability requirements placed on NFP [not for profit] organizations by Victorian Government systems, processes, structures and functional relationships' (State Services Authority, 2007:1). The aim of the review, in part, was to identify how to reduce the regulatory burden on these organizations whilst 'maintaining appropriate levels of accountability and transparency' (State Services Authority, 2007:1). This would then enable non-profit organizations to focus more of their scarce resources on delivering services and programs. The Victorian Government recognized that regulations affecting non-profit organizations had been subject to relatively less scrutiny than regulatory regimes for business, in particular 'corporate regulation governing the creation, governance and operation of NFP entities' (State Services Authority, 2007:17).

While the review mirrored many of the concerns about incorporations legislation expressed in the 2005 study by The Allen Consulting Group discussed earlier, it also highlighted the significance of the problem. The review estimated there were more approximately 36,000 non-profit organizations in Victoria, of which more than 33,000 were registered as incorporated associations (State Services Authority, 2007). Almost 24% of these were sport organizations. The review cited part of the submission provided by the peak sport lobby group, the Sports Federation of Victoria (VicSport), in summarizing the burden the current regulatory regime posed for non-profit organizations:

> ... the unnecessary variations in state based association incorporation regulations creates unnecessary administration complications for NFP groups ... the standardisation of state-based associations incorporation requirements could easily improve accountability and transparency, while at the same time generating significant financial and human resource savings.
>
> (State Services Authority, 2007:71)

The second review that examined (in part) regulations affecting the Victorian non-profit sector completed in 2007 was commissioned by the Victorian Government to 'provide advice on the long-term sustainability of community organizations in the State' (Stronger Community Organizations Steering

Committee, 2007b:7). This review also called for state and territory governments to move towards national model legislation for incorporation requirements. Similar reviews of incorporation legislation and regulations have been conducted by other Australian States including New South Wales in 2003 and Queensland in 2006, which also recommend simplifying the legislation and accompanying regulatory requirements and costs for non-profit organizations.

Regulatory reform efforts in relation to the structures adopted by sport organizations are not restricted to Australia. In Canada, a 1999 report from the federal government initiated Voluntary Sector Task Force, entitled *Working Together*, cited regulatory reform as essential in order that 'the regulatory framework for the voluntary sector [be able to] balance two needs: the need to ensure public confidence in voluntary organizations and the need to ensure a supportive and enabling environment for them' (Voluntary Sector Task Force, 1999:45). At the time, the regulation of non-profit organizations, including sport organizations, was seen to be deficient in five areas: a lack of transparency in registration decisions; a need for a clearer compliance system that provided assistance to organizations to meet their compliance obligations, greater enforcement of those obligations and a clearer process of sanctions for non-compliance; greater support for the sector; dissemination of more information about the sector; and finally, a clearer definition of what constituted a charitable or non-profit organization (Voluntary Sector Task Force, 1999). Much like the Australian reviews, the Canadian Task Force report posed a number of questions about the regulatory system in place for non-profit organizations, including 'whether it is desirable, appropriate or urgent to have a common legal framework for non-profit organizations; the relationship between federal and provincial statutes; and conflicts between organizational law and charity/equity law' (Voluntary Sector Task Force, 1999:48).

This reform agenda led to a report published in 2003 entitled *Strengthening Canada's Charitable Sector* that proposed a number of changes to the regulation of organizational practice among non-profit organizations. These included the peak regulatory body adopting a more educational role for the sector, increasing its visibility to the sector, being better resourced, having expanded powers and a better communication strategy for its activities. It also recommended a greater commitment towards coordinating the various regulatory efforts of federal and provincial agencies for non-profit organizations (Voluntary Sector Initiative, 2003).

These examples of regulatory reform efforts from Australia and Canada illustrate the effect inappropriate regulation of organizational structures can have on non-profit sport organizations. Imposing unnecessary administrative complexities on these organizations simply adds further work that distracts them from their mission and soaks up scarce resources that could be otherwise used to deliver services to their members and the public. Closely allied with this problem of overly complex regulation of organizational and legal structures are issues associated to complying with government funding and financial reporting requirements, which are explored in the following section.

GOVERNMENT FUNDING COMPLIANCE

The federal sport agencies of countries such as Australia, Canada and the UK have all invested heavily in a range of intervention strategies designed to influence the operations of National Sport Organizations in relation to elite sport development. The impact on NSOs of receiving increased funding from government sport agencies to support elite sport has been well-documented (Green & Houlihan, 2005; Papadimitriou, 1998). Green and Houlihan (2005:179) noted that when governments introduce significant public funding targeted towards the achievement of elite sport outcomes NSOs readily accept the funds, though such acceptance 'comes at a price ...[as]... once an organization has adjusted to high public subsidy the extent of resource dependence can leave little option but to follow the shifts in government priorities'. The argument we wish to make in this section is not, however, about the distribution of funding between elite or community level sport, the increased level of resource dependency that now exists between the State and NSOs or how NSOs go about delivering elite sport outcomes. Rather, we wish to explore the impact that entering into such funding arrangements has had on the compliance burden experienced by sport and the associated increased reporting requirements.

In order to receive federal government funding, NSOs in countries such as Australia, Canada and the UK must meet certain minimum criteria. For example, Canadian Heritage, the federal government department in which Sport Canada resides, uses the Sport Funding and Accountability Framework (SFAF) to 'identify which organizations are eligible for Sport Canada contributions under the Sport Support Program – in what areas, at what level and under what conditions' (Sport Canada, 2007). The SFAF process involves two steps: first, establishing eligibility to receive funding; and second, once they are eligible, undertaking an assessment that 'evaluates their size, scope, performance and potential, and ranks them according to their contribution to the goals of the Canadian Sport Policy in the areas of participation, excellence, capacity and interaction' (Sport Canada, 2007). In order for an NSO to achieve eligibility, it must meet all the criteria in Section A (General), as well as all criteria in either Section B (National) or Section C (International). Figure 2.1 lists the criteria that NSOs must fulfil to achieve eligibility.

Section A: General

A1. The sport meets the criteria outlined in the Sport Canada "Definition of Sport": (Annex A1)

    As the Governing Body for its sport in Canada:

A2. The NSO is the single national governing body for all aspects of the sport in Canada, including its disciplines and events. (Annex A2)

A3. The NSO has a volunteer leadership structure that is democratically elected by the membership. (Annex A3)

A4. The NSO has a constitution, by-laws and objects that are written and available in both official languages.

A5. The NSO is incorporated under Part II of the Canada Corporations Act. (Annex A5)

A6. The NSO has independently audited financial statements for each of the last 4 fiscal years. (Annex A6)

*A7. The NSO is committed to providing its members with technically and ethically sound and safe sport programs and content based on established long term athlete development principles. (Annex A7)

*A8. The NSO has a multi-year plan, ratified by the Board of Directors. This plan should identify measurable outcomes across the full range of sport development and be based on the NSO's Long Term Participant/Athlete Development Model. (Annex A8)

*A9. The NSO is formally committed to the principle of technically and ethically sound coaching education and conduct. (Annex A9)

*A10. The NSO is formally committed to the principle of technically and ethically sound officiating education and conduct. (Annex A10)

*A11. The NSO has formally adopted the 2004 Canadian Policy Against Doping in Sport and the related Canadian Anti-Doping Program.

*A12. The NSO has a formal policy on Official Languages that complies with Sport Canada contribution guidelines on Official Languages. (Annex A12)

*A13. The NSO has a formal policy or policies demonstrating commitment to equity and access, notably for women, persons with a disability and Aboriginal peoples as athletes, coaches, officials, volunteers and leaders. (Annex A13)

*A14. The NSO has a formal policy on athlete centeredness and can demonstrate the direct involvement of high-performance athletes in decision-making. (Annex A14)

*A15. The NSO formally recognizes the fundamental role and importance of certified coaches through their involvement in athlete development programs and in the technical direction of national team programs.

*A16. The NSO has a formal policy on harassment and abuse, including procedures for the reporting and for the investigation of complaints. (Annex A16)

*A17. The NSO has an internal Appeal process consistent with established principles of due process and natural justice and containing a provision that allows disputes to be referred to the alternate dispute resolution services of the Sport Dispute Resolution Centre of Canada.

*Non-funded NSOs that do not currently have these plans and policies are required to develop and formally adopt these requirements. Eligibility, and subsequent assessment, will be conditional to Sport Canada approval of documentation substantiating compliance in all these areas.

Section B: National Scope Criteria

NSOs that are national in scope, according to the criteria outlined below, have a significant number of active members and affiliated constituents across Canada. NSOs are actively engaged with their Provincial/Territorial constituents in aligning and harmonizing their strategic plans, programs and activities based on long term athlete development principles to provide a technically and ethically sound and safe sport experience for more Canadians.

B1. The NSO has a minimum of 3000 registered members: (Annex B1)

B2. The NSO has a minimum of 8 affiliated Provincial or Territorial Sport Organizations (P/TOs): (Annex B2)

B3. The NSO has a National Championship in which a minimum of 6 P/TOs compete regularly in at least one category: (Annex B3)

FIGURE 2.1   *SFAF criteria for Canadian NSOs to achieve eligibility for funding.*

(Continued)

Section C International Scope Criteria

NSOs that have an international scope, according to the criteria outlined below, have access to a significant level of international competition (regular calendar of competition) sanctioned by an International Federation that complies with the World Anti-Doping Code. NSOs are actively involved, through their national team program(s), in the selection, long-term development, coaching and support of Canadian athletes for the purpose of achieving podium performances at Olympic, Paralympic and/or World Championship (WC) levels and have a proven track record of success and/or a demonstrated potential for future success.

C1. The NSO is affiliated with the International Federation (IF) for its sport and recognized by the International Federation as the governing body for its sport/discipline in Canada. (Annex C1)

C2. For Olympic and WC-only sports: The International Federation has a minimum of 35 member countries and the IF has accepted, or set a date to accept, the IOC/WADA World Anti-Doping Code; and/or for Paralympic sports: The sport is on the competition program of the Paralympic Games and has accepted, or set a date to accept, the IPC/WADA World Anti-Doping Code. (Annex C2 for non-Paralympic AWAD sports)

C3. For Olympic and WC-only sports: the IF has a minimum of 35 member countries of which a minimum of 20 countries must have competed in each of the past 4 Senior World Championships, including qualifying competitions. (Annex C3a); and/or for Paralympic and WC-only sports for athletes with a disability: the sport is on the official competition program of the 2008 Paralympic Games and since 2000, a minimum of 8 countries must have competed in each of the past 4 world competitions (Senior World Championships and/or Paralympic games). (Annex C3b).

C4. For Olympic sports: the NSO has had at least one top 16 and top half finish in one Olympic event in 50% of all Olympic Games and Senior World Championships since January 2000; or For non-Olympic sports: the NSO has had at least one top 16 and top half finish in one event in 50% of all Senior World Championships since January 2000; and/or for Paralympic sports the NSO has had at least one top 8 and top half finish in one Paralympic event in 50% of all Paralympic Games and World Championships since January 2000; or for non-Paralympic sports for athletes with a disability: the NSO has had at least one top 8 and top half finish in one event in 50% of all World Championships since January 2000.

(Sport Canada, 2007)

FIGURE 2.1   Cont'd

Havaris and Danylchuck (2007:34) described the combination of the SFAF and the implementation strategy adopted by individual NSOs as the 'cornerstone of each NSO's funding relationship with the Government of Canada'. Furthermore, the accountability relationships that develop in relation to this agreement are directly related to the 'organizational development and success' of an NSO (Havaris & Danylchuck, 2007:34). The analysis of the impact of the SFAF on NSOs conducted by Havaris and Danylchuck (2007) also found that NSOs developed strategic plans targeted towards the achievement of goals important to both the NSO and Sport Canada. However, in relation to the compliance burden associated with the SFAF for NSOs, they found that although the amount of funding received by NSOs varied, they were all subject to the same SFAF eligibility and reporting processes, despite significant differences in the capacity of the NSOs to service those requirements.

The eligibility criteria used by other government sport agencies such as the Australian Sports Commission (ASC, n.d.) and SPARC (SPARC, 2008a) also involve a similar level of documentation and evidence. UK Sport has adopted a system of 'funding triggers' that require NSOs to comply with addressing or developing specific governance and management systems such as financial reporting, board member training and adopting an anti-doping code in order to access ongoing funding payments (UK Sport, 2008). The efforts of sport funding agencies to introduce more transparent criteria for funding has arguably imposed a greater compliance burden on sport organizations. In many ways this is understandable in light of the significant public funds being invested in sport and the importance of protecting the interests of key stakeholders such as the members, the general public and the government. Using a framework reported in the review of not-for-profit regulation discussed in the previous section (State Services Authority, 2007:27), the following key stakeholder interests in financial reporting associated with sport funding can be identified:

- NSO members: require accurate financial information to consider the direction of the organization generally or to take action to constrain the board;

- General public: accountability to the public is warranted on the grounds that NSOs receive public funds, are part of the social infrastructure and play a key role in the community;

- Government as policymaker, regulator and funder: require information to assess performance and suitability for future funding, to develop future policy on funding sport, and to ensure compliance with funding requirements and to maintain trust in the sector.

In summary, it is clear that the federal governments of Australia, Canada, New Zealand and the UK have all adopted the approach of forcing their NSOs to meet a range of conditions in order to receive government funding. These conditions have had a direct impact on their organizational practices such as having a volunteer leadership structure that is democratically elected by the membership, adopting a formal incorporated structure, auditing their financial records, providing their services to members in an ethical and equitable manner, adopting long-term strategic planning processes, committing to coach and official development, agreeing to abide by a national anti-doping code separate to any that might be requested by an International Sport Federation and structuring their sport competition and delivery structures to meet minimum geographic distribution requirements on a national basis. The compliance burden that these requirements impose on NSOs and their members should not be underestimated.

GOVERNANCE REQUIREMENTS

The final area in which government policy affects organizational practice is the development and dissemination of corporate governance guidelines for NSOs by federal sport agencies (cf. ASC, 2007; SPARC, 2004; UK Sport, 2004). These guidelines are an important element of several Commonwealth countries' attempts to improve the corporate governance structures and systems within NSOs and their member organizations. Hoye and Cuskelly (2007) argued that the development of these guidelines by governments was driven by a desire (in part) to protect their investments by ensuring that the NSOs that were delivering government-funded elite sport programs were governed effectively. This is evident in the fact that 'the notion of excellence in sport management and governance has become an increasingly prevalent part of government sport policy and is one of the four pillars of the [2007] Australian government's sport policy, Backing Australia's Sports Ability' (Hoye & Cuskelly, 2007:26).

In Australia, the ASC has adopted a direct interventionist strategy of trying to improve the governance of NSOs. The Governance and Management Improvement Program (GMIP) is administered by the ASC and is designed to direct, assist and support NSOs in addressing strategic governance and organizational issues. The GMIP includes activities such as reviewing NSO constitutional and structural arrangements; providing advice on policies, processes and procedures used by NSOs in areas such as financial management, risk management, insurance, information technology and people management; and directly facilitating strategic and business planning, amalgamations, mergers and change management issues (Hoye & Cuskelly, 2007).

The ASC also publishes *Governance Principles: A good practice guide for sporting organizations* that articulates core governance principles that NSOs should adopt in the following six areas: board composition, roles and powers; board processes; governance systems; board reporting and performance; member relationship and reporting; and ethical and responsible decision making (ASC, 2007). While the ASC claims it does not advocate one governance model over another, a condition of being recognized as an NSO is that the sport must show that it has 'formally committed to a governance structure that is consistent with the ASC's governance principles of best practice' (ASC, n.d.:3). In addition, an umbrella body that seeks to be recognized by the ASC must show that it has 'formally committed to a governance structure that is consistent with the ASC's governance principles of best practice and which protect the interests of all parties' (ASC, n.d.:4). In effect, the ASC is regulating the type of governance structures that NSOs and other sport organizations should utilize by restricting access to the government funding pool.

UK Sport, the agency responsible for high-performance sport also focusses on governance improvement among NSOs. In 2004, UK Sport published the *Good Governance Guide for National Governing Bodies*, designed to assist NSOs with a wide range of governance issues including roles, responsibilities and liabilities of board members; the role of the board chair; board member training, performance and evaluation; conflicts of interest; the role of the CEO; constitution or articles of association; the purpose and conduct of meetings; planning and risk management; stakeholder participation; and compliance issues. As noted earlier in this chapter, UK Sport has adopted a system of 'funding triggers' that require NSOs to comply with specific governance requirements in order to continue being funded, a system that would appear to be even more stringent than that used by the SC.

SPARC also operates a similar program of direct intervention in the governance of NSOs. SPARC's program is entitled the Leadership and Governance Program, which offers much the same services as the ASC's GMIP. SPARC also published their own version of sport governance guidelines *Nine Steps to Effective Governance* (SPARC, 2004) that are designed to 'assist NSOs in areas such as the role of the board, work planning, meeting structures and procedures, strategic planning, the Board – CEO relationship, performance monitoring for the organization, board performance, succession planning and the induction process for new board members' (Hoye & Cuskelly, 2007:26). SPARC does not tie any funding conditions to the adoption of these governance guidelines. In a similar vein, the SFAF utilized by Sport Canada discussed earlier in this chapter, while being a very comprehensive set of criteria for funding, does not explicitly require Canadian NSOs to adopt any particular governance structure or system, bar some requirements for geographic spread of membership and use of democratic election processes.

In summary, it is apparent that the Australian and UK sport agencies have adopted very direct regulatory measures that affect the nature of the governance structure and systems that are adopted by their respective NSOs. While SPARC offers a very comprehensive set of resources that NSOs can adopt for improving their governance, the adoption of these are not tied to funding access conditions, nor does Sport Canada impose such conditions. These examples further illustrate the various efforts of governments in seeking to regulate the organizational practices of sport organizations.

CONCLUSION

This chapter has examined the impacts of a range of regulatory policies that have affected the way sport organizations conduct their activities, specifically the structures adopted by non-profit sport organizations, compliance obligations associated with the receipt of public monies to support their activities and corporate governance systems. The policies concerned with incorporation and legal structures have not been developed specifically for sport, rather they are generic policies designed to facilitate the activities of all non-profit organizations. Conversely, federal sport funding agencies have developed a range of policies that seek to regulate and control the nature of non-profit sport organizational practices, in particular governance systems, financial accountability measures and compliance with other sport-specific policies such as adhering to anti-doping codes of practice. The rationale of the majority of government policies reviewed in this chapter can arguably be interpreted as attempts to protect government investment in sport through various funding schemes, and this has led to an increased compliance burden in terms of meeting organizational practice requirements.

It is also evident that the sport sector, specifically national and provincial/state governing bodies, are not central to the policy communities that devise these regulatory policies. While they are certainly at the forefront of dealing with the increased compliance burden associated with these policies, they are not involved in the design of the generic organizational structure requirements, governance standards or financial reporting systems beyond the normal sort of operational level consultation between government agencies and sport about procedural matters. This (in part) is explained by the type of regulatory strategies employed by governments in this area which, using the framework from Baldwin and Cave (1999), include command and control strategies (fixed set of organizational structure options), disclosure strategies (detailed reporting to government agencies), and to a certain degree, the use of direct action by central sport agencies by providing principles and frameworks for the adoption of good governance guidelines for sport organizations to adopt.

These policies present a number of challenges for sport organizations. Firstly, they have resulted in a greater level of accountability and general compliance burden for NSOs to manage so that they can access government funding. The capacity of an NSO to deal with these burdens is arguably dependent on the quality of volunteers and staff at their disposal. Secondly, they have imposed restrictions on the legal and governance structures that sports might seek to adopt. Finally, these policies tend to maintain the resource dependency that exists between NSOs and federal government sport agencies. The impact of government policy on sport organizations, whether it be sport policy or housed within other spheres of government, is not restricted to affecting their organizational practices. Chapter 3 explores further examples of direct government intervention by way of regulatory policies, specifically how some sporting activities that present inherent risks for participants and spectators such as boxing, combat sports, motor sport, shooting and sport parachuting are subject to direct regulation by government.

Regulation of Sport Activity

One of the few scholars to address the impact of governments directly intervening in the regulation of sport activity was Sárközy (2001), who explored the conditions under which the state can regulate sporting activity, a domain of civic activity that until the 1980s had largely been subject to self-regulation by independent governing bodies of sport. Sárközy (2001) argued that the increasing level of government intervention in sport came about as a result of the increasing commercialization of elite sport and thus the need to protect the interests of athletes and corporations involved in professional sport, the importance of countries securing large scale sport events for both economic and political gain, and the increasing level of public interest in the benefits from sport participation. The increased level of government intervention we see today is even more significant given the fact that:

> *Sport governing bodies are powerful organizations; they regulate particular niches of everyday life in much the same way as might be expected of the State. They lay down rules that affect not only the on-field activities of sportspersons, but also affect the commercial transactions which they may conduct, their employment relationships, personal conduct and drug use. Governing bodies engage in licensing, control safety standards and have significance powers to exclude individuals from their sport. One might wonder whether such activities would not ordinarily be carried out by organs closely related to the State – yet it must be remembered that, for the most part, sports governing bodies are private associations and not elements of the State. These private, self-regulating associations generally grew up during the late nineteenth century as sport developed out of disparate and localised games in to the codified and uniform packages that exist today. While government may have been generally supportive of regulation of sports, because of the increased orderliness and control it brought to them, it took no significant part in the regulatory process.*
>
> (Gardiner et al., 2006:179)

There is no doubt that the 'hands off' approach to regulation in sport has passed. As noted in the introductory chapter, governments are involved in regulating many aspects of sport, including sport activity itself. There are a number of sports that present inherent risks for participants or spectators such as boxing, combat sports, sport parachuting, horse racing, motor sport and some forms of hunting that are subject to direct regulation by government. For example, the sport of professional boxing not only presents several safety concerns for participants but is also at risk of malpractice from promoters and others who might seek to profit from the activity. The absence of an appropriate governing body to enforce adequate regulatory control over participants or officials in some instances has led to governments enacting specific regulations aimed at controlling the manner in which certain sport activities are conducted. Indeed, Gardiner et al. (2006:102) argued that 'the major role of the State in sport continues to lie in the regulating and prohibiting of sporting activities'. As Gardiner et al. (2006) explain, this role presents fundamental difficulties for governments who must decide what sport activities should be prohibited and to what extent should others be regulated, if at all, and all the while attempting to balance the interests of individuals with an interest or investment in those activities versus the wider interests of the community. Governments need to balance the libertarian views of some versus those who believe governments' role is to intervene to prevent individuals harming themselves or others.

The purpose of this chapter, therefore, is to review the regulatory regimes that exist in several sports across a number of jurisdictions in order to identify the reasons cited by government for undertaking such direct intervention in regulating sport activity, to identify the centrality of sport in determining the nature and extent of such interventions, the variety of regulatory instruments used and to make some assessment of their efficacy in mitigating risks while enabling the sport activity to persist.

BOXING AND COMBAT SPORTS

The groups of sports that have arguably attracted the most attention from governments in relation to the regulation of their respective sport activities include boxing and combat sports (i.e. contact forms of martial arts such as kickboxing or other forms of combat sport contests where the intention is to strike, hit, grapple with, throw or punch the other contestant). In many jurisdictions there is a distinction made between the public regulation of professional boxing and combat contests versus governments allowing amateur contests to be self-regulated, the rationale being that there are fundamental differences:

> *Amateur fighters do not compete for prize money and are more likely to be required to use specific equipment or protective wear such as headgear. Professional fights sometimes require match injuries to be more severe before the referee will stop the competition and knockouts may score more highly than other blows and may even be a fighter's objective.*
> (Department of Local Government, Planning, Sport and Recreation [Queensland], 2007:6)

The key issues of concern to regulators seeking to control professional boxing and other combat sports include: (1) ensuring the safety of participants, (2) improving the standard of event management, including minimising the risk of malpractice, and (3) improving the standard of record keeping, specifically the reporting of injuries to participants. Lobby groups such as Sports Medicine Australia (SMA) and the Australian Medical Association have repeatedly called for a ban on all forms of boxing. SMA has argued since 1992 that there is 'irrefutable evidence that professional boxing leads to chronic brain injury' (SMA, 1997:1). In the absence of a total ban on boxing, the SMA policy on the safety of boxing stipulates that such an activity (and other combat sports) should be subject to clear regulations for participants providing consent to be involved, for the provision of medical assistance, ongoing training and education of officials and regular medical clearances for participants. Governments are also concerned with reducing the risks of malpractice in relation to the staging of professional bouts (i.e. 'fixing' the results, promoters forcing participants to compete with injuries, etc.).

Governments are also concerned that the fragmented nature of the boxing and combat sports industry precludes the ability of a single governing body to effectively address these regulatory issues. The reality of the situation was highlighted in a discussion paper on safety for boxing and combats sports prepared by the Queensland State Government:

> *The combat sports industry is extremely diverse. While it includes many broadly known categories such as boxing, karate, judo, kung fu, taekwondo, aikido, kickboxing, jujitsu, silat, hapkido, tang soo do, savate and others, it also includes numerous variations of these and other lesser known codes. Clubs and associations teaching these sports are not currently subject to any accreditation or regulatory system that is inclusive of all, or even the majority of participants.*

> *The industry is therefore very fragmented and uncoordinated,*
> *making it unlikely that a voluntary regulatory regime would be*
> *consistently implemented or monitored.*
> (Department of Local Government, Planning, Sport and Recreation,
> 2007:7)

This view was supported by a more recent review of boxing and combat sport regulations conducted by the Victorian State Government:

> *It should be noted that the boxing and combat sports industry is*
> *relatively fragmented and rules could vary considerably. There is also*
> *no overarching representative or rule making body for these sports.*
> *Typically, self regulation suits industries that are unified and have*
> *strong common interests (e.g. the Code of Conduct for Marketing*
> *Retail Energy in Victoria, the Alcohol Advertising Beverages Code).*
> *In addition, professional boxing and combat sports carry moderate to*
> *high risks for contestants. These risks can result in catastrophic*
> *consequences if not well-managed. Self-regulation would also result*
> *in government losing control over emerging combat sports such as*
> *cage fighting events.*
> (Sport and Recreation Victoria, 2008:36–7)

The most recent amendments to the Victorian legislation in this area with the passing of the *Professional Boxing and Combat Sports (Amendment) Act 2007* even included provision for the government, via its Professional Boxing and Combat Sports Board, to 'cancel or suspend a contestant's registration if it considers that the person lacks the required skills, using a comprehensive checklist, including the contestant's defensive skills, mobility and tactical awareness' (Sport and Recreation Victoria, 2007b:1). The legislation also enabled the Government to prohibit caged combat sports as explained in the media release from the Minister for Sport and Recreation Mr Merlino:

> *I have never approved and will not be approving any combat sport*
> *competitions staged in cages ... I believe the spectacle of two*
> *competitors in caged combat style competition does not meet the*
> *community's standards of what is acceptable for professional combat*
> *sports in Victoria.*
> (Sport and Recreation Victoria, 2007a:1)

The majority of Australian State and Territory governments have had regulations in place for boxing and combat sports since the 1970s, often enacted as the result of growing concerns regarding boxing injuries.

The majority of these regulations have undergone a number of reviews in more recent years, with the result that 'while they vary in scope and application, NSW, Western Australia, South Australia and the Australian Capital Territory all have dedicated laws regulating professional boxing and/or martial arts/combat sports. Only Queensland, Tasmania and the Northern Territory do not have specific regulatory controls' (Sport and Recreation Victoria, 2008:13). The common elements of the regulatory approach of those states with regulations has been to specify the need for participants to obtain a licence and be registered as a fighter or contestant, trainer, promoter, match-maker, timekeeper, referee or judge; for fighters to undergo medical examinations before and after bouts, and for the provision of medical assistance and supervision at bouts. In most cases, these regulations also establish a board, authority or commission to carry out the licensing, monitoring and enforcement activities associated with the regulations.

A similar provincial-based regulatory regime operates in Canada, with the majority of Provincial Governments enacting legislation and associated regulations to control professional boxing whilst allowing a non-profit association to govern the amateur participants in their respective jurisdictions. In some cases the regulatory power rests at the city level; for example, the City of Edmonton empowers a Boxing and Wrestling Commission to regulate boxing, wrestling and full contact karate competitions. The focus of the Canadian regulations are very similar to those in Australia, with an emphasis on ensuring participant safety and adequate probity of events accomplished through a licensing regime, supported by monitoring and enforcement by an Authority or Commission.

South Africa passed national legislation in 2001, the South African Boxing Act, establishing an independent regulatory body, Boxing SA, whose members are appointed by the South African Minister of Sport. Boxing SA is responsible for administering a comprehensive set of regulations regarding the conduct of professional boxing, including registration requirements for boxers, officials, managers, promoters, matchmakers, trainers, seconds and agents; the setting of fees, sanctioning of bouts, rules for competition and the roles and duties of all individuals associated with the conduct of the sport. The 115-page set of regulations (Sport and Recreation South Africa, 2004) enables Boxing SA to fulfil its statutory mandate to 'regulate, control and exercise general supervision over professional boxing at tournaments in the Republic' (Boxing South Africa, 2008). Figure 3.1 illustrates the stringent regulations imposed on individuals who wish to be registered as a boxer in South Africa.

In contrast, the level of government intervention in boxing in New Zealand is relatively minor: 'Boxing or wrestling organizations submit

Registration requirements for boxers

(1) In order to be registered as a boxer, an applicant shall, subject to the provisions of regulation 2(1)

    (a) be older than 18 years but younger than 35 years in the case of a first registration: Provided that a boxer who has not participated in a boxing contest for a continuous period of 12 months or more shall be deemed to be a first registration;

    (b) submit in writing to Boxing SA his or her history as a boxer, with full supporting evidence;

    (c) at the request of Boxing SA, report to a gymnasium determined by Boxing SA in order to have his or her boxing ability tested by a person designated by Boxing SA;

    (d) submit himself or herself, at his or her own expense, to a medical examination by a registered medical practitioner and submit the results of the examination to Boxing SA in the form set out in Annexure F, which medical examination shall include a test for the Human Immune-deficiency Virus (HIV-infection) and Hepatitis B and, in the case of a female boxer, a breast and pelvic examination; and

    (e) submit himself or herself, at his or her own expense, to a medical examination contemplated in paragraph (d) annually when applying to renew his or her registration, or at any other time when requested thereto by Boxing SA.

(2) A certificate of registration contemplated in regulation 2(1) shall not be issued to a boxer if he or she suffers from any of the following medical conditions:

    (a) High blood pressure (hypertension amounting to a reading higher than 140/80 taken over several readings);

    (b) an organic heart disease or a history of cardiac surgery;

    (c) a lung disease;

    (d) retinopathy, a retinal detachment or a history of eye surgery;

    (e) defective vision: both eyes not less than J10 for myopia or 20/100 for hyperopia;

    (f) herniae of the abdomen or organomegaly (liver or spleen) or palpable masses in the abdominal region;

    (g) absence of one kidney or evidence of a renal disease;

    (h) physical deformity or other medical condition that, in the opinion of Boxing SA or its medical advisors, may lead to bodily injury or may affect the boxer's ability to adequately defend himself or herself;

    (i) a brain disease, brain injury or a history of brain surgery;

    (j) evidence of disease of the nervous system;

    (k) an enlargement of the thyroid or lymphatic glands or active thyroid disease;

    (l) he human immuno-deficiency virus infection;

    (m) hepatitis B surface antigen;

    (n) pregnancy in the case of a female boxer;

    (o) evidence of breast disease or in the case of a female boxer a history of breast surgery ;

    (p) any other disease or medical condition which, in the opinion of Boxing. SA or its medical advisors, may constitute a risk to the health of the boxer, his or her opponents, or the boxer and his or her opponents, as the case may be.

(3) Boxing SA shall annually, in the case of a boxer's application for the renewal of his or her registration, review his or her application, and if, in the opinion of Boxing SA, the boxer has endured excessive punishment, Boxing SA may, despite the boxer undergoing a positive neurological investigation, refuse his or her application for renewal

(4) Boxing SA shall annually, in the case of an application by a boxer for the renewal of his or her registration who is 35 years or older for registration, require the boxer to submit himself or herself, at his or her expense, to the medical examinations and tests that Boxing SA deem appropriate in order to determine whether it is in the best interests of his or her mental or physical well-being to continue boxing.

(5) A boxer may assume and use a ring name, but the right to use any ring name is subject to the approval of Boxing SA and may be refused by Boxing SA either at the time of the boxer applying for registration as a boxer or at any time thereafter should Boxing SA, on reasonable grounds, deem it undesirable for the boxer to use or to continue using such ring name.

FIGURE 3.1 *Excerpt from South African Boxing Act, 2001 Regulations.*

their rules and standards to the Minister and if they are approved, those organizations can hold boxing and wrestling contests' (Department of Local Government, Planning, Sport and Recreation, 2007:11). There is no separate government regulatory agency to which participants or officials must register or seek a licence as this function is performed by the approved governing bodies, nor does the New Zealand government regulate other combat sports (Department of Local Government, Planning, Sport and Recreation, 2007). The lack of direct government intervention is even more marked in the UK, where boxing is self-regulated by the British Boxing Board of Control. The government does not intervene in any way in the conduct of the sport, leaving the British Boxing Board of Control to manage all 'arbitration and disciplinary procedures; revision, upgrading and application of rules and regulations; appointment of referees and timekeepers; and licensing of people involved in boxing' (Department of Local Government, Planning, Sport and Recreation, 2007:12).

In summary, governments in the major Commonwealth nations have adopted a variety of approaches and levels of involvement in regulating boxing and combat sports. Government intervention varies from the setting of direct regulations administered by an independent body (South Africa), a focus on regulating the safety and probity issues associated with these sports (Australian and Canada), having little direct involvement beyond approving organizations' rules and regulations (New Zealand), or indeed, having no public regulatory function whatsoever (UK).

RACING

The regulation of thoroughbred horse racing, harness racing and greyhound racing in Australia has traditionally been on the basis of private regulatory arrangements between racing and wagering organizations with an overarching public regulatory system focussed on licensing the general activities of these organizations. There is no specific national legislation governing the regulation of racing in Australia and the long history of state legislative control over racing regulation has remained unchallenged by the Commonwealth. The central regulatory function of Australia's State and Territory governments in relation to racing (as distinct from wagering activities that are explored in detail in Chapter 5) has been to prohibit proprietary racing while licensing specific non-proprietary clubs to hold race meetings. A Principal Club (usually the first established or largest club) was empowered to control racing activities in their respective state or territory. The Principal Clubs of the eight states and territories of Australia met regularly as the Australian Conference of Principal Racing Clubs (now known as the Australian Racing Board) to formulate and adopt the Australian Rules of Racing. In addition to conducting race meetings at their own racecourses, the Principal Clubs had ultimate responsibility to enforce the Australian Rules of Racing for other clubs in their respective state (Hoye, 2006a).

The key policy instrument employed by Australian State and Territory governments in controlling racing has been through specific racing legislation. In Victoria, for example, the *Racing Act 1958* stipulates (in part) where race meetings can be held (only on licenced race courses), the length and type of races, the procedures and conditions for appeals in relation to the outcome of races, the requirements for individuals to be licenced as participants, governance arrangements for each racing industry and even the requirement for participants to abide by the Australian Rules of Racing. Specifically, the main purpose of *Racing Act 1958* is to:

- Regulate the conduct of race meetings and betting at meetings,

- Provide for the licensing of racing clubs and racecourses,

- Provide for the issue of permits for minor race meetings and betting activities,

- Provide for the registration of bookmakers and their clerks,

- Establish Harness Racing Victoria, Greyhound Racing Victoria, Racing Appeals Tribunal and the Bookmakers and Bookmakers' Clerks Registration Committee, and

- Recognize the role of Racing Victoria Limited as the controlling body of thoroughbred racing (Department of Justice, 2009).

A unique element of the government intervention in this sport is the creation of a statutory body to hear appeals against penalty decisions passed down by the governing body of the sport. For example, in Victoria, the government operates the Racing Appeals Tribunal that operates as a higher authority for appealing decisions which in some cases may involve suspensions and fines. This is in stark contrast to most other sports, where the appeals mechanism is provided for under the control of a sports' respective governing body, rather than being referred to a statutory authority.

In Canada, the racing industry is regulated by provincial racing commissions. For example, the Ontario Racing Commission governs, directs, controls and regulates horse racing in the Province of Ontario (Ontario Horse Racing Industry Association, 2009). A similar situation operates in

New Zealand with the New Zealand Racing Board overseeing all aspects of racing across the three codes, including operating a Judicial Control Authority – the government-operated body that conducts inquiries into any breaches of the rules of racing (New Zealand Thoroughbred Racing, 2008).

In contrast to the federalist system of regulating racing in Australia and Canada and the direct national government control in New Zealand, horse racing in the UK is regulated by a single national organization, the British Horseracing Board (BHB). The BHB decides where and when races are to be held, how finances are to be distributed within the racing industry, and liaises with commercial organizations for betting and licensing functions but not disciplinary functions (British Horseracing Board, 2004). The BHB is a company limited by guarantee with board members elected to represent the interests of various stakeholders, including breeders, trainers, racecourses, owners and the original governing body for racing in the UK, the Jockey Club. The private regulatory role of the BHB reflects what occurs in most other sports, where key stakeholders or members elect people to represent their interests in a democratic system and to oversee the regulation of the sport.

The rationale for direct government involvement in racing by way of regulation and prohibition can be attributed to governments, in some jurisdictions, wishing to ensure the highest standards of integrity operate within racing in order to preserve public confidence in the activity, to ensure high levels of probity exist within a sport dependent on wagering to fund its operations, and to protect a significant stream of government taxation revenue associated with the wagering on racing.

SPORT PARACHUTING

Sport parachuting or skydiving is arguably one of the world's highest risk sports, and has traditionally been self-regulated by international and national governing bodies. At the international level the sport is regulated by the International Parachuting Commission (IPC) of the Federation Aéronautique Internationale (FAI), which oversees all air sports. One of the central roles of the IPC is to 'assemble, analyse and disseminate information and statistics on parachuting in member countries which will contribute to the improvement of parachuting, parachuting equipment, training methods, international standards and safety' (FAI, 2008:2). One of the IPC's largest organizational members, the United States Parachute Association (USPA), represents the interests of more than 31,000 regular parachutists. The US Federal Government, via the 'Federal Aviation Administration recognizes USPA's successful leadership role in the self-regulation of sky-diving' (USPA, 2008). The USPA supports and promotes skydiving competition and provides recommendations for skydiving training and instructional rating programs, and licences the operations of 'more than 250 parachute jumping businesses who have pledged to follow USPA's Basic Safety Requirements' (USPA, 2008). USPA Group Member skydiving schools also pledge to offer skydiving training taught and supervised by USPA-rated staff. USPA-issued skydiving licences are recognized internationally through the IPC. A similar system of private regulation provided by a national governing body that is recognized by national governments operates in most countries of the world.

An important test of the ability of the sport to remain self-determining was recently played out in Canada. The actual sport activity is regulated by the Canadian Sport Parachuting Association (CSPA) (the equivalent to its US counterpart, the USPA) and is Canada's representative to the IPC. The CSPA was incorporated in 1956 for the purpose of promoting safe, enjoyable sport parachuting through cooperation and adherence to a set of self-imposed rules and recommendations (CSPA, 2008). The Canadian Associates of Professional Skydivers (CAPS) is also recognized by the Canadian government as a provider of private regulation of parachuting activities. Until early 2008, the Canadian Federal Government's involvement in regulating sport parachuting was limited to regulating access to controlled airspace to make parachute descents and licensing of aircraft and the pilots of the aircraft used in the sport (Government of Canada, 2008). In May 2008, Transport Canada, the agency responsible for regulating aviation in Canada, amended the Canadian Aviation Regulations to introduce provisions to 'protect the public against parachute training schools that are unable to satisfy stringent parachute training standards' (Government of Canada, 2008).

The regulatory impact analysis statement that accompanied the introduction of the new regulations in March 2008 provided the following explanation of the rationale for government intervening in the regulation the sport:

> *At present, the two parachuting organizations in Canada (Canadian Sport Parachuting Association and Canadian Association of Professional Skydivers) and the parachute training units assert that the student parachutist training units voluntarily comply with the standards, procedures and technical recommendations of the parachuting organizations. However, currently these organizations have no right to monitor or enforce compliance with their standards. Inquests into deaths of student parachutists have indicated that the*

training units at which those students who died obtained their training and conducted their first solo jumps may not have been following the standards of the organizations. This is an unsafe situation. These proposed Regulations will serve as a deterrent to those who may be tempted not to comply with the standards established by the parachuting organizations.

(Government of Canada, 2008)

In effect the regulations did not materially alter the regulation of the activity, it simply made it mandatory that 'parachute training will be required to be conducted in accordance with the current standards, procedures and technical recommendations established by one of the parachuting organizations that has been recognized by the Minister' (Government of Canada, 2008). In other words, it implemented a series of penalties for non-compliance that the government perceived would ameliorate the inability of the existing sport governing bodies to effectively regulate against non-compliance. The response from the governing bodies (CSPA and CAPS) was to refute the need for such regulation, citing a decrease in the number of fatalities under the existing regulatory system as proof of its effectiveness. This example of heightened government intervention into regulating sport illustrates the reluctance of sport to be subject to such regulatory measures due to their belief in the merits of self-regulation.

MOTOR SPORT

The vast majority of motor sport activity is regulated by non-profit associations such as the Motor Sports Association (MSA) in the UK, or the Confederation of Australian Motor Sport in Australia. Organizations such as these operate a regulatory system of permits and licences for competitors and their motor vehicles, officials and racetracks and circuits. However, in some Australian jurisdictions, additional government regulations apply for the provision of public safety at motor vehicle sports events. For example, 'licenses and/or permits to conduct motor racing events in NSW are obtained through NSW Sport and Recreation under the Motor Vehicle Sports (Public Safety) Act 1985 or the Mount Panorama Motor Racing Act 1989' (NSW Sport and Recreation, 2009d). This government agency issues licences to motor vehicle racing grounds that have addressed a set of minimum requirements in regard to the safety of spectators, competitors and officials and specifically 'prohibits the conduct of motor vehicle racing except on licensed grounds, which have to meet stringent safety conditions'

(NSW Sport and Recreation, 2009d). Separate licensing conditions apply to events planned to be held on public roads which are granted by the NSW Roads Traffic Authority and NSW Police Service under separate Road and Transport Legislation.

One other form of regulation associated with motor sport in Australia is focussed on enabling the safe conduct of major motor sport events on public roads and limiting access to areas central to the management and operation of a motor sport event. For example, the South Australian Motor Sport Regulations 1999 stipulate a wide set of powers for the government led South Australian Motor Sport Board to conduct motor sport events quite separate to any governing body such as the Confederation of Australian Motor Sport (South Australia Government, 1999).

BLOOD SPORTS

The final example of direct regulation by government of a sporting activity that we have selected to highlight is the sport of fox hunting, one of the 'blood sports' defined by Gardiner et al. (2006:121) as 'sports where the animal becomes pitted against human in a test of athletic excellence by use of a gun, other instrument or animal agency'. Gardiner et al. (2006) provided a summary of the status of the regulation of blood sports in Britain in 2006 which we have reproduced in modified form in Table 3.1. The table highlights that some blood sports are prohibited outright, including fox hunting, while others are allowed under certain regulations. Gardiner et al. (2006:121) noted that this regulatory framework had developed 'often in a piecemeal and arbitrary way', with regulations being developed in response from vigorous and sustained campaigning on specific issues. Fox hunting

Table 3.1 Regulation of Blood Sports in Britain

Sport	Lawful	Legal Prohibition or Qualification
Angling	Yes	*Salmon and Freshwater Fisheries Act 1975; Control of Pollution (Angler's Lead Weight) Regulations 1986*
Deer hunting	Yes	*Deer Act 1991*
Hare coursing	Yes	*Hares Act 1848; Protection of Animals Act 1911*
Mink hunting	Yes	*Protection of Animals Act 1911*
Bird shooting	Yes	*Wildlife and Countryside Act 1981; Games Act 1831 and Games Act 1971*
Cock fighting	No	*Cock fighting Act 1952; Protection of Animals Act 1911*
Dog fighting	No	*Protection of Animals Act 1911; Protection of Animals (Amendment) Act 1911*
Badger baiting	No	*Protection of Badgers Act 1992*
Fox hunting	No	*Protection of Animals Act 1911*

is no exception with its legality being questioned over many years with two opposing views, those who oppose it on moral grounds and the rights of animals versus those who wish to preserve a traditional way of life in the country. The current prohibition on fox hunting came in to force in 2005 after a long and bitter campaign.

CONCLUSION

These examples of varying degrees of government intervention to directly regulate or prohibit sporting activities illustrate a number of arguments for and against sports maintaining the ability to self-regulate. Baldwin and Cave (1999) argued that the case for self-regulation in any activity rests on two assumptions. The first is that private independent governing bodies have more expertise in the conduct of their respective activities and thus this technical knowledge makes them more effective regulators. The second assumption is that:

> *Self-regulators, with their easy access to those under control,*
> *experience low costs in acquiring the information that is necessary to*
> *formulate and set standards. They, furthermore, have low*
> *monitoring and enforcement costs and they are able to adapt their*
> *regimes to changes in industrial conditions in a flexible and smooth*
> *manner because they act relatively informally and tend to enjoy the*
> *trust of the regulated group.*
>
> (Baldwin and Cave, 1999:127)

Aside from these arguments about effectiveness and efficiency, the costs of self-regulation are also generally borne by those involved in the regulated activity rather than taxpayers. In relation to the sport examples reviewed in this chapter, the majority of governments have determined that in the case of boxing and combat sports, the disparate nature of the industry has not facilitated the establishment of governing bodies for the various disciplines that have the requisite expertise or resources to effectively and efficiently regulate their activities. There is also some evidence of this reasoning in the case of sport parachuting in Canada.

Baldwin and Cave (1999:126) also argued that the case against self-regulation centres on issues related to 'mandates, accountability, and the fairness of procedures'. Regulations devised by sport governing bodies can be criticised for being the product of an undemocratic process that may not serve the public interest. In addition, Baldwin and Cave (1999:129) argued that 'as far as enforcement is concerned, it has been alleged that self-regulatory bodies have an especially poor record in protecting the public interest through enforcing standards against errant members'. This lack of mandate for sport governing bodies to regulate to protect public safety at motor sport events or to ban fox hunting in order to serve the public interest goes some way to explaining government regulatory intervention in these areas.

Government regulatory intervention in the sport of horse racing certainly seems to be linked to the potential lack of accountability that self-regulation might engender. As Baldwin and Cave (1999:130) posit

> *the key problem in identifying the proper level and form of accountability lies in deciding whether the self-regulation at issue is a matter of private control (a matter of resolution between members) or whether it is governmental (in so far that it affects the public interest) and merits democratic (or judicial) accountability accordingly.*

The interdependence of wagering and horse racing (further explored in Chapter 5) would suggest that the important public interest in controlling access to racing in order to ensure high standards of probity and to preserve public confidence in the sport are key motivating forces for government to directly regulate elements of this sport (and other forms of racing).

The final criticism of self-regulation, as argued by Baldwin and Cave (1999:132), is that it can be considered unfair 'in so far as non-members may be affected by regulatory decisions to which they have poor or no access. Past experience suggests that self-regulators have a sporadic, unstructured, and patchy record of consulting those with interests in the working of their systems'. From the examples we have reviewed, we have not uncovered any evidence that sport governing bodies have been subject to such criticisms, and thus been a motivating factor for governments to regulate sport activities directly.

In terms of the first of our four questions we sought to address in this chapter (i.e. what are the reasons cited by government for undertaking such direct intervention in regulating sport activity) we can conclude that governments have done so to overcome concerns about the effectiveness and efficiency with which some sports can self-regulate their activities (boxing and combat sports, and to a certain extent sport parachuting); a lack of a mandate for sport governing bodies to regulate their activities in the public interest (motor sport safety and fox hunting); and a lack of accountability in allowing horse racing to completely self-regulate their activities.

In relation to our second question – the centrality of sport in determining the nature and extent of such regulatory interventions – it is evident that in some cases, such as in boxing and combat sports, that government has led the development of the regulatory regime in the absence of a coherent 'voice' from the sport. In others, such as sport parachuting and fox hunting, the sport governing body has been absolutely central to the development of the regulatory system, and while it may not agree with the final form of the regulations, it has been centrally involved in the debate. In other sports, such as horse racing and motor sport, the governing bodies have also been intimately involved and generally supportive of the development of government regulations.

Our third question is concerned with the variety of regulatory instruments employed by government. Again, using the framework from Baldwin and Cave (1999), these have ranged from command and control strategies (outright prohibition of fox hunting and certain types of combat sports, as well as motor sport safety requirements), market harnessing controls (in the form of licensing participants to engage in boxing, combat sports, and horse racing), and the use of direct action through forming Authorities or Commissions to carry out these licensing functions.

Finally, we need to address the question of the efficacy of these regulatory interventions. In the majority of cases these regulatory interventions appear to mitigate risks while still facilitating people's involvement in the sport activity (bar fox hunting). At this basic level, the intervention by government to regulate the access to or conduct of these sport activities has allowed these activities to carry on in the absence of effective private regulatory regimes. This has certainly been the case for boxing and combat sports in the majority of the jurisdictions reviewed here, and the regulatory burden imposed on the sports of horse racing, motor sport and sport parachuting do not appear to be overly burdensome to prevent people enjoying these sports as spectators, facilitators or participants. What remains to be seen is the development and impact of future government regulatory interventions on sport as sport continues to evolve as a commercial and social institution.

CHAPTER 4

Regulating Safe Sport Environments

An increasing area of government policy intervention in sport can be broadly identified as attempts to improve the environment in which people can participate safely in sport. In Australia, these policies fall under the banner of 'member protection' and are focussed on issues such as the prevention of abuse, harassment and discrimination. A particular focus of these policies in some jurisdictions, such as the UK, has been on protecting children. We should point out that government policy intervention in these areas is not limited to sport, but highlight that the particular context of sport, with high numbers of children participating, its dependence on volunteers for service and program delivery, individual's emotional investment as coaches, players, parents, spectators, officials and administrators and the very nature of sporting competition heightens the potential for the incidence of behaviours such as abuse, harassment or discrimination. As a result, many national and sub-national governments have developed specific regulatory policies aimed at ensuring the safety of people participating in sport.

One of the foremost authors in this field, Celia Brackenridge, offered an explanation for why it had taken so long for sport to become the subject of such direct government intervention when she argued that:

> *It is still common for sport organizations to be seen as existing outside the regulatory and moral frameworks which operate in other spheres of institutional life. It could be argued that this status of 'moral isolation' is a product of the historical roots of the voluntary sector in sport in the UK. The moral imperative was an important part of the original raison d'être of many sport organizations. Nineteenth century bourgeois ideology permeated the institutions of sport and was reinforced in their self-regulatory amateur codes so there was thought to be no need for other regulatory incursions by the state.*
>
> (Brackenridge, 1994:288)

The failure of this self-regulatory framework to protect people involved in sport was highlighted in the 1990s through a series of cases worldwide where coaches and others in positions of authority within sport organizations were convicted of systematic and long-term abuse of people under their care. The acceptance by sport organizations that they were ill equipped to deal with such matters was slow. Boocock (2002:99) argued that in relation to child abuse in sport, the lack of willingness to address the issue at any level was 'supported by denial ("it doesn't happen in this sport"), blaming or externalising ("it's someone else's fault") and minimisation ("it's not a big issue")'. Despite the early reluctance of sport to fully engage in issues of child abuse, discrimination or harassment, they are now subject to a variety of regulatory policies. In the Australian context, these are described by the Australian Sports Commission (2009b) as:

> *Practices and procedures that protect an organization's members – both individual members such as players, coaches and officials, and the member organizations such as clubs, state associations, other affiliated associations and the national body. Member protection involves protecting members from harassment, abuse, discrimination and other forms of inappropriate behaviour; adopting appropriate measures to ensure the right people are involved in an organization, particularly in relation to those involved with juniors; providing education and training; and promoting and modelling positive behaviour.*

The purpose of this chapter is to review the regulatory regimes focussed on the broad area of member protection in sport in order to identify the government rationale for undertaking such regulatory action, to identify the extent to which sport organizations have been central to determining the nature and extent of such interventions, to identify the variety of regulatory instruments used and to make some assessment of their impact on sport organizations. The chapter focuses on policies in two areas: child protection and discrimination. It should be noted that the majority of policy development and associated research or evaluative efforts have focussed on the issue of child protection in sport (cf. Brackenridge, 1994, 2002, 2003, 2004; Brackenridge et al., 2004, 2005), which is the main focus of this chapter.

CHILD PROTECTION

The work by Brackenridge, particularly during the 1990s, highlighted the extent of the policy problem associated with child protection in sport. Brackenridge (1994:290) noted that in relation to the extent of child sexual abuse generally, official statistics underestimate the scale of the problem, but the consensus (at that time) was that child sexual abuse is either of epidemic proportions or, at the very least, a 'significant issue'. Some nine years later, Brackenridge (2003:3) argued that the context of 'sport offers prime sex offending opportunities' and that data from three countries (Canada, Norway and Australia) illustrated that 'sexual exploitation is a serious issue for sport' (Brackenridge, 2003:9).

Malkin, Johnston, and Brackenridge (2000:151) noted that 'it is not only the child who might suffer when abuse occurs: the institution of sport itself is brought into question'. They cite the example of coaches and other officials possibly being tainted by wrongful allegations or people being dissuaded from participating in sports that become infamous for abuse as further imperatives for sports to be subject to regulatory policy and to engage in addressing the issues. The focus of child protection policies should therefore not be confined to merely protecting athletes. Brackenridge (2003:10) outlined the following four dimensions of protection that sport organizations should address in relation to sexual abuse:

1. Protecting the athlete from others – that is, recognizing and referring anyone who has been subjected to sexual misconduct by someone else, whether *inside* sport (by another staff member or athlete) or *outside* sport (by someone in the family or peer group);

2. Protecting the athlete from oneself – that is, observing and encouraging good practice when working with athletes in order to avoid perpetrating abuse;

3. Protecting oneself from the athlete or others – that is, taking precautions to avoid false allegations against oneself by athletes or their peers or families;

4. Protecting one's profession – that is, safeguarding the good name and integrity of sport, coaching and sport science.

Child protection policies should also not be focussed explicitly on concerns about sexual abuse. The ASC (2006:1) defined child abuse as comprising the following:

1. Sexual abuse/sexual misconduct – any sexual act or sexual threat imposed on a child including exposure to pornographic material, sexual touching, voyeurism and child prostitution. Sexual abuse often involves a progression in behaviour from fondling to intercourse.

2. Physical abuse – non-accidental injury to a child. This may include severe shaking, bruising, biting, scalding, throwing a child, injury caused by excessive discipline, poisoning, suffocation or strangulation.

3. Emotional abuse – behaviours that may psychologically harm a child. This behaviour tends to be a chronic behavioural pattern that undermines a child's self esteem or impairs a child's wellbeing or development. It may include constant criticism, rejection, withholding praise and affection, threats or unreasonable demands.

4. Neglect – where a child is harmed by the failure to provide them with the basic physical and emotional necessities of life. This may include inadequate supervision of young children for long periods, failure to provide adequate and proper food, clothing, personal hygiene or medical attention.

Malkin et al. (2000:153) argued that the structure of sport was 'not conducive to the recognition or implementation of child protection policies' and that sport organizations tend to 'only see the good in what they do and fail to recognize their weaker areas'. They concluded that NSOs should look to their respective national sport agencies for assistance and that they should only receive government funds on the condition that they implement an effective child protection policy. These arguments were echoed by Cense and Brackenridge (2001:72), who wrote that 'in order to prevent those who want to abuse children/athletes from doing so, action from outside sport is needed'. In other words, sport organizations would be unable to effectively protect their participants (members) without government regulatory intervention and support. We now turn to reviewing the development of government policy in relation to child protection in sport within three jurisdictions: the UK, Australia and Canada.

United Kingdom

Early attempts to introduce some form of self-regulation in the area of child protection in the UK were noted by Brackenridge (1994:293): 'ethical codes have been introduced by some sports organizations as part of their efforts to professionalise and formalise organizational behaviour'. She argued that the codes, which aimed to control or constrain behaviour of sport organization members and to exclude those individuals who were unable or unwilling to abide by the code, were relatively ineffective in preventing child abuse. The introduction of the Children Act 1991 'focussed attention on the legal rights of children' (Brackenridge, 1994:294), but the legislation did not require (at that time) sport organizations to undertake police screening of people wishing to be employed as coaches or appointed as voluntary sport leaders (Brackenridge, 1994).

Boocock (2002:100) noted that in the late 1990s individual National Governing Bodies 'approached the NSPCC [National Society for the Prevention of Cruelty to Children] and National Coaching Foundation (now SportsCoach UK) to develop child protection policies, training and a number of resources', but argued that the work of the task force 'lacked co-ordination and political support'. Boocock (2002:100) candidly admitted that at the time, even the lead national sport agency, Sport England, 'shared the attitudes of denial, blame and minimisation' regarding the extent of child abuse in sport. The first indication that government was serious about the development of specific policy in this area was the establishment of the National Task Force for Child Protection in Sport in 1999 by Sport England and the subsequent production of an Action Plan for Child Protection in Sport. Brackenridge (2002:104) argued that this was created in response 'to lobbying and pressure from grass roots sport for a central, one-stop shop to co-ordinate child protection enquiries and information'. Brackenridge also highlighted that in 1999 only about half of English NGBs had a child protection policy in place but that a year later almost all of the 58 funded NGBs had one. This was largely in reaction to a new funding criterion from the Department for Culture, Media and Sport (DCMS) that 'grant aid for an NGB became contingent on it demonstrating to Sport England that an active CP [child protection] policy was in place' (Brackenridge, 2002:104). Sport England also introduced minimum operating standards for child protection. Brackenridge (2002:104, 105) concluded that 'not surprisingly, the policy lever exerted by the funding criterion had a dramatic effect on policy activity at the national level in voluntary sport'.

The flow on effect to club and local level sport, however, was uncertain and Brackenridge (2002:105) argued that most NGBs developed their policies in the absence of any empirical data on the nature and extent of child abuse in their respective sports, and thus considered it unlikely that sport clubs would develop 'evidence-based policy'. Indeed, Brackenridge (2002:103) stated that 'child abuse in youth sport has become a 'moral panic' in British society but there is evidence of a child protection policy vacuum between national and club level'. A degree of policy disconnect was also evident between national sport agencies as argued by Williams (2003:79): 'the autonomy of the Sports Councils has resulted in England and Wales being out of step with each other to the extent that while Sport England funded governing bodies have to have basic child protection standards in order to receive funding, Welsh organizations can still choose whether they have them or not'. The situation in the later part of 2001 was that while Sport England had made it a requirement for NGBs to develop a child protection policy, these policies were not well informed by evidence or consistently implemented and applied within sport organizations throughout the UK.

Arguably the most important policy decision by Sport England in regard to child protection was to partner with the NSPCC to create the Child Protection in Sport Unit (CPSU) in 2001. The CPSU is 'a partnership between the NSPCC, Sport England, sportscotland, Sport Northern Ireland and the Sports Council for Wales [and was] founded in 2001 to co-ordinate and support sports organizations' implementation of the 2000 National Action Plan for Child Protection in Sport' (NSPCC, 2009a). The mission of the CPSU is to 'safeguard the welfare of children and young people under 18 in sport and to promote their well-being' (NSPCC, 2009a). Their main roles are to assist sports and other organizations to 'recognise their responsibility to protect children and young people left in their care, develop strategies and standards to protect children and young people, identify and respond to adults who are a threat to children and young people, and develop child protection knowledge and skills among all staff and volunteers' (NSPCC, 2009a).

The work of the CPSU is outlined in their most recent strategy document for the period 2006–2012 (CPSU, 2006). This strategy operates in the wider context of the UK Government's policy on improving the lives of children as articulated in the policy statement *Every Child Matters: Change for Children*, published in 2004. This policy identified five key outcomes for children and young people: to be healthy, to stay safe, to enjoy and achieve, to make a positive contribution and to achieve economic well-being (Department for Education and Skills, 2004). The CPSU strategy focuses on improving awareness and communication about child abuse and associated preventative measures in sport, the development of evidence about the prevalence and incidence of abuse in sport, the development of a framework of policies, standards and systems that sports can implement to protect children, increasing the capacity and competence of people involved in sport to deal with child protection issues, and striving to integrate initiatives by sport organizations with other agencies and organizations (CPSU, 2006). A cornerstone of the CPSU strategy has been the development of a set of *Standards for Safeguarding and Protecting Children in Sport* (CPSU, 2007). Different versions have been established by each Home Nation 'appropriate to the legislation and structure in each country [and] although the structure of the standards assessment process may differ, the principles are consistent' (NSPCC, 2009b). The version for England is summarized in

Table 4.1	Summary of CPSU Standards for Safeguarding and Protecting Children in Sport
Standard	**Description**
1. Policy	Any organization providing services or activities for children and young people under the age of 18 should have a child protection policy. This is a statement of intent that demonstrates a commitment to safeguard children involved in sport from harm.
2. Procedures and systems	Procedures provide clear step-by-step guidance on what to do in different circumstances. They clarify roles and responsibilities, and lines of communication. Systems for recording information and for dealing with complaints are also needed to ensure procedures are implemented and complied with.
3. Prevention	Measures to help minimize the possibility of children and young people being abused by those in a position of trust.
4. Codes of practice and behaviour	Codes of practice describe what is an acceptable standard of behaviour and promote good practice.
5. Equity	Measures to ensure the needs of all children and young people to be protected from abuse are addressed.
6. Communication	Ways of informing, consulting and listening to all relevant parties about how children involved in the sport are to be safeguarded.
7. Education and training	Opportunities to develop and maintain the necessary skills and understanding to safeguard children.
8. Access to advice and support	Arrangements made to provide essential information and support to those responsible for safeguarding children. Children and young people who are being abused are assisted to get help.
9. Implementation and monitoring	Action taken to ensure that the organization's intentions in relation to safeguarding children are taking place, and to monitor and evaluate action and effectiveness.
10. Influencing	Action taken by the organization to influence, encourage and promote the adoption and implementation of measures to safeguard children by partner organisations.

Source: CPSU (2007).

Table 4.1. These standards (and earlier versions since 2002) provide sport organizations with a framework in which to create safe sport environments and to help them benchmark against other organizations, and were developed after a wide consultative process.

These standards and the focus of the CPSU have been the subject of some criticism. Brackenridge (2004:334) argued that while the creation of the CPSU and associated policies has greatly enhanced the capacity of sport to address child abuse and increased the level of 'ethical reflection in sport', she also stated that an over-emphasis on child protection policy in the UK is potentially detrimental for other groups involved in sport:

It is important to recognize that a false hierarchy of inequalities favours nobody in the end. The relatively narrow focus of the CPSU on children, defined as under 18 years old, draws attention and resources away from those over that age boundary, including many people with disabilities and, especially, adult women in sport.

Brackenridge, Bringer and Bishopp (2005:272) also argued that the standards demand sport organizations 'record and monitor allegations of abuse, yet very few sport organizations have robust case-recording and management systems in place'. So while the policies and associated standards are very well intentioned, in order for them to be effective, sport organizations need to enhance their capacity for better data management and reporting in relation to child protection.

Australia

Efforts by Australian national and state/territory governments to develop policy in relation to child protection in sport were arguably just as slow as those in the UK. Leahy, Pretty, and Tenenbaum (2002:17) highlighted that aside from processes implemented in 2000 by the NSW State Government, 'in Australia, legal and regulatory processes related to sexual abuse prevention, which operate in other public sectors such as health and education, are conspicuously absent in the sport and recreation sector'. The problem of a lack of meaningful regulation was highlighted by Leahy et al.'s (2002:31) study that illustrated 'the high prevalence rates of sexual abuse within the sport environment in Australia' despite the existence of self-regulation in the form of 'coaching codes of ethics and policy guidelines'. The major difference in the development of child protection policies in the UK and Australia was that, in Australia, child abuse was considered as part of a wider policy agenda addressing harassment in sport. The ASC led the development of a series of guidelines for coaches, athletes, organization and administrators focussed on harassment and abuse in sport in the late 1990s. Leahy et al. (2002:32) argued that while these were important resources, the significant 'apathy and systemic inertia, which has for so long characterised the Australian sport industry's approach to child protection in sport' was, in 2002, a formidable obstacle that was yet to be overcome.

Much like the UK situation with sport organizations subject to different policy and procedural requirements between home nations, the legislative power in this area rests with the various Australian state and territory governments, with the result that the regulatory regime varies between jurisdictions. However, there are four common elements to the state and territory regulations regarding child protection and sport: (1) mandatory reporting requirements for individuals to report reasonable suspicions of child abuse, (2) requirements for organizations to screen individuals who work or volunteer with children, (3) requirements to develop organizational-level policy and procedures to deal with child protection issues and (4) in some cases, government sport agencies have 'introduced funding criteria that requires sporting organizations to develop and implement policies and procedures to promote positive and respectful behaviours and to meet obligations relating to harassment, discrimination and child protection' (ASC, 2006:3).

To illustrate how these government policies impact on sport, we now provide a brief review of the NSW Government policy on child protection in sport. The policy delivery agency is NSW Sport and Recreation, part of the NSW Department of the Arts, Sport and Recreation. Their website states their policy as:

NSW Sport and Recreation is committed to a coordinated and comprehensive approach to promoting the protection of children and ensuring that their safety, welfare and wellbeing is maintained at all times. We're here to help sporting and recreation organizations create safe environments for children and young people.

(NSW Sport and Recreation, 2009a)

What do you need to do as an organization?
- Establish a Child Protection Policy
- Ensure all employees and members are aware of your policy and procedures
- Identify child-related employment positions (paid and unpaid)
- Decide on record-keeping procedures associated with the Working With Children Check
- Report any relevant completed disciplinary proceedings against an employee in the course of their employment to the Commission for Children and Young People. Relevant disciplinary proceedings involve child abuse, sexual misconduct involving children or acts of violence directed at children or occurring in the presence of children. (NB: this does not include allegations proven to be false, misconceived or vexatious).
- Nominate a Child Protection Officer
- Run child protection awareness sessions for your staff

What do you need to do administratively?
- Register with NSW Sport and Recreation to get an Employer ID Number
- Always keep records secure and treat information as highly sensitive

What do you do for current staff (paid or unpaid) in child related employment?
- All staff must sign a Prohibited Employment Declaration

What do you do about new staff in child related employment?
- Add information to recruitment packages for identified paid child related positions
- Prospective staff need to sign Prohibited Employment Declarations and Working with Children Check Consent forms
- Screen the preferred applicant for new paid employment
- Conduct structured referee checks on the preferred applicant
- If you decide not to employ someone based on the Working with Children Check, inform the person involved and the Commission for Children and Young People

FIGURE 4.1   *NSW Sport and Recreation Child protection policy requirements for sport organisations. Source: NSW Sport and Recreation (2009c).*

The policy requires sport organizations to adopt a number of measures in relation to child protection under the Children and Young Persons (Care and Protection) Act 1998 who are outlined in Figure 4.1. A key element of these requirements is that sport organizations appoint a Child Protection Officer that coordinates all of an organization's child protection activities and conveys a clear message about the importance of child protection to the organization's members. In addition, all sport organizations must ensure that individuals (paid and voluntary) undergo a Working with Children Check 'to ensure, as far as possible, that people who may pose a risk to children are not employed in

Identify and analyse risk of harm
The organization develops and implements a risk management strategy. This includes a review of existing child protection policies and practices to determine how child-safe and child friendly the organization is and the development of strategies to minimize and prevent risk of harm to children.

Develop codes of conduct for adults and children
The organization has codes of conduct that specify standards of conduct and care when dealing and interacting with children, particularly those in the organization's care. The organization also has codes of conduct to address appropriate behaviour between children. These codes set out professional boundaries, ethical behaviour and unacceptable behaviour.

Choose suitable employees and volunteers
The organization takes all reasonable steps to ensure that it engages the most suitable and appropriate people to work with children. This is more likely to be achieved using a range of screening measures. Such measures aim to minimise the likelihood of engaging (or retaining) people who are unsuitable to work with children. If a criminal history report is obtained as part of their screening process, the organization ensures that the criminal history information is dealt with in accordance with the standards developed by the Chief Executive of the Department for Families and Communities.

Support, train, supervise and enhance performance
The organization ensures that volunteers and employees who work with children or their records have ongoing supervision, support and training such that their performance is developed and enhanced to promote the establishment and maintenance of a child safe environment.

Empower and promote the participation of children in decision-making and service development
The organization promotes the involvement and participation of children and young people in developing and maintaining child safe environments.

Report and respond appropriately to suspected abuse and neglect
The organization ensures that volunteers and employees are able to identify and respond to children at risk of harm. The organization makes all volunteers and employees aware of their responsibilities under the Children's Protection Act 1993 if they have suspicion on reasonable grounds that a child has been or is being abused or neglected.

FIGURE 4.2 *South Australia Child protection requirements for sport organizations. Source: Play by the Rules (2009b).*

roles where they have direct, unsupervised contact with children' (NSW Sport and Recreation, 2009c). The government also offers free training to sport organizations in relation to understanding their obligations and provides a range of information resources about child protection issues.

In an attempt to standardize the approach of state and territory governments to issues such as child protection in sport (and other issues such as harassment, discrimination and inclusive sport environments), the Play by the Rules organization was established through a collaboration between the 'Australian Sports Commission, Human Rights and Equal Opportunity Commission, all state and territory sport and recreation and anti-discrimination agencies and the Queensland Commission for Children, Young People and Child Guardian' (Play By The Rules, 2009a). This organization performs a similar role to the UK CPSU in terms of providing information on mandatory reporting and screening issues. It highlights that 'South Australia and the Northern Territory are the only states where individuals who work in sport are required by law to report any suspicions they may have that a child or young person is at risk of harm' (Play By The Rules, 2009c). The majority of states (Queensland, NSW, Victoria and Western Australia) require people working or volunteering in sport to have a Working with Children Check. In regard to sport organizations developing specific risk management strategies focussed on child protection, only Queensland, South Australia and Victoria have legislated for this requirement. The South Australian requirements are summarized in Figure 4.2 and highlight the significant administrative burden this places on sport organizations.

Canada

In contrast to the policy initiatives evident in the UK and Australia, there has been very little progress in Canada toward the development of specific policies aimed at child protection in sport, or any substantial empirical research efforts. Kerr and Stirling (2008:310) summed up the Canadian situation when they stated that 'despite the advances made in politically affirming the rights of the child in sport, policy developments specifically on the protection against relational child treatment in sport are lacking'. While recognizing the lead role played by the UK and Australia in this policy area, they noted that only 'preliminary developments [in Canada] have been made with respect to the mandated reporting of relational abuse in sport' (Kerr & Stirling, 2008:311). They concluded that the self-regulatory policies and codes of ethics established in Canada by sport organizations such as the Coaching Association of Canada were inadequate and specifically that 'the child-protection policies established so far in Canadian sport are lacking in accountability and universality' (Kerr & Stirling, 2008:311).

In summary, the examples from the UK, Australia and Canada highlight the reluctance of sport to acknowledge the existence of child abuse in sport until relatively recently and the general inability of sport-governing bodies to deliver effective self-regulatory regimes for child protection. The role of government is fundamental to supporting sport in tackling this issue through various regulatory measures such as direct legislation, the provision of policy templates and guidelines, educational resources and funding support to undertake screening of individuals involved in children's sport.

DISCRIMINATION

Under the broad umbrella of member protection policies, the second area we have selected to review is that of racial discrimination. In the UK, the topic of racial discrimination in sport had arguably only been seriously addressed by government since 1998 when Sport England, in conjunction with the Commission for Racial Equality (CRE), established the Sporting Equals program. Prior to that government intervention was restricted to public awareness campaigns targeting racism in sports such as football and rugby league (Long, Robinson, & Spracklen, 2005). While the lead government agency, Sport England, had funded and supported groups facilitating greater equality for women and people with disabilities, the Racial Equality Action Group (also funded by Sport England) felt that 'progress on racial equality had not been as quick as the progress being made' (Long et al., 2005:44) in these other areas. In 2000, Sporting Equals produced the *Racial Equality Charter for Sport*, a statement on racism in sport, and followed that with a framework document *Achieving Racial Equality: A Standard for Sport*. The Standard provides sport organizations with guidelines to tackle racism in sport through three action areas: (1) commitment, policy and planning; (2) participation and public image; and (3) administration and management. These were assessed on three levels of achievement for each area: preliminary, intermediate and advanced. While the standard was available for all sports, intensive support to help sports reach these various levels of achievement was only provided by Sporting Equals to those sports funded by Sport England (Long et al., 2005). Sport England later made it a proviso of receiving funding that sport organizations had to at least have reached the preliminary achievement level by March 2003. Long et al. (2005:46) argued that the poor record of sports achieving this standard prior to the threat of funding cuts indicates 'sport's unwillingness to lead and the resistance of the White community to change'.

In November 2004 'a new Equality Standard was published, which embraced gender and disability as well as race and ethnicity' (Spracklen, Hylton, & Long, 2006:292). This meant that sports were being asked to adopt a generic approach to addressing the issue of discrimination, rather than the previous sport-specific framework. Spracklen et al. (2006:300) argued that the lack of real progress toward eradicating discrimination in sport under either of these frameworks highlighted a fundamental problem of 'the limitation of intervention'. They argued that some people viewed the policy as 'an imposition by the Government, through Sport England, of a performance management framework of audit and inspection' (Spracklen et al., 2006:300). The reality was that most sports included statements about addressing discrimination in their policies, but these never filtered down to actual changes in organizational practice. Spracklen et al.'s (2006:302) criticism of this policy approach is centred on the fact that the policy 'demands evidence of action but not evidence of change'. In other words, the policy requires sport organizations to demonstrate they have changed their policies to address discrimination but the 'lack of sustained and systematic monitoring of participation and involvement' prevents sports from demonstrating real changes in who participates in their respective sport, or alternatively, being criticised for a lack of real progress in relation to discrimination. Shaw (2007:430) also criticises the dependence on an audit culture evident in the policy and argued that 'the bureaucratisation of equality is at odds with process-oriented research in this area and falls short of providing cultural and structural change within organizations'.

In Australia, as was the case for child protection, racial and other forms of discrimination in sport have been addressed as part of a broader suite of member protection policies and the legislative power in this area rests with the various Australian state and territory governments, with the result that the regulatory regime varies between jurisdictions. However, the ASC's harassment-free sport strategy 'assists the sports industry address discrimination, abuse and other inappropriate behaviours by helping sports to create safe, respectful and harassment-free sport environments' (ASC, 2009a). The strategy was first developed in 1996:

> *In response to increased litigation in relation to discrimination, harassment and abuse in sport; increased media attention given to the issue; growing concerns that sport may not be aware of and/or meeting its legal and ethical obligations and Government*

legislation... [and currently includes]...a mandatory requirement for national sporting organizations funded by the Australian Government to develop and implement a policy that addresses harassment, discrimination and child abuse.

(ASC, 2009a)

While no empirical research has been conducted on the efficacy of this policy, there are similarities in the way the ASC requires NSOs to establish policies on discrimination as a condition of receiving government funding, in much the same way that Sport England requires its funded NGBs to meet the Equality Standard conditions.

CONCLUSION

In the previous chapter we reviewed the arguments for and against sports maintaining the ability to self-regulate the conduct of their actual sporting activity. These same arguments about sports having a lack of mandate, a potential lack of accountability and a poor track record of self-regulation certainly seem to apply in relation to member protection policies, specifically in the areas of child protection and discrimination. The first of our four questions we sought to address in this chapter is what are the reasons government gets involved in direct regulation of member protection. We conclude that governments have done so to overcome concerns about the willingness and capacity of sport-governing bodies to self-regulate in relation to these difficult issues, a lack of a mandate for sport-governing bodies to regulate the behaviour of their members in the public interest and a lack of accountability sport organizations have in relation to self-regulating the behaviour of people involved in their organizations. To effectively combat issues such as child abuse, sport organizations require government intervention in terms of assisting them undertake screening of individuals involved in their sport (i.e. Working with Children or Police Checks) and to provide a mechanism where inappropriate behaviours can be reported to a judicial authority (i.e. mandatory reporting processes).

Our second question focuses on establishing whether sport has been central in determining the nature and extent of such regulatory interventions. It is evident that in relation to child protection in the UK, the lead sport agency shared a lack of initial willingness to fully engage in the issues with the sport-governing bodies and only initiated real change after significant pressure from certain sections of the sport industry. Sport has thus far tended to rely on government agencies and other non-profit groups, such as the NSPCC, to provide advice as to what form of policy development they should undertake themselves, and (in Australia at least) have been some-what reluctant to overcome what some have described as apathy and systemic inertia about developing effective self-regulation in the area. In relation to discrimination and harassment in sport, sports have also been largely on the receiving end of government led initiatives, and while they have been consulted about the mechanics of any regulatory actions, they could not be considered as central to the development of regulatory policy.

The third question we have sought to answer is to identify what are the variety of regulatory instruments employed by government. In terms of the Baldwin and Cave (1999) framework, these have ranged from command and control strategies (legislating to force sport (and other) organizations to engage in practices such as mandatory reporting and screening), mandating self-regulation (requiring sport organizations to develop their own policies and procedures in relation to child protection and discrimination or face the withdrawal of government funding support), and the use of direct action through forming Agencies or Commissions to carry out a range of information and other support work for sport organizations on these issues.

Our final question relates to the impact on sport of these regulatory policies. In simple terms, they obviously impose a significant compliance burden on sport-governing bodies to develop policies and procedures in these areas, to report progress to funding agencies, to create data management systems to monitor cases of child abuse and discrimination or harassment and for individuals to undertake training and development programs. As noted by Spracklen et al. (2006), there was some feeling that these regulatory actions were an imposition on sport, and indeed, the need for sport organizations to undergo significant cultural change to be able to effectively meet the challenges of these policies at the lower levels is evident. There is also a question of the capacity of sport-governing bodies to effectively cope with the data management and reporting requirements of these regulatory regimes, particularly among the smaller sports (Brackenridge, 2005).

CHAPTER 5

Gambling and Sport

The intersection of gambling and sport is an increasingly important area of public policy, particularly as gambling represents one of the fastest growing revenue streams for sport organizations, second only to broadcast rights (Sellenger, 2006). Governments also reap significant taxation returns from licencing wagering and betting operators associated with sport. Forms of gambling can be divided into two categories: gaming activities (games of chance such as lotteries, keno, electronic gaming machines and raffles) and wagering (betting money on the outcome of a horse race, sporting contest or other event). Using examples from Australian, Canadian, New Zealand and UK jurisdictions, this chapter explores three broad areas of policy that affect the gambling and sport industries. First, the desire to ensure integrity in the conduct of sporting competitions through both governments and sport governing bodies regulating the activities of individuals and organizations involved in playing, officiating or administering sporting competitions on which betting fields might be made. Second, the development of regulatory systems for wagering and betting operators by governments, in order to control illegal betting activities and to capture taxation revenues. Third, ways in which public policy has evolved to fund specific sport events and sport organization activities through the development of national and state/provincial lotteries and the more recent moves to protect the interests of sport organizations in capturing product fees for the provision of sporting product to wagering and betting operators. In addition to exploring these policy areas, the chapter also reviews the degree of policy coherence and convergence evident across Australia, Canada, New Zealand and the UK and identifies some future policy challenges in the area of sport and gambling. But initially, the scale of wagering and sport betting markets in those four jurisdictions is defined.

The Australian Productivity Commission (1999) defined sports betting as wagering on local, national or international sporting events (other than horse and greyhound racing), with bookmakers and Totalisator Agency Boards (TABs). TABs provide punters the opportunity to engage in parimutuel betting such that the wagering operator places all bets on any particular betting contingency (i.e. outcomes or placing of a single race) into a pool, deducts a commission at a pre-determined rate and the remainder is then treated as a dividend pool that is divided equally amongst successful bettors. Sports betting was largely illegal in Australia until the 1980s when a limited amount of sports betting was legalized through the state-owned TABs and bookmakers operating on course at horseracing meetings (Australian Institute for Gambling Research, 1999). The 1990s saw the emergence of licenced sports betting agencies (commonly known as corporate bookmakers) based in the Northern Territory (NT) and the Australian Capital Territory (ACT) (Australian Institute for Gambling Research, 1999). The view of the Productivity Commission (1999) was that the expansion of sports betting in Australia was the result of a wider liberalization of gambling policy by state and territory governments and the emergence of internet technology to facilitate secure financial transactions between punters and sports betting providers. In addition, the July 2003 *Report of the Betting Exchange Task Force* to the Conference of Australasian Racing Ministers (2003) stated that legal sports wagering is now firmly entrenched in all Australian states and territories. Statistics gathered by the Queensland Government Office of Economic and Statistical Research (2006) also shows a steady increase in sports betting turnover across Australia. Total gambling turnover in Australia exceeded $AUD 142.8 billion in 2004–2005, up from $AUD 36.9 billion in 1992–1993 with the majority of this expended on gaming machines and casinos (Office of Economic and Statistical Research, 2006). The proportion of gambling turnover associated with wagering on thoroughbred horse racing across Australia in 2004–2005 was approximately 11% or $AUD 15.6 billion and on sports betting approximately 1% or $AUD 1.7 billion (Office of Economic and Statistical Research, 2006). Hewett (2006:23) noted that sports betting in Australia had grown 'at an extraordinary rate of nearly 30 per cent a year over the past several years'.

However, not all jurisdictions are as liberal or structured in their approaches to gambling as Australia. For example, in Canada, betting directly on the outcome of single sports events is illegal, although most provincial governments operate lotteries based on sports competitions. However, the most recent data show that wagering on horse racing is a far smaller proportion of overall gambling revenue (measured as wagers less prize payouts, before operating expenses deducted) as compared to Australia with only about 3.0% or $CAN 405 million of $CAN 13.3 billion earned via wagering in 2005–2006 (Canadian Partnership for Responsible Gambling, 2007). As is the case in Australia, the bulk of Canadian gambling revenue is derived from either government-owned or licenced electronic gaming machines and casinos.

Sports betting was introduced in New Zealand in 1996 and has enjoyed consistent growth since then with turnover increasing from $NZ 4.8 million to $NZ 131.5 million in 2006–2007 (Department of Internal Affairs, 2007). Turnover of wagering on horse racing for 2006–2007 was $NZ 1.3 billion (Department of Internal Affairs, 2007). Much like Australia, sports betting and wagering as a proportion of all gambling expenditure was approximately 13.3% or $NZ 269 million out of a total of $NZ 2 billion in 2006–2007 (Department of Internal Affairs, 2007). The bulk of gambling expenditure is associated with electronic gaming machines and casinos.

The UK gambling market, in stark contrast to Australia, Canada and New Zealand, is dominated by the sports betting and wagering sector and the government-owned national lottery. Total gambling turnover in the UK was approximately £GBP 91.5 billion in 2005–2006. About 38% of this can be attributed to sports betting and wagering and another 25% to the national lottery (Davis, 2007).

In three of these four jurisdictions (Australia, New Zealand and the UK) it is apparent that sports betting, and to a lesser extent wagering on horse racing, has grown at a significant rate over the last 10–15 years. In Canada, there is mounting public pressure to legalize sports betting as the gambling market has matured to the limits of current regulatory arrangements rather than through any slackening of consumer demand for gambling (Azmier, 2005). There is no doubt that the sports betting and wagering markets are continuing to grow, and together with the associated issue of governments turning to general gambling taxation revenues and specific lotteries to fund sporting developments, presents a number of policy issues. We now turn to reviewing the first of three policy issues at the intersection of sport and gambling.

INTEGRITY PROTECTION

Forrest and Simmons (2003) noted that the integrity of sport has been the subject of some debate since the 1700s. They cited Munting (1996) who described how the laws of cricket and golf were codified in 1744 in order to satisfy the needs of bookmakers to operate with consistent rules to enable disputes over bets to be settled by an appropriate governing body. The infamous Black Sox baseball scandal, where eight players from the Chicago White Sox were accused of throwing the 1919 World Series against the Cincinnati Reds and were subsequently banned for life from professional baseball, is described as the 'most notorious example of betting-related corruption' in sport by Forrest and Simmons (2003:606). More recent examples of claims of match fixing in professional cricket and tennis in the 1990s and 2000s and of point shaving in US college basketball and football highlight the continual problem of protecting the integrity of sport (Forrest & Simmons, 2003). Fitzgerald (2007) cited an example of a 'rugby league team not taking a conversion attempt 13 seconds before full time...even though it made no difference to winning or losing the game itself, it affected payouts to those punters who had bet on the points spread in that game' as poor self-regulation by sports in this area. Failing to ensure sporting, competitions are conducted under appropriate rules and that players, officials and administrators do not act outside those rules to affect game outcomes or team performance, can lead to a lack of public confidence in the integrity of sporting leagues, teams or individual are athletes. This lack of confidence is likely to result in lower fan interest and attendance, lower tickets sales, lower merchandise revenues, diminished broadcast rights value and a reduction in the amount individuals willing to bet on competition outcomes.

Concerns over integrity in sports betting in the UK were highlighted in 2006 when the Department of Culture, Media and Sport (DCMS) hosted an Integrity in Sports Betting Conference to launch a voluntary code of practice for sports governing bodies that would assist them protect the integrity of their respective sport. The 10-point plan included provisions to regulate the behaviour of sport participants in relation to betting, to ensure sport governing bodies provided information to statutory authorities that might be investigating sports betting activities associated with their sport and to encourage sport governing bodies to enter into information-sharing agreements with sports betting operators. It also stipulated that sport governing bodies would appoint an individual to be responsible for sports betting matters and that sports should seek to share integrity provision best practice with other sport governing bodies (Gambling Commission, 2007a). The objectives of the plan were to encourage sports to be proactive in developing ways to protect the probity of betting on sports, to safeguard participants and consumers and to develop relationships between government regulators, sports governing bodies and sports betting operators. The UK Gambling Commission reported that by mid-2006, 12 sport governing bodies had committed to the 10-point plan, including the sports that attract the majority of betting such as cricket, football, horse racing, tennis and the two rugby codes (Gambling Commission, 2007a).

In March 2007, the UK Gambling Commission released its *Integrity in Sports Betting Information Sharing* paper. This was the start of a consultation process among the Commission, major sport governing bodies and sports betting providers to explore how to better regulate activities associated with sports betting. The Commission's consultation process explored a number of core issues, including reviewing the existing sports integrity models in sports such as horse racing, greyhound racing, football and cricket. The review highlighted, unsurprisingly, that the two racing codes had long-established integrity models in place and invested considerable funds in maintaining integrity. In cricket and football, the increased costs of integrity protection were noted to divert funds away from grassroots sport development. As the amount gambled on these sports increases, the sport governing bodies believe that the costs of policing integrity issues ought to be borne as a contribution from the income generated from betting on the sport rather than from general revenue.

The review also noted that the Association of British Bookmakers (ABB) considered that 'there is no evidence of systematic failings in the protection of the integrity of sport as a substantive problem' (Gambling Commission, 2007a:6). The Gambling Commission agreed with this assessment when it noted in its final policy position paper that 'the evidence points to the number of incidents giving cause for concern about integrity in sports betting being low' (Gambling Commission, 2007b:1). Arguments to impose tighter regulation on sports betting transactions through more stringent auditing and risk assessments were dismissed by the ABB and not imposed by the Gambling Commission for fear that 'extra regulation may encourage sports betting operations to relocate offshore' (Gambling Commission, 2007b:1) with a resultant loss of taxation revenue.

The only other jurisdiction that has developed direct regulation in the interests of ensuring integrity in sports betting is the State of Victoria in Australia. The major professional sporting codes in Australia formed a group called the Coalition of Major Professional Sports (COMPS) in late 2003 with the aim of providing a collective voice for those sports most affected by sports betting policy. COMPS comprised the Australian Rugby Union (ARU), National Rugby League (NRL), Tennis Australia, Football Federation Australia (FFA), Cricket Australia (CA) and the Professional Golf Association Tour of Australasia (PGA Tour). The largest professional sport organization in Australia, the Australian Football League (AFL), remains aligned to COMPS, but is not a formal member. COMPS concerns with sports betting policy and the associated regulatory framework prior to 2006 focussed on two central issues: firstly, maintaining integrity of their sporting product in relation to sports betting activities, and secondly, ensuring sporting organizations 'receive a fair share of revenue wagered on their respective sports' (COMPS, 2006:2). In response to pressure from COMPS regarding regulatory reform of sports betting, the Victorian State Government released a discussion paper on the regulation of sports betting in March 2006 (State of Victoria, 2006). The discussion paper noted that at that time there was no legislative requirement that wagering operators be authorized by the controlling bodies of sport or that wagering and sport organizations should cooperate to ensure sports betting was subject to high standards of integrity.

The discussion paper outlined three issues concerning the development of integrity systems in sports. The first was the general lack of rules, codes of conduct and disciplinary procedures within sports other than racing that were designed to control the behaviour and activities of players, officials and administrators in relation to sport betting. The second was the absence of incentives in place for sports to develop such rules and codes, in particular the lack of product fee revenues from wagering operators to finance their development and implementation. The third issue was whether integrity concerns should be subject to public or private regulation. In other words, should sport governing bodies be responsible for regulating sports betting or should a government agency be responsible.

The resulting legislation, the Gambling and Racing Legislation Amendment (Sports Betting) Act 2007, and accompanying regulations, the Gambling Regulation (Sports Betting Fees) (Amendment) Regulations 2007 came into effect in late 2007. Together they represented major changes to how sports betting was regulated in Victoria, including provisions for wagering operators to pay product fees to sport organizations (discussed later in this chapter) and addressing integrity protection. The new regulatory regime required sport governing bodies to apply to the Victorian Commission for Gambling Regulation to be a 'controlling body' for sport. Controlling bodies are responsible for the following:

1. managing sports events or competitions;

2. ensuring adequate integrity controls are in place;

3. allocating sufficient resources to enforce integrity controls;

4. implementing appropriate processes to report on matters relevant to the betting market and

5. developing policies on sharing information with sports betting providers.

While the Victorian legislation is a step in the right direction towards improving integrity protection for sports betting, it only applies to sport events held in Victoria and assumes that sports betting revenues received by sports controlling bodies from product fees paid by sports betting operators will be used to develop these integrity systems. Sports betting operators also conduct their business on a national or international scale so this state-based legislation further complicates the regulatory regime across Australia. This issue was recognized by the State of Victoria (2006:17), which stated that 'sports betting takes place across jurisdictional boundaries and that, to be truly effective, any regulatory regime should be part of a national approach that provides for consistency between the states and territories'.

In summary, the spectre of potential problems with the integrity of sports betting has led to recent changes in government policy in the UK and Australia. While there is arguably little evidence of systemic corruption in the conduct of sport, the potential for loss of public confidence in sport and subsequent negative impacts on revenue for sport organizations that might result from sports betting scandals, would have serious consequences for most sport organizations. The increased financial costs associated with monitoring, education and enforcement of integrity systems in sport would seem to be insignificant relative to the potential losses that sports might be forced to bear from betting scandals affecting public confidence in their sport.

REGULATION OF WAGERING AND BETTING PROVIDERS

There are four types of wagering and sports betting providers: totalisators, on-course bookmakers operating at racecourse meetings, corporate bookmakers operating off-site from racecourses, and the newest type, betting exchanges. This section briefly outlines how each of these are regulated in the Australian, Canadian, New Zealand and UK markets and the associated public policy issues associated with regulating their operation.

All Australian state and territory governments have granted their respective TABs an exclusive licence to conduct wagering and sports betting in retail agencies, hotels and clubs and over the telephone and internet with the result that in each jurisdiction, the respective TAB operator enjoys a monopoly. The TABs in all states except NSW pool their sports betting under the TAB Sportsbet brand managed by TABCORP Limited, the privatized Victorian TAB. The privatized NSW TAB, TAB Limited, conducted sports betting under the SportsTAB brand until mid 2004, when it was acquired by TABCORP. The SportsTAB brand is still used in NSW, but is now managed by TABCORP, which has effectively created a national TAB pool for sports betting. While all of the privatized or state-run TABs offer fixed odds sports betting on sporting events, the sports betting market is dominated by corporate bookmakers based in the NT and the ACT. Sports betting taxation revenue for state and territory governments has also increased, more so for the states with multiple sports betting providers, but revenue returns differ markedly between the states and territories because of different rates of taxation (Australian Racing Board, 2007). These differences in regulations, taxation rates and the sports betting products offered by the TABs in each jurisdiction also extends to the way in which bookmakers are licenced.

As of 30 June 2007, there were 638 on-course bookmaker licences issued across Australia for the three codes of racing (thoroughbred, harness and greyhounds), the majority of which were issued in the major racing states of New South Wales (220), Victoria (181) and Queensland (112) (Australian Racing Board, 2007:10). There were also 10 licenced corporate bookmakers in the NT, and six in the ACT (Australian Gaming Council, 2007). The power to issue bookmaking licences differs between each of these jurisdictions. In NSW, Victoria and Queensland, the racing governing body is empowered to issue bookmaker licences (including sports betting), while this function remains in the hands of state or territory regulatory agencies in those jurisdictions where the horse racing industry is relatively smaller (South Australia, Western Australia and Tasmania) or negligible (ACT and NT). Hoye (2006b:158) argued that 'this could be due to governments accepting the regulatory role in the absence of the controlling body for racing being able to perform the function, or governments (in the case of the NT and ACT) wishing to control the licencing function in order to maximise taxation revenue by creating opportunities for corporate bookmakers to offer wagering and betting on activities conducted in other states of Australia'. It should also be noted here that none of these jurisdictions have seen fit to empower sport governing bodies with any role in the processes to licence bookmakers. The newest form of wagering operator to be granted a licence to operate in Australian jurisdictions has been betting exchanges, a form of wagering where punters can bet with each other through a third-party provider. The first of these was Betfair, a company that was granted a licence to operate onshore by the Tasmanian Government in 2006. This in effect enabled it to receive bets (including sports betting) from any person in Australia via the internet.

The majority of gambling activity in Canada is government owned and operated (Azmier, 2005). The remainder, including betting on horse racing and some sports-based lotteries, is regulated by each provincial government. This regulation extends to licencing racetracks to be able to conduct racing and wagering activities and the licencing of teletheatres (off-track betting locations operated by racetracks). In many ways, the federalized regulatory system in place in Australia is replicated in Canada, but the Canadian system remains heavily controlled by provincial government agencies rather than some licencing functions being devolved to governing bodies as is the case in licencing bookmakers in Australia.

In many ways, the regulatory system in place in New Zealand could be considered 'leading edge' with a single agency, the New Zealand Racing Board (NZRB), acting as the regulator and provider for all racing, wagering and sports betting activities. The NZRB is established under a single piece of national legislation and is charged with running the TAB, the country's sole provider of betting on racing and sport and maximizing wagering and sports betting profits for the benefit of racing and other sports. The NZRB returns a proportion of every dollar spent on wagering and sports betting back to the relevant sporting code. There are no bookmakers licenced in New Zealand, thus all wagering and sports betting is conducted via the NZRB.

In contrast to the federalist systems of regulating wagering and sports betting in Australia and Canada, the UK system is more like the New Zealand centralized model. Under the Gambling Act 2005, the Gambling Commission regulates all commercial gambling in Great Britain, apart from spread betting and the national lottery (Gambling Commission, 2007c). This extends to betting on horse racing, football or other sporting events. The Commission's stated objectives in regulating these activities are to keep crime out of gambling, to ensure that gambling is conducted fairly and openly and to protect children and the vulnerable from being exploited by gambling (Gambling Commission, 2007c). In fulfilling this role, the Commission issues licences in three areas:

1. General betting licencees are able to offer facilities for betting as premises-based bookmakers (off-course) and on tracks (on-course), as well as by remote means (for example by telephone or over the internet).

2. Pool betting incorporates racecourse, football and other sports pool operators as well as 'fantasy football' type competitions. It can be conducted in person, for example the Tote accepts pool bets on tracks and in high street betting shops, or remotely, such as through an internet betting site run by one of the football pools operators.

3. Betting intermediaries facilitate the making or acceptance of bets between others. Remote betting intermediaries, often called betting exchanges, generally operate through the internet (Gambling Commission, 2007d).

While there appears to be a huge variation in the systems employed for regulating wagering and sports betting in these four jurisdictions, they are each tackling similar public policy issues. The first is to restrict access to the wagering and sports betting markets, either by stipulating the type of wagering or betting allowed or by creating monopolies to make it easier to regulate operators and to maximize taxation revenues. The second is to control what have become an increasingly wider range of legalized gambling activities through the creation of strict licencing regimes and centralized monitoring agencies. In many ways, the schema developed by Miers (2004) to describe the 'British model of commercial gambling regulation' can be used here as a basis to portray the regulatory system for wagering and sports betting. The first element is to regulate the probity of suppliers by requiring individuals and organizations to hold a licence qualifying them to work or operate within the industry. The second is to regulate the supply of wagering products and services by restricting where and when such activities can take place. The third is to regulate what wagering or sports betting products are permissible, such as the type of events on which people can bet and specifying the medium through which people can bet (i.e. telephone, internet, retail outlet). The fourth element is to regulate who is allowed to place bets. The final element is to secure compliance to these conditions via the actions of regulatory agencies, the imposition of penalties for breaching licence conditions and inspection and auditing of wagering and sports betting activities.

The two-tiered layers of government in the UK and New Zealand have arguably made it easier to achieve these policy aims through national legislation and agencies, while the federalist systems of Australia and Canada have led to a more fractured approach at the provincial and state levels. What is common in all the jurisdictions, however, is the attempt to maintain the integrity of the sport and associated wagering and betting activities in order to protect the interdependent financial interests of sport governing bodies, wagering operators (of all types) and governments.

FUNDING SPORT THROUGH GAMBLING DISTRIBUTIONS

As highlighted earlier, one area that until recently had been a 'policy vacuum' was the absence of legislative requirements in most jurisdictions for sports betting operators to pay product fees to sport governing bodies in exchange for the use of their sport as a market for betting. The exceptions are New Zealand, where sports betting operators have been required since 1996 to pay product fees to sport governing bodies in return for profiting from betting on their sport product and the recent regulatory reforms in Victoria, Australia. Forrest and Simmons (2003:603) noted that 'team sports are less well placed than racing to capture part of any surplus generated by betting because the existence of these sports does not typically depend on betting interest'. In other words, their popularity as a sporting contest in itself will be enough to generate fan interest and thus ticket and merchandise sales and the sale of broadcast rights income. Forrest and Simmons (2003) also noted that any move to introduce legislative requirements for domestic sports betting operators to pay product fees might simply drive them offshore in the modern globalized betting market. At the same time, however, they recognized that sports betting is the fastest growing form of gambling, that sport governing bodies are not unaware of this trend and that they are moving to secure access to this new revenue stream.

The recent reforms to sports betting legislation in Victoria were discussed earlier in this chapter. Part of these reforms focussed on addressing the concerns of sporting organizations and that they should receive a product fee from wagering operators. These concerns were expressed in the COMPS submission to the Victorian State Government discussion paper on sports betting:

> ... we note that all members of COMPS, and indeed the majority of sporting organisations in Australia, are not-for-profit organisations, charged with the responsibility of reinvesting all surplus revenues back into the relevant sport, from grass roots to high performance, and into the specific infrastructure which supports it. Furthermore, it should be noted that each of the sports represented by COMPS, and Australian sporting organisations more generally, currently expend substantial funds and resources in promoting, conducting and developing their sports throughout Australia, and in ensuring the processes which touch upon integrity are maintained and effectively implemented. The betting product that is produced by sports, whether it is a tennis match or a rugby union fixture, is currently being utilised by various wagering operators across Australia without any mandated or consistent compensation back to the sport.
>
> (COMPS, 2006:5, 6)

This argument was accepted and the subsequent regulatory reforms in Victoria now require sports betting operators to negotiate product fee payments with sport governing bodies. Such moves, however, may require sports to adapt their game design to maximize the revenue returns from new forms of gambling. As Forrest and Simmons (2003:605) highlight, 'matches divided into quarters would provide windows for betting on the result while, if betting on penalties became popular, there may be a demand for rule changes that would increase the number of penalty decisions'. The future possibility of sports adapting their rules to meet the requirements of betting providers mirrors the changes sports have made to accommodate broadcast partners, which suggests that sports may have to be similarly flexible to increase their betting-related revenues (Forrest & Simmons, 2003).

The second policy concern associated with the funding of sport from gambling activities is the hypothecation of gaming distributions for community and elite sport development such as the use of national lotteries to fund sport. As noted by Forrest and Simmons (2003:599), many governments permit forms of gambling, but seek to appease 'those who regard the activity as distasteful or immoral by earmarking all or part of the associated tax revenue to sectors with a more favourable image, such as education, health care, culture, or, of course, sport'. Citing examples from Hong Kong, China, Sweden, Canada and Britain, Forrest and Simmons (2003:599) argue that 'many jurisdictions employ revenue from hypothecated lottery or other gambling taxes to build infrastructure required for hosting international events, or to train elite athletes, or to improve facilities for recreational sportsmen and sportswomen'.

One of the largest national lotteries, the UK National Lottery, is the preferred gambling medium of UK citizens. With half the funds retained for the operation of the lottery, distributions to treasury and allocations to five nominated causes, of which sport is one, the lottery effectively acts as a sport tax for those people who buy lottery tickets. The funds have been used to support the operation of UK Sport, the agency responsible for elite sport development, and for general community sport development through the sports councils. In the most recent financial year, a total of over 301 million pounds was provided to the sports councils (National Lottery Distribution Fund, 2007). In addition, the funds have been used for major facility and stadia developments for Commonwealth and Olympic Games. Indeed, the 2012 London Olympic Bid was based on substantial funding for the Games being made available from the lottery distributions (Forrest & Simmons, 2003). Arguably, the lottery could be seen to be a windfall for sport that is not sustainable 'given secular decline in sales of lottery products' (Forrest & Simmons, 2003:602). Forrest and Simmons (2003) argue that one alternative could be to do away with the hypothecation to sport and allocate funding to sport from general government revenues in order to avoid major projects being funded that might not otherwise be supported in the absence of such a 'regressive tax'.

The impact of the lottery funding scheme has also had some unintended consequences (Garrett, 2004). Based on research into the behaviour of sports clubs that had received funding via the UK National Lottery, Garrett (2004:27) found evidence that the conditions of lottery funding with which clubs had to comply were, at times, 'inconsistent and incompatible with the long established norms and values'. In addition, the reporting requirements for receipt of lottery funding might outweigh the financial benefits that clubs might accrue from such funding opportunities. The danger is that if such schemes, driven by a desire to demonstrate accountability for the distribution and use of funds, impose overly bureaucratic compliance and reporting requirements on sports clubs, it may be that 'only the larger, more professionalized and formalized voluntary sport clubs feel they are able to manage a project and produce the required outcomes' (Garrett, 2004:28). This would thus result in a narrower distribution of lottery funding and impact on sport development at the community level.

CONCLUSION

This chapter has explored three of the more important policy issues concerning the relationship between sport and gambling, namely efforts to ensure integrity in the conduct of sporting competitions, regulating wagering and betting operators, and the funding of sport lotteries and the capture of product fees by sporting organizations from wagering and betting operators. The examples provided from the Australian, Canadian, New Zealand and the UK jurisdictions on each of these policy issues enable us to draw several conclusions in relation to our questions concerning the rationales governments have used to justify policy intervention in this area, the centrality of sport organizations in the policy community, the type of regulatory strategies employed by government and the existing (or likely) impact of these regulatory policies on sport organizations.

Firstly, while there are marked differences in the structure of the regulatory regimes in each of the jurisdictions, there is a degree of coherence in how they regulate access to the wagering and sports betting markets and the level of controls imposed on wagering and sports betting operators. For example, all jurisdictions impose licence conditions on individuals and organizations wishing to operate a wagering or sports betting operation in order to maximize probity and thus consumer confidence in wagering products.

Secondly, the rate of sports betting growth in each of these jurisdictions is similar and represents one of the fastest growing forms of gambling in each country. Policy makers in each country are thus conducting reviews of sports betting and developing policy solutions as the globalized sports betting market expands. There is evidence therefore of a degree of policy learning and associated convergence as each jurisdiction monitors regulatory reforms and policy developments in other countries. Some similarity in how they deal with common issues of probity, licencing, internet-based technology developments and protecting sports governing bodies rights to product fees would appear to be inevitable. In relation to the regulatory rationales identified by Baldwin and Cave (1999), governments are intervening in this policy area to address the issues of monopoly markets (i.e. licencing sports betting and wagering operators), windfall profits (i.e. transfer some of the profits on sports betting and wagering to fund sport development and infrastructure), information inadequacies (i.e. informing consumers about sports betting operations and reporting requirements) and distributive justice and social policy (through restricting access to sports betting and wagering markets by undesirable individuals).

Thirdly, in terms of the regulatory strategies outlined by Baldwin and Cave (1999), governments have employed a wide range in relation to their intervention into the relationship between gambling and sport. These include command and control strategies (legislation to prohibit certain activities or to re-distribute the profits of wagering and sports betting), disclosure requirements (requiring sports betting transactions to be totally transparent), franchising (limiting the number of wagering licences available in certain jurisdictions) and direct action (state agencies to conduct wagering and sports betting operations).

The fourth conclusion is that there appears to be an increase in the lobbying power of sport governing bodies with policy makers that is more congruent with the growth of the sports betting market and the associated potential increases in taxation revenues for governments. In this sense, sport seems to be positioned as a much more central member of the policy community associated with wagering and sports betting. There is evidence that the arguments put forward by Hoye (2006b) that sporting codes lack any serious regulatory policy input to wagering and sports betting policy may be losing some legitimacy. Hoye (2006b:169) stated that 'the racing industry has dominated the policy landscape with its high level of technical knowledge of gambling, wagering and sports betting and well established political clout with government'. This, at least in Australia, could be attributed to the 'lack of an inclusive policy forum that enables sporting organisations to liaise with state and territory governments on the issue of sports betting, in comparison to the long standing relationships between government and racing industries in regulating racing activities and establishing the TABs from the 1960s (Painter, 1991)' (Hoye, 2006b:169). The recent regulatory reforms in Victoria, Australia and the more inclusive policy communities evident in New Zealand and the UK suggest that sport could now be described as more central to policy development in the area of sports betting than previously considered.

Finally, there remain significant policy challenges in the intersection of sport and gambling. As stated at the start of this chapter, the continued increase in popularity of sports betting over other forms of gambling will result in sports betting revenues being second only to broadcast rights revenues for the major sporting codes. This increased dependence will require sport organizations to develop robust systems to ensure integrity in their sport and protect consumer confidence in their sporting product. Sport organizations will have to increase their knowledge and capacity to deal with changes in sports betting technologies and formats and the associated policy issues of integrity and protection of intellectual property rights associated with the provision of data to wagering and sports betting operators. Sport organizations will also need to work with regulators to ensure they retain control of their sport from wagering and sports betting operators. It is clear that the intersection of sport and gambling will continue to present sports, wagering operators and governments ongoing policy challenges that will require cooperative efforts to ensure their mutually interdependent interests are protected.

CHAPTER 6

Media Regulation

A further area of regulatory policy associated with sport we have selected to explore focuses on government intervention in the relationship between sport and the media, specifically broadcast television. Media organizations have become essential partners for professional and non-profit sport organizations. The breadth and depth of the coverage that media organizations provide their sporting partners is of such significance that it has the capacity to influence the social and commercial practices of millions of people. Their financial relationship is also significant, so much so that sport and the media are often regarded as interdependent (Wenner, 1998). One of the consequences of the ways in which the social, commercial and financial aspects of the relationship between sport and media organizations have developed is that governments around the world have increasingly sought to intervene through direct regulation in order to protect consumers and the efficiency of the sport media market.

Motta and Polo (1997:327) noted that the broadcasting industry is 'neither purely competitive nor entirely regulated'. The sport broadcasting industry is no different, with different types and intensity of regulation applied in a variety of national and pan-national contexts. The media industry's ever-changing complexity and diversity is such that governments often find it difficult to apply regulatory frameworks that adequately meet their policy objectives and allow the market to function as efficiently as possible. The sport media landscape is also often regarded as a separate component of the much broader media landscape because of its special features: significant audience appeal, vigorous competition between broadcasters, relatively cheap production costs, and a mutually reinforcing web of promotion between different types of media (modes and relationship to the sport).

Hoehn and Lancefield (2003:566) noted that the 'pre-eminent position of sports programming in a channel's offering and as a key driver of a TV delivery/distribution platform has forced governments to intervene in media merger proposals, sports-rights contract negotiations, and disputes among

TV distribution systems over access to content'. The importance of sport has been enhanced by a shift in the broadcasting industry paradigm, from one in which content, such as sport, was competing for broadcast time on media outlets that were scarce, to one in which a multitude of outlets and forms are competing for scarce content (Cowie & Williams, 1997). In the latter paradigm a range of products are considered to be 'premium content', with sport often viewed as the most valuable because it not only attracts large audiences, but is relatively cheap to produce and its commercial potential is often not hindered by cultural and language barriers.

The importance of sport to both the modern media industry and consumers has resulted in government seeking to regulate the relationship between sport and broadcast media in four major areas. First, government regulation attempts to prevent the broadcast rights to sport events migrating exclusively from free-to-air television to pay or subscription television. Second, governments have developed regulatory policy aimed at ensuring that sport and media organizations do not engage in anti-competitive behaviour in the buying and selling of these broadcast rights. Such behaviour can lead to monopolies being created that will necessarily restrict supply, which in turn will raises price to a level that will exploit consumers (New & LeGrand, 1999). Third, governments regulate to prohibit certain types of advertising being associated with sports broadcasting, such as tobacco advertising. Finally, government regulation attempts to limit or prevent any negative consequences of the vertical integration of the sport and media industries, such as the purchase of a sport team or league by a media organization. This chapter examines each of these policy areas, drawing on examples from a number of countries, in order to identify the reasons cited by government for undertaking such direct intervention in regulating the relationship between sport and the media, to identify the centrality of sport in determining the nature and extent of such interventions, the variety of regulatory instruments used and to make some assessment of their impact on sport.

SALE OF BROADCAST RIGHTS

The competition between broadcasters to secure the rights to sport events is based on their perceived value in

(i) generating advertising and programme sponsorship revenue, particularly by attracting the most difficult to reach, and high-disposable-income consumer group, the 16–34 ABC1 males;
(ii) driving subscription penetration and reducing churn by building loyalty, and, increasingly, driving interactive revenues (such as

betting) in digital pay-TV and online distribution markets, which can also have positive spillover effects to the broadcaster's overall brand, as well as demand for other content and products; and (iii) achieving public-service obligations, including the coverage of a wide range of sports, minority sports, and 'national games'.

(Hoehn & Lancefield, 2003:554)

The value of sport rights, specifically broadcast rights for football, are derived from what are considered to be their unique characteristics:

First, football is an ephemeral product as viewers are often only interested in live broadcasts. Next, substitution is very limited, because viewers who want to see a given football event are unlikely to be satisfied with the coverage of another event. Finally, the exclusive concentration of rights in the hands of sports federations reduces the number of sellers on the market.

(Toft, 2003:47)

The value of sport broadcast rights has grown considerably over the last 15 years and as Hoehn and Lancefield (2003:556) argued, 'major rights have tended to migrate to pay-TV platforms in Europe and premium cable and satellite services in the USA'. The policy response by various governments to protecting the interests of broadcasters, sport organizations and consumers has been varied but, as Noll (2007:400) highlighted, governments have tended to focus on three issues related to sports rights:

whether pay-TV should be allowed to capture rights to events that historically have been broadcast on free-to-air stations, whether rights to team sports should be sold by leagues or by teams, and whether a single buyer should be permitted to acquire all of the rights to a major sport. Reflecting conflicting views about these issues, different leagues around the world have adopted different policies and practices regarding the sale of broadcast rights and the distribution of the revenues from rights fees among their members.

The first of these issues, the migration of rights from free-to-air TV to pay TV is addressed in the next section. The remaining two issues are central to determining the value of rights as Noll (2007:419) concluded:

The performance of sports broadcasting depends on the market structure for rights, which in turn is determined by two competition policy decisions. The first is whether the power to sell rights is reserved for teams or given to leagues. The second is the policy of national governments with respect to competition in broadcasting.

In the European market, the objective of the European Commission is to prevent sport leagues, clubs and broadcasters engaging in anti-competitive behaviour. Their view is that 'effective competition in these markets is likely to improve the functioning of broadcasting markets and give viewers access to TV services that are reasonably priced, innovative, of good quality and with a variety of offers' (Toft, 2003:47). The selling of rights by leagues such as the Union of European Football Associations (UEFA) on behalf of their member clubs to a single broadcaster in each EU state was considered, in 2003, to contravene the Commission's policy on competition:

> *The joint selling arrangement which UEFA initially notified meant that all TV rights were sold to a single free-TV broadcaster in each Member State and on an exclusive basis for periods up to four years. Some rights could be sub-licensed to a pay-TV broadcaster, subject to UEFA's prior consent and against payment of 50% of the sublicensing fee to UEFA. Sub-licensing arrangements can do little to alleviate the restrictive effects of a joint selling arrangement. Football clubs had no access to exploit any TV rights. Neither UEFA nor the football clubs exploited Internet or mobile telephone rights. The notified arrangement thereby contained most of those negative aspects of joint selling which it is the Commission's policy to counter.*
>
> (Toft, 2003:48)

The Commission's objections centre on their view that this form of 'packaging and manner of sale of football TV rights can distort the competitive process by favouring the business methods of particular broadcasters or by raising barriers to entry on the market' (Toft, 2003:48). So, while the Commission acknowledges that the joint selling of sport broadcasting rights is an accepted practice and in many instances facilitates exclusivity, which in turn maximizes the return that sport leagues and their clubs can achieve, they consider that joint selling also facilitates long-term contracts and if the broadcaster is dominant in the marketplace, this can lead to market foreclosure. Their response has been to influence the selling arrangements used by leagues such as UEFA by insisting on shorter contract periods, the sale of discrete parcels of rights rather than the entire league 'bundle' and enabling clubs to sell certain rights if leagues are unable to sell them.

Nicholson (2007) noted that various European governments responded differently to the challenge of regulating the practice of joint or collective selling of sports rights by their respective national leagues. France enabled the national football federation to be the sole authority responsible for the sale of broadcast rights (Cave & Crandall, 2001; Rumphorst, 2001). In direct contrast, the Netherlands competition authority prohibited the joint selling of rights by the Dutch Football Association. In Italy, a similar ban on the collective selling of live rights by the national football federation was imposed in 1999 by the Italian competition authority (Tonazzi, 2003). However, the collective sale of highlight packages was allowed due to the logistical difficulties in selling these rights on an individual basis (Rumphorst, 2001).

This tension between leagues or clubs being empowered to sell broadcast rights is most evident in the United States. Nicholson (2007:89) noted that

> *Court rulings in 1953 and 1960 determined that league wide television contracts that benefited the collective at the expense of the rights of individual teams were a violation of the Sherman Act. In response, the government enacted the Sports Broadcasting Act in 1961, which gave sport leagues the ability to offer rights as a package to a national network on the grounds that it was in the interest of spectators and the leagues' health and competitive balance (Cave & Crandall, 2001; Sandy, Sloane, & Rosentraub, 2004). As a result, the National Football League (NFL) signed its first national television contract in 1962, which was worth US$4.7 million annually.*

Such direct government regulatory intervention in the United States via the creation of the Sports Broadcasting Act has allowed the National Football League to offer collective rights to national networks since 1962 (Nicholson, 2007). Cave and Crandall (2001) noted that no other professional sport in the US relies solely on national rights and that the NFL has the highest proportion of total revenue derived from broadcast rights. Nicholson (2007) argued that a governing body's capacity to limit or prevent the sale of individual rights by teams to local and regional broadcasters is related to their ability to argue that collective selling of rights is necessary to maintain competition within the league. In reality, this is a difficult argument to sustain with the result that almost all basketball, baseball and hockey teams in the United States sell individual broadcast rights rather than their leagues maintaining control over the collective rights (Noll, 2007).

The other issue related to the sale of sports rights is the extent to which broadcasters can monopolize sports rights by purchasing them via extended contracts or through controlling the majority of the market. In relation to this, the International Competition Network's 'Unilateral Conduct Working Group' reported in 2008 that foreclosure, in which competition is weakened when the actions of a dominant business or organization hinder or eliminate actual or potential competitors in the marketplace, is more likely when businesses are able to enter into arrangements of exclusivity and when these arrangements are long term. In the sport broadcasting context, the issue of foreclosure is most significant when media organizations are able to obtain the exclusive rights to premium sport content. In the Italian response to the Unilateral Conduct Working Group Questionnaire on predatory pricing and exclusive dealing, they cite the example of where a major broadcaster displayed anti-competitive behaviour:

> *Telepiù, the incumbent firm in pay-TV market, signed long-term contracts for exclusive broadcasting rights with a significant share of Italian soccer teams. The Authority first ascertained the existence of Telepiù's dominant position in the Italian pay-TV market, as indicated by its market share (the entire market through 1997, 93 per cent of all subscribers at the end of 1998 and 82 per cent at the end of September 1999). The Authority concluded that Telepiù had violated Article 82 of the Treaty. It was found that the acquisition of exclusive rights to top sports events for a lengthy period, just at the time when the conditions for effective competition in pay TV were being established (entry of a new operator, the approaching expiry of Telepiù's exclusive rights to league matches), reinforced its dominant position and raised the already high barriers to entry into the relevant market, so making likely a harm to consumer welfare. The Authority also deemed Article 82 of the Treaty to be violated by the clause according a right of pre-emption to Telepiù or its subsidiaries for acquisition of exclusive rights for the period following the expiration of initial rights, as this would enable the dominant firm to further prevent competitors from gaining access to the most important program contents.*
>
> (Autorità Garante della Concorrenza e del Mercato, 2008:15–16)

Efforts by governments to prevent such behaviour are again mixed. In Italy for example, regulation 'prohibits a single broadcaster, irrespective of distribution platform, from owning the rights to more than 60 per cent of live football matches' (Hoehn & Lancefield, 2003:562). This is in contrast to Germany 'where the government intervened to ensure that the collective sale of premium football was exempted from national competition law' (Hoehn & Lancefield, 2003:562). In countries such as Australia, New Zealand and the UK, no such restrictions on the purchasing rights of media companies exist.

ACCESS TO SPORT BROADCASTS

As noted earlier in this chapter the migration of rights from free-to-air TV to pay TV has also been subject to a high degree of government intervention. Prior to the introduction of pay-per-view or subscription TV, the general public was able to access sport via the state and commercial free-to-air broadcasters. The public benefits of this system have generally been considered to be of social and cultural significance. Nicholson (2007) argued that governments have assumed that the migration of sport from free-to-air to pay television will cause market failure, whereby the cost imposed on the sport product, which was previously delivered at no cost, is likely to result in significantly less people having access to the product. Many governments regard sport events of national and international significance to be merit goods, where community demand for the product is high because of social benefits, 'but the normal market cost would be intolerable for an individual consumer' (Michael, 2006:63). The government intervention in this instance has come in the form of protecting some rights for sport events being sold to the highest bidder without first testing whether free-to-air broadcasters wish to purchase the rights. In member states of the European Union these legal measures are enshrined in something that Parrish (2008:82) claims is 'where issues of sporting autonomy, commerce and public interest collide' – the Television Without Frontiers Directive (the Directive), and a later revision known as the Audiovisual Media Services Directive (AMSD). The Directive was established in 1989 and then amended in 1997. Article 3a of the 1997 version of the Directive states

> *Each Member State may take measures in accordance with Community law to ensure that broadcasters under its jurisdiction do not broadcast on an exclusive basis events which are regarded by that Member State as being of major importance for society in such a way as to deprive a substantial proportion of the public in that Member State of the possibility of following such events via live coverage or deferred coverage on free television. If it does so, the Member State concerned shall draw up a list of designated events, national or non-national, which it considers to be of major importance for society. It shall do so in a clear and transparent manner in due and effective time. In so doing the Member State concerned shall also determine whether these events should be available via whole or partial live coverage, or where necessary or appropriate for objective reasons in the public interest, whole or partial deferred coverage.*

The European Commission argues that events such as the FIFA World Cup, the European Football Championship and the Olympic Games are of major importance to society. Article 3a of the Directive is therefore designed to prevent instances where events such as these are broadcast exclusively on pay television. Under Article 3a, individual member states are able to construct a list of events that should be made available for purchase by free-to-air broadcasters. Individual country lists reflect different national sporting and cultural preferences. For example, Austria's includes the FIS World Alpine skiing championships and the World Nordic skiing championships, Belgium's includes football and cycling, while the list for Ireland includes culturally specific events such as the All-Ireland Senior Inter-County Hurling Finals, Irish Grand National, Irish Derby and the Nations Cup at the Dublin Horse Show.

Listed events in the UK are divided into group A and group B events, depending on their perceived importance (see Figure 6.1). Like many European nations, the UK's Group A listed events comprise sport events that are considered to be of global importance, such as the Olympic Games, the FIFA World Cup Finals Tournament and the Rugby World Cup Final; regional importance, such as European Football Championship Finals Tournament; and local importance, such as the FA Cup Final, the Grand National and the Wimbledon Tennis Finals. The UK Television Broadcasting Regulations of 2000 state that Group A events must be made available for acquisition by a free-to-air broadcaster and that the channel or broadcaster must have a minimum 95% penetration. By contrast, Group B events are those that may not be broadcast live on an exclusive basis unless an adequate provision has been made for secondary coverage. The minimum acceptable service in this respect is edited highlights or delayed coverage of the event of at least 10% of the event or 30 minutes of coverage for an event of 1 hour or more in duration, whichever is greater.

A similar approach is adopted by the Australian government through part seven of the Australian Broadcasting Services Act of 1992 that gives the responsible government minister the power to protect the free availability of certain types of programs. In reality, the list, known as the anti-siphoning list, comprises sporting events which are considered to be nationally significant (see Figure 6.2). Like the UK listed events, this list gives free-to-air broadcasters the first option to purchase the rights to these events, but does not compel them to do so. If no free-to-air broadcaster purchases the rights to an event, the event is automatically delisted 12 weeks prior to its commencement (previously 6 weeks), at which time the rights are able to be purchased by a pay television provider. The Australian regulations also contain anti-hoarding provisions, which essentially provide

The revised list of sports events protected under Part IV of the Broadcasting Act 1996
Group A (Full Live Coverage Protected)
- The Olympic Games
- The FIFA World Cup Finals Tournament
- The European Football Championship Finals Tournament
- The FA Cup Final
- The Scottish FA Cup Final (in Scotland)
- The Grand National
- The Derby
- The Wimbledon Tennis Finals
- The Rugby League Challenge Cup Final
- The Rugby World Cup Final

Group B (Secondary Coverage Protected)
- Cricket Test Matches played in England
- Non-Finals play in the Wimbledon Tournament
- All Other Matches in the Rugby World Cup Finals Tournament
- Six Nations Rugby Tournament matches involving home countries
- The Commonwealth Games
- The World Athletics Championship
- The Cricket World Cup - the Final, Semi-finals and matches involving home nations' teams
- The Ryder Cup
- The Open Golf Championship

FIGURE 6.1   *List of protected events, UK. Source: DCMS (2009).*

protection against commercial free-to-air television networks acquiring the rights to broadcast sport events, but then not exercising these rights. The anti-hoarding provisions are required in large part because of the extent of the anti-siphoning list, both in terms of the number of sports, but also the number of single games or matches within a single event (e.g. the number of matches at Wimbledon).

In 2001, the Australian Broadcasting Authority (ABA, now the Australian Communications and Media Authority) reviewed the anti-siphoning provisions on behalf of the government. The ABA (2001:13) concluded that 'Australia's anti-siphoning scheme and its list of events are both more extensive and restrictive than those in operation overseas'. The explanatory statement to the Broadcasting Services (Events) Notice (No. 1) 2004, claims that industry reaction to the ABA's report was generally negative. In other words, neither the free-to-air commercial broadcasters nor the pay television providers were satisfied with the outcome of the review. The report recommended some changes to the list, including the deletion and addition of certain events, as well as the extension of the anti-siphoning provisions for a period of 5 years (ABA, 2001). According to the government, following the release of the report it was lobbied by free-to-air commercial

Olympic Games

1.1 Each event held as part of the Olympic Games.

Commonwealth Games

2.1 Each event held as part of the Commonwealth Games.

Horse Racing

3.1 Each running of the Melbourne Cup organised by the Victoria Racing Club.

Australian Rules Football

4.1 Each match in the Australian Football League Premiership competition, including the Finals Series.

Rugby League Football

5.1 Each match in the National Rugby League Premiership competition, including the Finals Series.
5.2 Each match in the National Rugby League State of Origin Series.
5.3 Each international rugby league "test" match involving the senior Australian representative team selected by the Australian Rugby League, whether played in Australia or overseas.

Rugby Union Football

6.1 Each international "test" match involving the senior Australian representative team selected by the Australian Rugby Union, whether played in Australia or overseas.
6.2 Each match in the Rugby World Cup tournament.

Cricket

7.1 Each "test" match involving the senior Australian representative team selected by Cricket Australia played in either Australia or the United Kingdom.
7.2 Each one day cricket match involving the senior Australian representative team selected by Cricket Australia played in Australia or the United Kingdom.
7.3 Each one day cricket match involving the senior Australian representative team selected by Cricket Australia played as part of a series in which at least one match of the series is played in Australia.
7.4 Each World Cup one day cricket match.

Soccer

8.1 The English Football Association Cup final.
8.2 Each match in the Fédération Internationale de Football Association World Cup tournament held in 2006.
8.3 Each match in the Fédération Internationale de Football Association World Cup tournament held in 2010.

Tennis

9.1 Each match in the Australian Open tennis tournament.
9.2 Each match in the Wimbledon (the Lawn Tennis Championships) tournament.
9.3 Each match in the men's and women's singles quarter-finals, semi-finals and finals of the French Open tennis tournament.
9.4 Each match in the men's and women's singles quarter-finals, semi-finals and finals of the United States Open tennis tournament.
9.5 Each match in each tie in the Davis Cup tennis tournament when an Australian representative team is involved.

Netball

10.1 Each international netball match involving the senior Australian representative team selected by the All Australian Netball Association, whether played in Australia or overseas.

Golf

11.1 Each round of the Australian Masters tournament.
11.2 Each round of the Australian Open tournament.
11.3 Each round of the United States Masters tournament.
11.4 Each round of the British Open tournament.

Motor Sports

12.1 Each race in the Fédération Internationale de l'Automobile Formula 1 World Championship (Grand Prix) held in Australia.
12.2 Each race in the Moto GP held in Australia.
12.3 Each race in the V8 Supercar Championship Series (including the Bathurst 1000).
12.4 Each race in the Champ Car World Series (IndyCar) held in Australia.

FIGURE 6.2 *Anti-siphoning list of events, Australia 2006–2010. Source: ACMA (2009).*

broadcasters that wanted the list extended for ten years, in order to provide commercial certainty in rights negotiations. On the other hand, pay television providers lobbied to have the list reduced in size, or an alternative regulatory regime imposed (such as a dual rights scheme).

The ABA's investigations not only revealed that the anti-siphoning provisions were highly contentious, but that there was little agreement within the sport and broadcasting sectors about the purpose and impact of the regulations. For example, the Australian Football League (AFL) argued in its submission that the anti-siphoning provisions were anti-competitive, that they prevented sport organizations from maximizing their revenue and that they should be abolished entirely. Similarly, the Women's National Basketball League argued that a proposal to include the League's finals on the anti-siphoning list would curtail its ability to negotiate a suitable broadcast rights deal. The notion that sport organizations could be disadvantaged by the anti-siphoning provisions was also raised by the Sport 2000 Taskforce, when it argued in its review of the Australian sport system at the end of the 1990s that the removal of the anti-siphoning laws would be likely to significantly increase the TV broadcasting revenues of the major sports (Commonwealth of Australia, 1999). Subsequently, in submissions to a Senate Committee investigation into the anti-siphoning provisions, the AFL, National Rugby League (NRL) and National Basketball League (NBL) all claimed that the regulations did not allow sports to maximize the benefits of rights negotiations (Commonwealth of Australia, 2005). By contrast, the Confederation of Australian Motor Sport submission to the ABA suggested that the list served motor sport well, while Tennis Australia wanted to safeguard the free-to-air coverage of the most popular tennis tournaments and matches, but also wanted to enable pay television operators to acquire the rights to lesser events. Sport Industry Australia took the middle ground by recognizing that public interest was served by the anti-siphoning list, but argued for a new system in which sport organizations could negotiate with free-to-air and pay television broadcasters as required.

In 2003, the Australian Competition and Consumer Commission (ACCC) presented a report to government on the impact of emerging market structures on competition in the communications sector. As part of its investigations, the ACCC (2003:72) examined the anti-siphoning provisions, and concluded that the 'potential costs of the current anti-siphoning regime include: possible reduction in the number of sports programs that may be broadcast; less choice for consumers; less competition between FTA and pay TV broadcasters in both acquiring rights and at a retail level; and increased barriers to entry for pay TV operators'. In many respects the ACCC's conclusion mirrored the Australian Productivity

Commission's (2000:444) finding that 'the anti-siphoning rules are anti-competitive and that the costs of the current scheme to sporting organizations, the broadcasting industry and the community as a whole, exceed their benefits' and its subsequent recommendation that 'broadcasters in one form of broadcasting should not be allowed to acquire the broadcast rights of sporting events of major national significance to the exclusion of those in other forms of broadcasting'. In 2003 the ACCC recommended that a dual rights regime be adopted in place of the existing anti-siphoning provisions, but in 2004 the government resolved to extend the existing anti-siphoning regulations, because they best achieved the original intentions of the legislation, which was to ensure free-to-air access to significant sporting events. One of the arguments since 1992 has been that pay television penetration has not been sufficient to justify allowing the potential migration of sporting events, yet in the UK it has been demonstrated, in particular through the example of British Sky Broadcasting (BSkyB) and their acquisition of rights for the English Premier League, that the migration of sport events can be an important driver of pay television take-up. Thus, the rationale and implementation of the Australian regulations have created what is essentially an anti-competitive catch-22 for pay television broadcasters.

Two of the most influential and outspoken actors in the sport broadcasting policy community in Australia are two industry organizations that represent free-to-air commercial television broadcasters (FreeTV, previously the Federation of Australian Commercial Television Stations) and pay television broadcasters (Australian Subscription Television and Radio Association, ASTRA). Both these organizations have been vocal in support of and in opposition to the anti-siphoning regulations respectively, through formal mechanisms such as government and government agency enquiries, as well as informal publicity and promotional campaigns. Both have established websites to advocate their case and encourage the Australian public to contact their local member of Parliament in support of their causes. The information provided by both organizations is essentially contradictory; ASTRA claims that of the 1300 events on the anti-siphoning list, only 23% are covered live by free-to-air broadcasters, while FreeTV claims that 838 events are actually matches at the Australian Open and Wimbledon tennis tournaments and that free-to-air coverage of the AFL, NRL, cricket and motor sports is substantial.

In short, the anti-siphoning law protects the interests of commercial free-to-air broadcasters through ensuring that sport is available to the Australian population at little cost rather than via pay television. The Australian government has therefore placed pay television operators at a commercial disadvantage. When pay television was introduced to Australia in 1995, free-to-air television networks expressed concerns that pay television would capture the rights to sport and free-to-air television would lose advertising revenue. In 2002 pay television advertising revenue was less than \$AUD100 million, while free-to-air advertising exceeded \$AUD2,000 million.

ADVERTISING CONTENT ASSOCIATED WITH SPORT BROADCASTS

Governments also seek to regulate media content in order to protect their citizens, most commonly referred to as 'the consumers'. Perhaps not surprisingly, governments are most concerned about media content that has the potential to cause harm. For example, the Canadian Television Broadcasting Regulations of 1987 note that a licensee shall not broadcast

> *any abusive comment or abusive pictorial representation that, when taken in context, tends to or is likely to expose an individual or a group or class of individuals to hatred or contempt on the basis of race, national or ethnic origin, colour, religion, sex, sexual orientation, age or mental or physical disability ... nor ... any obscene or profane language or pictorial representation.*
> (Canadian Department of Justice, 1987)

Governments also seek to regulate which types of content are appropriate for broadcast at particular times of the day, with a view to protecting particular segments of the community and children in particular. In many nations governments have applied classification standards, which categorize television programs and films on the basis of their content (most commonly the amount and degree of sex/nudity, violence and profane language). In the case of films these standards are used to prevent access to people on the basis of their age, while in the case of television they are used by broadcasters to determine when they are able to be broadcast, as well as provide parents with a guide to regulate their children's viewing.

Governments also seek to regulate media content in order to maximize benefits that accrue to citizens or consumers. The Canadian Broadcasting Act of 1991 refers to the purpose of the Canadian broadcasting system as being to:

> *safeguard, enrich and strengthen the cultural, political, social and economic fabric of Canada (and) encourage the development of Canadian expression by providing a wide range of programming that reflects Canadian attitudes, opinions, ideas, values and artistic*

> *creativity, by displaying Canadian talent in entertainment*
> *programming and by offering information and analysis concerning*
> *Canada and other countries from a Canadian point of view'.*
>   (Canada Department of Justice, 1991)

Similarly, one of the aims of the Australian Broadcasting Act of 1992 is 'to promote the role of broadcasting services in developing and reflecting a sense of Australian identity, character and cultural diversity'. Local content regulations are the most prominent form of regulation in this context and serve to both enshrine and protect a nation's cultural values. In Canada, public and private broadcasting licensees are required to devote 60% and 50%, respectively, of evening broadcasts (between 6 pm and midnight) annually to Canadian programs. Similarly, the Australian Content Standard requires 55% Australian content during evening broadcasts on commercial television stations, with specific sub-quotas for Australian children's programs, documentaries and drama. Being relatively cheap to produce in comparison to other programming genres, sport events are important in assisting broadcasters reach these quotas.

Government regulation of media content as it relates to sport is apparent in both of the categories summarized above: harm mitigation and benefit maximization. Sport organizations tend not be to be involved in the policy communities formed to develop policies and regulation to mitigate harm in the media, and in general the impact of these regulations on sport organizations, although there are important exceptions, is low. On the other hand, in order to maximize social and cultural benefits available to media consumers, broadcasting policies across a range of nations often focus on sport organizations and events. Sport organizations are often heavily involved in the policy communities that coalesce to debate and develop these policies and regulations, although it is clear that they are rarely the most influential.

As previously noted, government regulations designed to minimize the potential harm to consumers through exposure to media content generally have little influence on sport organizations. There are, however, notable exceptions, although it is evident that the regulations are not applied consistently across national jurisdictions. Harm mitigation regulations that have the greatest impact on sport organizations are in the area of prohibitions on tobacco advertising and sponsorship. In this context, government regulation of media content is designed to mitigate the harm that consumers do to themselves by consuming products advertised through the media, rather than consumption of media itself. The content regulations that govern tobacco advertising are akin to content regulations or standards regarding alcohol advertising, but are inherently different to content regulations that govern appropriate levels of sex or violence in the media (despite arguments that exposure to sex and violence might make people more predisposed to sexually deviant or criminal behaviour).

The Australian government effectively banned all tobacco advertising on radio and television in 1976 through amendments to the Broadcasting and Television Act. A further amendment in 1990 made it illegal to advertise tobacco products in newspapers and magazines. One of the unintended consequences of these regulations was that tobacco companies began allocating far more of their promotional budgets to sporting events, leagues and teams, as a way of maximizing their public exposure and circumventing advertising regulations. Rothmans sponsored motor racing, Marlboro sponsored the Australian Open Tennis Championships, Escort sponsored the Victorian Football League, Winfield sponsored Australian Rugby League, while Benson and Hedges secured the marketing rights for international cricket played in Australia (Stewart, Nicholson, Smith, & Westerbeek, 2004). In response, the Australian government, through the Tobacco Advertising Prohibition Act of 1992, not only made it illegal for Australian media organizations to broadcast or publish a tobacco advertisement, but also made it illegal for tobacco companies to sponsor sport. As a result of this legislation Australia became one of the 'darkest' markets in the world for tobacco manufacturers and one of the first democracies in the world to ban tobacco advertising and sponsorship (Chapman, Byrne, & Carter, 2003). The concept of a 'dark market' is a euphemism used by British American Tobacco executives, which refers to the dichotomy between media and no media and restrictive advertising regulations that make it impossible to use standard marketing practices across major media outlets (MacKenzie, Collin, & Sriwongcharoen, 2007).

The Australian Tobacco Advertising Prohibition Act allowed existing tobacco sponsorships to run for the duration of their contract, which meant that most tobacco sponsorship of sport in Australia was eliminated by the end of the 1990s. The impact of the Tobacco Advertising Prohibition Act on Australian sport organizations was significant. It was estimated that the value of tobacco sponsorship of sport in the early 1990s was $AUD20 million, which represented approximately 30% of all private sport sponsorship in Australia (Furlong, 1994). However, the Act also contained provision for sporting or cultural events of international significance to be granted an exemption if it was likely that the event would not be held if an exemption was not granted. Most notably, Australia's round of the Formula One Grand Prix was granted an exemption until 2006 on the grounds that a ban would have meant the event would not have continued, such was the importance of tobacco sponsorship to Formula One.

As a result of the Tobacco Advertising Prohibition Act of 1992, Australia was regarded as being in the vanguard of tobacco advertising regulators. In many respects this was a result of its stance on sport sponsorship. Of all the national tobacco advertising regulations introduced throughout the world in the 1990s, very few banned tobacco sponsorship of sport. As a result, in many developed countries with highly commercialized sport systems, tobacco companies focussed their promotional activities on sport and sport organizations subsequently benefited from artificially inflated sponsorship revenues. For example, the advertising of tobacco products in Canada was banned under the Tobacco Products Control Act of 1988, but the tobacco sponsorship of sport was allowed until 2003. However, the Canadian ban on tobacco sponsorship of sport contained no provision for exemptions, meaning that it could be argued that the Canadian government's regulations were even stronger than Australia's. As a result of the 2003 regulations, the Canadian round was dropped from the international Formula One Grand Prix circuit in 2004. This decision was consistent with Formula One's role in lobbying against tobacco advertising controls and negotiating exemptions from national laws and prohibitions.

In Europe, a directive banning tobacco advertising and sponsorship was first proposed in 1989; it was adopted in 1998, before being annulled in 2000. A subsequent European Commission directive was proposed in 2001, which eventually took effect in 2005. Neuman, Bitton, and Glantz (2002) have argued that the significant delay between the initial proposal and adoption, as well as the annulment, were due in large part to the sustained lobbying and strategic tactics of tobacco companies such as Phillip Morris and British American Tobacco. They identified that one of the strategic tactics employed by the tobacco companies was establishing alliances with groups that represented industries throughout Europe, including Formula One Racing, a sport organization that benefited substantially from tobacco advertising. Corporate documents obtained by Neuman et al. (2002:1328) revealed that Phillip Morris established a program in the early 1990s to strengthen relations with the then 300 Formula One journalists, 'in order to sensitize them to the issue and make them react against the proposals of restrictive legislation'. Neuman et al. (2002) did not analyse the relative successes of the variety of tactics employed, however, it is clear that sport organizations such as Formula One played a relatively minor role in what was a very large policy community, particularly when compared to other actors such as national governments, the World Health Organization, the World Bank, major national and regional health agencies, tobacco companies, media organizations and (what became) the European Union.

Sport organizations might rarely be influential actors in the policy communities that develop regulations that determine whether and how tobacco products can be advertised, but there are examples where sport has been deliberately used to subvert government regulations and been drawn into the policy community by default. In these instances sport's significant media coverage, as well as its existence as a product in its own right (that can be sponsored and named), result in the role of sport and sport organizations being highly ambiguous. The use of sport sponsorship by tobacco corporations in Thailand is a good example of sport's ambiguity in terms of media regulation, as well as the often unintended consequences of government regulations. In 1992, the same year in which Australia adopted its Tobacco Advertising Prohibition Act, Thailand enacted legislation that comprehensively banned tobacco advertising. According to MacKenzie et al. (2007), transnational tobacco corporations attempted to undermine the regulations because they considered Thailand an important growth market and feared it would become a regional model of tobacco control. One of the primary ways in which the tobacco corporations attempted to do this was through sport sponsorship. Through their analysis of British American Tobacco's internal corporate documents, MacKenzie et al. (2007) argued that the company sponsored regional sport teams and events in order to exploit what was considered a loophole in the government regulations (which primarily dealt with national media), as well as attempted to influence the way in which the events and competitions were covered in the media (in order to safeguard their investment). One of the unintended consequences of the Thai legislation was that sport teams and events, particularly in motorsport, received additional financial and political support that would not have been expected or warranted, which in turn raised issues of equity and morality. Unfortunately, sport organizations are often no more than pawns in a larger battle between health regulators and tobacco corporations, and arguably will continue to be so as long as they accept tobacco sponsorship.

Although in many instances tobacco advertising regulations throughout the world have resulted in an ambiguous role for sport, broadcasting standards regulation and its relationship to sport are even less well defined. For example, the Hong Kong Broadcasting Authority's (HKBA, 2007) code of practice for television broadcasting contains guidelines for various types of content. The code of practice notes that real-life violence takes many forms, including physical violence in which blows are exchanged and that 'the depiction of violence on television should be handled with extreme care by the licensee' and that 'the degree and type of violence and the detail which can be shown depend upon context and the service on which it is shown' (HKBA, 2007:18). The vast majority of the violence section of the code of practice appears to regulate the dramatic representation of violence in television broadcasting, rather than violence in other areas of television programming. While it might be assumed that sport is a 'context' in which violence is deemed acceptable, the degree and type of violence is likely to vary depending on the sport and the individual contest. In this respect the broadcast of kickboxing or ultimate fighting during hours when children are likely to be watching might be considered unacceptable or at very least dubious in light of the code of practice.

MEDIA OWNERSHIP

The final area of government regulatory intervention in relation to sport and the media is in the area of preventing the vertical integration of the sport and media industries, whereby sport franchises are purchased by broadcast corporations. Hoehn and Lancefield (2003) and later Nicholson (2007) used the case of the UK Competition Commission blocking the takeover by media company BSkyB (a News Corporation subsidary) of the high-profile football club Manchester United in the late 1990s to highlight government's concerns of such vertical integration effects on consumers. On October 29, 1998, the British Secretary of State referred the proposed acquisition of football club Manchester United by the United Kingdom Competition Commission (formerly the Monopolies and Mergers Commission). In its final report the Commission noted that BSkyB was

> *A vertically integrated broadcaster which buys TV rights, including those for sporting events, makes some of its own programmes, packages programmes from a range of sources into various channels, and distributes and retails these channels to its subscribers using its direct-to-home satellite platform as well as selling them wholesale to other retailers using different distribution platforms.*
>
> (Competition Commission, 1999:3)

At the time of the inquiry, BSkyB was essentially the only provider of premium sports channels on pay television, and as a result of the limited number of sports rights available to the market BSkyB's high market share delivered it an effective monopoly. Any acquisition of Manchester United by BSkyB was therefore likely to enhance its ability to raise prices above competitive levels with impunity. The Commission noted that the influence of the highly successful Manchester United team over other premier league clubs would lead to excessive influence over other clubs to support the sale of rights to BSkyB. The notion that BSkyB could be both a club owner and a bidder for the broadcast rights was just one of the anti-competitive impacts of the proposed merger that led the Commission to conclude that it should be prohibited. Nicholson (2007) noted that the decision of the Competition Commission to prohibit the purchase of the club by BSkyB was based mainly on the effects on competition between BSkyB and other broadcasters, but that it would also lead to undue influence over the football league.

CONCLUSION

The first of our four questions we have sought to address in this chapter is what are the reasons government has intervened in the relationship between sport and the media through regulatory policy? We conclude that governments have done so to overcome concerns about (1) the potential lack of competition in the marketplace through either sport governing bodies exerting control over the market by collective selling of rights or alternatively, media organizations enjoying a monopoly through the acquisition of the majority of rights to a particular league or event; (2) the potential loss to consumers of their 'free' access to viewing what are considered significant cultural events; and (3) the potential harm that may come to consumers through their exposure to inappropriate health or behavioural messages associated with sport broadcasts. To effectively combat competition issues governments have developed regulatory measures to restrict the conditions under which broadcast rights can be sold and purchased, the types of events that may be shown exclusively on pay TV, and the advertising of tobacco through many media forms associated with sport.

Our second question focuses on how central sport has been in determining the nature and extent of such regulatory interventions. In relation to policies designed to minimize harm, sport is rarely directly involved, and if they are, they are restricted to engaging as an interested lobbyist. In relation to the regulatory policies designed to maximize social and economic benefits, these are usually formed in consultation with sport organizations, although they remain on the margins of the debate as evidenced by the recent Australian reviews of the anti-siphoning list, where certain organizations argued for anti-siphoning to be dropped, or at least to have their events removed from the list, yet the government persisted in maintaining the current list.

The third question we have sought to answer is to identify the variety of regulatory instruments employed by government to achieve their policy objectives. These instruments have focussed on the broad issues of competition and content. In terms of the Baldwin and Cave (1999) framework these have been in two categories: command and control strategies and market harnessing controls. The use of command and control strategies is evidenced by governments seeking to regulate content in order to protect consumers via such actions as prohibiting tobacco advertising or sponsorship of sport, as well as seeking to regulate access to free-to-air sport broadcasts in order to protect consumers (i.e. anti-siphoning provisions which allow consumers access to content), although the supposed benefit is hard to quantify in this instance. Governments have also employed market harnessing controls such as allowing leagues an exemption from competition policy to enable them (in some instances) to act as a cartel and thereby prevent individual clubs auctioning off the rights, or ensuring that sporting leagues offer non-exclusive rights contracts to ensure competition between media organizations and prevent monopolies.

Our final question relates to the impact on sport of these regulatory policies. In simple terms, the listed events regulations mean that some sports are unable to maximize the value of their rights by not being able to auction them off to the highest bidder. As Parrish (2008:94) concludes:

> *Regulation diminishes the value of sports rights and this is a major concern for the governing bodies. Two public interest arguments must be balanced. The first is that of ensuring public access to major sporting events on free-to-air television. The second is allowing sufficient commercial freedom for the governing bodies to attain maximized revenues from rights in order to support re-investment in sport at all levels. Article 3a impacts upon these solidarity mechanisms by limiting the commercial freedom of the governing bodies. Therefore, regulation may potentially have the perverse consequence of penalising active participants at the grassroots of sport in favour of inactive television viewers.*

Similar concerns can be expressed for the effect on sport consumers:

> *This is reflected in the nature of the regime which affords consumers limited influence on the composition of national lists. It cannot be convincingly argued that the lists reflect actual consumer demand. As the ongoing debate within the 3a subsystem indicates, the nature of the regime and the content of the lists reflect the views of more*

powerful interests within the subsystem. The resulting compromise between these actors has resulted in very limited coverage of events which are assumed to be of major importance to the public.

(Parrish, 2008:95)

In other words, at least in relation to regulating the sale of broadcast rights, it can be argued that both sport and sport consumers are worse off than if no such regulations existed. In regard to other regulatory measures, such as restricting advertising of tobacco, the vertical integration of sport and media companies, or the packaging of rights, sports would consider themselves worse off because such regulations diminish the prospective value of their broadcast rights and access to much-needed revenues.

CHAPTER 7

School Sport and Physical Education

The final area of regulatory policy associated with sport we have selected to explore is physical education (PE). Sport is dependent on governments to support PE in order that future participants in sport have an adequate grounding in basic motor skills and physical activity. This chapter focuses on the complex relationship between sport and PE policy, using the UK as the primary example in order to identify the reasons government have sought to regulate in this area, to identify the centrality of sport in determining the nature and extent of such interventions, the variety of regulatory instruments used and to make some assessment of their impact on sport. In addition to applying the Baldwin and Cave (1999) framework for the analysis of these questions, this chapter also applies the work of Lukes (2005) and Foucault (1982) in the exploration of the particularly political nature of PE policy development in the UK.

THE UNEASY RELATIONSHIP BETWEEN GOVERNMENTS AND PHYSICAL EDUCATION

In many countries, there is considerable tension at the heart of the relationship between governments and school sport/PE. The history of state intervention in PE frequently exhibits a similar pair of characteristics: first, bouts of neglect alternating with periods of passionate concern and robust intervention and second, periods of scepticism about its value in the curriculum alternating with intense efforts to promote of PE as a subject possessed of transformative capacity for pupils, schools and local communities. Hardman (2002), in a survey of PE in European schools, records the ambiguity of governments towards PE and the range of educational and social problems it is used to address. He notes that PE/sport is an 'obligatory school curriculum subject in all [Council of Europe] member states for at least part of the schooling years for both boys and girls' (Hardman, 2002:3). However, while Hardman noted that all but two countries reported that PE was delivered according to statutory or adminis-trative guidelines, he also commented that 'actual implementation fre-quently does not meet with statutory ... obligations or expectations' (Hardman 2002:4). Among the indicators of neglect were the erosion of time allocated to PE/sport, lack of official assessment, diversion of resources away from PE/sport to other subjects and shortage of qualified staff. The decline in curriculum time allocated to PE/sport had been noted in England during the late 1990s (NAHT, 1999) and also in Sweden (Sollerhed, 1999). As regards its status relative to other subjects, Hardman concludes that PE/sport was accorded a lower status than other 'academic' subjects and that 'a pattern of prestige differentiation between other subjects and PE is generally discernible' (Hardman, 2002:5).

Somewhat paradoxically, school sport/PE is frequently identified as hav-ing a role in addressing complex social problems such as the social integra-tion of minority populations. Two-thirds of the countries in Hardman's survey identified this role for school sport/PE and, as will become evident later in the more detailed discussion of school sport/PE in England, other welfare-related roles of school sport/PE included improving community safety, boosting pupil self-esteem and improving youth behaviour. An even more pronounced paradox is that the prolonged periods of relative neglect and under-resourcing of school sport/PE contrast sharply with periods of intense political debate over the content of the subject. For example, Yamamoto (2009) noted how, in the 1920s, the PE division in the Japanese Ministry of Education was at the forefront of the militarization of PE and the promotion of the role of the subject in reinforcing the authoritarianism of the political system. The highly politicized nature of school sport/PE continued after World War II when America, as the occupying power, exer-cised tight control over the content of the PE curriculum with the intention of excluding the more overtly nationalistic sports, but was followed by a long period of marginalization. Park, in his analysis of sport policy in Korea, noted the strong association between PE and nation building in the 1960s and 1970s, and also highlights the later 'indifference towards school sport' (Park, 2009:167) in the 1990s (see also, Ha, & Mangan, 2002; Ok, 2004).

However, not all regulation is by the state as there are some countries where the highly politicized nature of PE had prevented or severely limited government or state involvement. In Ireland, for example, for a considerable part of the twentieth century, the Catholic Church was a dominant influ-ence in relation to the curriculum and both the Church and the Gaelic Ath-letic Association (GAA) were dominant influences in relation to sport policy. Between 1921 and 1939, there were a number of attempts to strengthen the position of PE in the curriculum all of which were unsuccessful due to Church opposition (Duffy, 1996). The reference in the draft of the Irish constitution to the role of the state in ensuring minimum standards of education, including PE, was removed due to pressure from the Catholic Church, which asserted the responsibilities of the family regarding all physical matters. The final draft of the constitution consequently referred to the 'inalienable right and duty' of the family in relation to 'the religious and moral, intellectual, physical and social education of their children' (Constitution of Ireland, 2004, Article 42). PE did not enter the curriculum until the mid-1960s, ironically at the prompting of the Catholic Church. However, from the 1960s until the early part of the present century, the government did little to promote the subject in part due to the competition for curriculum time and in part due to the opposition from the GAA to the introduction of sports into PE, which might challenge the dominance of Gaelic sport in the Irish society. In summary, PE in Ireland was tightly regulated, but by the Church and the GAA rather than by the state.

The experience of school sport/PE in England is not too dissimilar in that when the state sought to intervene in relation to PE and school sport it was, and continues to be, to reinforce a set of deeply embedded cultural values (mainly those associated with class, national identity and gender), although occasionally mediated by more immediate political or social contingencies (such as military preparation, economic development and social inclusion).

INTERESTS, POWER, REGULATION AND SCHOOL SPORT/PE

It is interests and the desire to further or protect them that result in the exercise of power in the form of regulation of actions. As is clear from the brief review of the politics of school sport/PE provided above, there are a range of interests seeking to regulate or influence policies including governments, religious organizations, sport organizations and PE professional bodies. However, the capacity to act on one's interests and exert regulatory influence depends on power. There are four broad forms of regulation that may be identified in relation to school sport/PE, which are informed by the discussions of the concept of power provided by Lukes (2005) and Foucault (1982).

The first form may be broadly defined as the use of incentives (an example of what Lukes refers to as 'one-dimensional power'), whereby the powerful (i.e. the resource rich) use their resources to shape the behaviour of the resource dependent. An example in relation to school sport/PE would be the use of government funds to create incentives, such as access to subsidized coaching or additional funding for sports clubs if they fulfil a set of criteria in relation to youth sport provision, to adopt a particular approach to school sport/PE or to include particular content. The second form of regulation also falls within Lukes' definition of 'one-dimensional power' and is the reliance on threats or sanctions. In most countries, the PE curriculum is reinforced by legislation or administrative regulations, the breach of which would incur some penalty. The third form of regulation is the erection of barriers that make the taking of particular actions or the raising of certain issues difficult. In many respects, this form of regulatory power is about controlling the parameters of debate about future policy direction, but can also be evident in debates about delivery processes for current policy. For example, certain issues may be kept off the policy agenda such as equal access to sport for girls or those with disabilities, the practice of non-competitive sport or the introduction of non-traditional sports. This is regulation through 'non decision-making', whereby 'demands for change in the existing allocation ... can be suffocated before they are even voiced' (Lukes, 2005:22,23). In this case, regulation is more subtle and empirically more difficult, but certainly not impossible, to detect.

The final form of regulatory power is also the most subtle insofar as it assumes a capacity on the part of the regulators to achieve their goals through the manipulation of the attitudes and values or, in Lukes' own words by 'influencing, shaping or determining [a person's] ... very wants' (Lukes, 2005:27). For example, a PE curriculum constructed around physical activity rather than sport or a curriculum that contains only non-competitive sport, are, in most countries, 'unthinkable'. This shaping of preferences may be the outcome of the efforts of a range of socializing agents including teacher training institutions, the media, sports organizations and politicians. Lukes' observation that this dimension of power can also be 'a function of collective forces and social arrangements [such as] ... the socially structured and culturally patterned behaviour of groups and practices of institutions' resonates strongly with the work of Foucault and those who have developed his work more recently such as Rose (1999), Rose and Miller (1992), and Dean (1999, 2007). The Foucauldian school of analysis would endorse Lukes' conclusion that 'Power is at its most effective when least observable' (Lukes, 2005:64). Consequently, the most effective form of regulation is self-regulation, where those whose behaviour is the target of regulation accept the behavioural requirements of the regulators: as Foucault argued 'to govern ... is to structure the field of action of others'

(Foucault, 1982:221). Thus, regulatory power is exercised not only by the 'ability to demand accounts' (Power, 1997:146), but also in the deep sense of obligation to provide them even if this involves 'divert[ing] resources from what they do to processes of accounting for what they do' (Clarke, Gewirtz, Hughes, & Humphrey, 2000:256).

A particularly valuable development of Lukes' third dimension of power concerns the concept of 'governmentality', which has been explored by a number of scholars (see for example Burchell, 1993; Dean, 1999, 2007; Raco & Imrie, 2000; Rose, 1999, Rose & Miller, 1992). Regulation is thus a process that 'does not only act upon people, but through them, harnessing their desires and choices to achieve the sought-after social order' (Davies, 2006:252). Attention is consequently focused on the kinds of knowledge and technologies through which social activity (school sport/PE) is regulated, and through which actors – teachers, school principals, coaches, club officers and young people – are constituted as self-disciplining subjects. The comment by Rose and Miller (1992:174) that 'Power is not so much a matter of imposing constraints upon citizens as of "making up" citizens capable of bearing a kind of regulated freedom' is an especially apt argument in relation to school sport/PE. As Raco and Imrie (2000:2191) comment, 'increasingly, government seeks not to govern society per se, but to promote individual and institutional conduct that is consistent with government objectives'.

Programs, such as the UK government's commitment to modernization, depict or represent spheres of activity in ways which are essentially self-validating. As Rose and Miller (1992:183) observe, 'they make the objects of government thinkable in such a way that their ills appear susceptible to diagnosis, prescription and cure by calculating and normalizing intervention'. Programmes are operationalized through the application of various technologies of government including audit, benchmarking, public service agreements, target setting and performance reviews and measurement. Audit, for example, is the process of producing auditable objects, a normative commitment that 'hardens into the routines of practice a new regulatory common sense' (Power, 1997:138). The net effect of the application of these technologies is to ensure that organizations are instrumental in their own self-government and engaged in the reflexive monitoring of their organization's actions such that they are able to 'account for what they do when asked to do so by others' (Giddens, 1995:35). It is with this layered and multiple conceptualization of regulation in mind that this chapter moves on to examine in more detail the English experience of regulated school sport/PE.

NATIONAL CURRICULUM FOR PHYSICAL EDUCATION

The British government's recent interest and regulatory intervention in school sport and PE has been shaped as much by interests located in a number of policy areas beyond education including sport, health, social inclusion and community safety as by debates within the education policy area. The impact of these multiple interests is evident in a number of still unresolved tensions such as those between PE and sport, between whole school objectives (behaviour, attainment and attendance in particular) and more sport-specific objectives and between the academic study of sport and the practice of sport.

Education policy in the UK from the mid-1960s to the late 1970s was dominated by debates over the structure of the secondary school system and the issue of the abandonment of selection at the age of 11. Relatively little attention was paid to questions of curriculum, which were generally seen as matters best determined at the school level with perhaps advice from the local education authority. However, while curriculum issues were largely uncontentious at the political level, they were the subject of intense debate at the professional level especially in relation to PE. During this period, there were debates about the purpose, content and pedagogy associated with PE which, rather than resulting in a more confident PE profession, seemed to lead to a loss of confidence and a prolonged period of self-doubt about the nature of the subject and its place in the school.

The nature and extent of the period of self-doubt is readily apparent from a review of the contemporary professional publications. For example, throughout much of the 1970s the *British Journal of Physical Education*, a leading publication for PE teachers, carried articles and editorials that expressed doubts about the lack of recognition of the contribution of PE (Britton, 1972; Quant, 1975), the worth of PE (Westthorp, 1974) and the marginal status of PE teachers (Dean, 1978). Carroll stated that PE was 'still regarded by many as unimportant' (Westthorp, 1974:103), while Quant concluded that the subject was 'at best, only of peripheral value in the school experience' (Quant, 1975:77). The generally marginal status of PE at this time was confirmed by the 1975 white paper, *Sport and Recreation*, which had scant reference to the place of PE in broader sport policy goals. As the *British Journal of Physical Education* noted in its editorial on the white paper, 'if PE teachers have thought that they had a fundamental part to play in the education of every child, that they provided an essential basis on which active life for work and leisure could be built for everyone, then, clearly, they have to think again' (Spectator, 1975:93)

However, if the peripheral role of the PE profession in debates on sport policy was in part due to the lack of a consensus among PE teachers about the relationship between sport and PE, then it was a weakness that persisted throughout the 1970s and 1980s and, to a considerable extent, remains unresolved today. Although many PE teachers were content to equate a satisfactory PE curriculum as one that put sport at the core, there were many others for whom sport was a distortion of good PE teaching and whose opinion was typified by Skinsley's observation that 'it is not the responsibility of PE teachers to produce the elite young sportspersons of national standard within school time and at the expense of the rest of the pupils in their school' (Skinsley, 1987:58).

Uncertainty and dissent within the profession were poor preparation for the period of turbulence into which PE was thrust from the late 1980s onwards. In the late 1980s, an emerging concern with the state of the health of young people and the perceived lack of success of elite sportsmen and sportswomen in England combined to push PE and school sport centre stage (cf. Evans, Penney, & Bryant, 1993:329; see also, Flintoff, 2003). The concern with children's health was reinforced by the far more emotive allegations made by some politicians and parts of the media that competitive school sport was in decline and that the PE profession was, if not culpable, then at least complicit. The concerns about the health of school children and the content of the PE curriculum broadly coincided with the government's plan to introduce a national curriculum and a parallel debate about the role of the government's sports agency, the Sports Council, in children's/school sport. However, the PE profession was ill-prepared for the turmoil and sustained period of governmental intervention that was to follow. As Kirk observed, the events of the mid- to late 1980s constituted 'a watershed in British physical education discourse, a new moment in the production of definitions of physical education' (Kirk, 1992:2).

The policy process around the production of the national curriculum for PE (NCPE) had three significant consequences for school sport and PE: first, it broadened the context within which PE was set beyond the confines of the education policy area to formally include sport; second, the tense, but long-established relationship between PE and sport came under intense scrutiny with sport eventually emerging as the more strongly supported (and regulated) partner; and third, the process introduced new policy actors which, though taking some time to establish themselves, were to have a significant impact on the emergence of the new regulated policy space of 'youth sport'.

The debate over the curriculum provided national sport organizations with a focal point for the growing unease experienced by some which had been prompted by a series of developments including the following: first, the perceived drift in curriculum content away from the practice of sport and the development of sport-specific skills and towards generic skills development (Her Majesty's Inspectorate of Education, 1978); second, the erosion of sport resources in schools as a result of the sale of playing fields and the loss of goodwill among teachers due to a dispute with the government over contracts in the mid-1980s; third; the broadening of the range of sports available in schools and the consequent challenge to the taken-for-granted security in the curriculum of the traditional summer and winter sports; and fourth, the decline in the birth rate, which had intensified the competition between governing bodies for talented young athletes. However, the passage of the 1988 Education Reform Act and subsequent disputes over the content of the NCPE not only activated national governing bodies (NGBs), but also prompted a number of other policy actors, including politicians, educationists and PE professional organizations, to consider their position in relation to sport and PE in schools (Evans et al., 1993; cf. Houlihan, 1991; Kirk, 1992; Murdoch, 1987, 1993; School Sport Forum, 1988; Talbot, 1993).

There were two stages in the process of determining the national curriculum that were crucial for PE: first, whether the subject would be included in the national curriculum; and second, if it was, what status would it be given and what would be the content. The inclusion of PE in the national curriculum was by no means a foregone conclusion. PE had come under sustained criticism from the radical right of the governing Conservative Party due to its perceived egalitarian character, which undermined the virtues of the market economy. Given the weight of radical right antipathy and the fact that PE had been excluded from the list of core and foundation subjects in an early consultative document, the eventual decision to include PE as a foundation subject was met with considerable relief within the profession and among NGBs. However, the relief was short lived as it soon became apparent that there was a substantial regulatory price to be paid for inclusion (Evans et al., 1993).

The PE Working Group, whose membership marginalized those voices deemed out of step with the government's right-wing priorities, was one of the last to be established and it soon became apparent that the Secretary of State for Education and the Minister for Sport had clear ambitions for PE curriculum design (Evans & Penney, 1995). The Interim report of the Working Group was rejected by the Education Minister on the grounds that it was too 'academic' and over-elaborate and gave too little emphasis to 'doing sport' (Talbot, 1995). The final version of the PE curriculum was published in 1991 and represented a compromise between the preferences of the government and the NGBs and those of the PE profession: the emphasis on 'doing' sport had been increased but the more reflective aspects of the interim draft of the curriculum were largely retained. The eventual

NCPE and its series of revisions in the intervening years have broadly maintained the accommodation between, on the one hand, the narrow concern with the development of sport specific skills and the attitudes and values their acquisition and practice were thought to produce and, on the other, a more holistic view of PE as the development of physical literacy and the acquisition of a series of personal and intellectual skills that could be transferred across the curriculum. However, the balance was clearly in favour of the former set of priorities. As Evans et al. concluded in their assessment of the NCPE, 'the NCPE now reinforces a very narrow and "traditional" definition of PE as comprising a set of separate and distinct areas of activity and openly accords the highest status to that area that has long dominated the PE curriculum in state schools, namely, competitive team games' (Evans, Penney, & Davies, 1996:7).

As was the case in so many policy areas reformed by the Conservative government in the 1980s, the rhetoric of deregulation and citizen empowerment belied the extent of centralist regulation. The introduction of the NCPE was reinforced through legislation and extended considerably the state's influence over school sport/PE. However, of equal significance was that the debate over the NCPE was the beginning of a long period of state intervention and regulation of school sport/PE in which the state deployed a wide range of regulatory forms and techniques. In short, successive governments have sought to establish new school sport policy spaces where delivery partners were more amenable to government regulation than the PE profession and where the definition of content was consequently more easily prescribed. Of particular importance was that, as well as determining the content of the NCPE, the government was also increasingly concerned to raise the profile of extracurricular sport, in large part responding to the growing unease among Conservative MPs regarding the current status of sport in schools and disquiet at the government's ambivalence towards the subject. During the late 1980s, but especially in the early 1990s, following John Major's appointment as Prime Minister, there were a number of proposals floated to increase opportunities for school sport including offering PE teachers additional payment to organize extracurricular activities and opportunities and altering their contract to require them to work outside curriculum time.

The government's concern to expand extracurricular sport was reinforced by the accumulation of evidence that foundation status for PE had had little impact on the steady erosion of timetable share allocated to the subject. Successive reports by the Secondary Heads Association (1987, 1990) and by Harris (1994) pointed to the steady decline in curriculum time for PE. Additional support for expanded extracurricular sport provision came from the newly active sports lobby, centred on the Central Council of Physical Recreation and supported by the governing bodies of the major traditional sports, whose influence was magnified due to the uncertainty and fragmentation within the PE profession. Further momentum was given to the drive for expanded extracurricular sport by the gradual involvement of the British Sports Council. Cautious not to be seen to be encroaching on the policy territory of the education ministry, one of the Council's first steps was to organize, with the support of the Department for Education and Science, a 'School Sport Forum' to investigate 'the place of sport in the school curriculum' (Department of the Environment/Department of Education and Science, 1986). Although the Council was on the periphery of the debate on the NCPE and the lobbying for increased extracurricular sport, it was gradually to take a much more central role in shaping and regulating children's experience of sport particularly following the publication of *Sport: Raising the Game* (Department of National Heritage, 1995).

The mid-1990s was a watershed in the involvement of government in school sport and PE. However, this was not because of its influence over the design and implementation of the NCPE, but paradoxically because it marked the time when government began to move away from attempts to shape the curriculum and concentrated its resources on creating an extra-curricular programme of sport that would be located beyond the influence of the PE profession. The PE curriculum, and the compromise between educationists and sports interests that it embodied, would continue to be corralled in the school timetable, while the centre of gravity of the fast-emerging policy space of 'youth sport' was moving organizationally, financially and politically beyond the school day.

FROM REGULATING CURRICULUM PE TO REGULATING YOUTH SPORT

According to Evans and Penney (1995; see also Penney, 1998), the appointment, in 1990, of John Major as Prime Minister gave added impetus to those groups arguing for the 'restoration' of competitive team sports to the school curriculum (cf. Penney & Evans, 1997; Penney, 1998). In 1994, John Major encouraged his Minister for Sport, Iain Sproat, to prepare a 'blueprint for the revitalising of school sport' (Evans & Penney, 1995:186) in which it was argued, inter alia, that every school should offer five core games, cricket, football, rugby, netball and hockey. This discourse of competitive team sport (reinforced by the increasing policy priority being given to elite sport success) was further strengthened in 1995 with the publication of the Conservative government's policy statement, *Sport: Raising the Game*. In the foreword to the policy statement, the Prime Minister expressed his intention to 'reverse [the] decline and put sport back at the heart of school life' (Department of National Heritage, 1995:7).

John Major's government began the process of widening the range of regulatory instruments adopted in relation to school sport and PE and moving beyond the reliance on legislation (NCPE) and inspection (by Her Majesty's Inspectors of Schools) to embrace other instruments based on financial incentives and, more significantly, peer pressure designed to redefine the characteristics of a 'good school'. For example, Major's government introduced specialist sports colleges that were secondary schools, which were given additional resources to enable them to act as centres of innovation in the teaching of PE. Each sports college would have a 'family' of secondary and primary schools to which it would disseminate good practice. A second example was the introduction of Sportsmark, which was a kite mark scheme for schools, the award of which indicated that the school had met a series of criteria (in terms of facilities, staff expertise and programmes) in relation to school sport/PE provision.

It is against this background of increasing, and increasingly diverse, state intervention in school sport/PE that a New Labour administration was elected in 1997 committed to making 'education its ... top priority' (Bache, 2003:300). Education indeed remained high on the government agenda, as did school sport and PE, which not only maintained its political salience, but also emerged as a significant cross-departmental vehicle for the administration's broader social policy objectives. The linkages between school sport and PE and these broader social policy objectives were evident in the Labour Party's sport policy statement, *A Sporting Future for All* (Department for Culture, Media and Sport [DCMS], 2000:7), and reinforced in *Game Plan* (DCMS/Strategy Unit, 2002:14). Targets, initially announced in *A Sporting Future for All*, were to appoint 600 School Sports Coordinators (SSCos) and to increase to 110 the number of specialist sports colleges, 'which will have an explicit focus on elite sport' (DCMS, 2000:8). These plans were reinforced in 2003 in the cross-departmental publication, *Learning through PE and Sport* (Department for Education and Skills [DfES]/DCMS, 2006), which launched the national PE, school sport and club links strategy (PESSCL), which contained eight programmes, including plans to increase the number of specialist colleges to 400, a Gifted and Talented programme, a plan to increase the links between schools and community sports clubs and to increase the number of SSCos working in School Sport Partnerships (DfES/DCMS, 2006:2). Considerable resources were allocated to support these policy developments, financed substantially by the exchequer, with additional funding from the National Lottery's New Opportunities Fund (NOF). The government's PESSCL strategy, summarized in *Learning through PE and Sport*, noted that

> the Government is investing £459 million to transform PE and school sport. This funding is on top of £686 million being invested to improve school sport facilities across England. Together, this means that over £1 billion is being made available for PE and school sport, and all schools in England will benefit in some way.
>
> (DfES/DCMS, 2006:1)

Notwithstanding that much of this 'additional' funding was simply making good the long-term erosion of spending on PE, the fact that this money was unencumbered by prior commitments provided the government with an important lever to effect policy change in connection with school sport. Moreover, with the appointment of Sue Campbell (chief executive of the Youth Sport Trust) as non-political adviser to the DfES and DCMS and the development of the School Sport Alliance (a joint advisory and coordinating committee comprising the DfES, DCMS, NOF and the Youth Sport Trust), the status of, and coordination between, PE and sport policy has never been closer (cf. Flintoff, 2003). Indeed, in the late 1990s, sport and physical activity for young people emerged as one of the central policy themes within the government's wider social inclusion agenda (cf. DCMS/ Strategy Unit, 2002; Flintoff, 2003). However, the incorporation of school sport/PE into the government's social policy objectives was challenged by the increasing prominence of elite sport and the associated concerns with the reinforcement of a culture of competitive sport and the practicalities of talent identification and development. While the PESSCL strategy resulted in PE and school sport becoming more closely aligned, this took place within a broader realignment of both PE and school sport with the imperatives of elite sporting success. School PE and sport, defined by place and educational purpose is, arguably at least, being challenged by youth sport, defined by the requirements of an increasingly complex talent identification and development structure and driven by the national priority for international sporting success. At the very least, there is now a dual regulatory process in place the contradictions of which are being, temporarily at least, masked by generous financial incentives.

Central to this process of dual regulation are the Qualification and Curriculum Authority (QCA) and the Office of Standards in Education (Ofsted). The QCA has been instrumental in defining outcomes for 'high quality' school sport/PE, (for example in terms of pupil commitment, enjoyment, skills development confidence, a desire to improve and willingness to take part in a range of competitive sports) and also in providing guidance on how progress towards sport/PE outcomes can be measured (for example, through discussions with pupils, analysis of registers of participation and pupils' activity logs and analysis of 'smart card' log-ins) (Department for Education and Skills, 2004, 2005). Ofsted, in its series of assessments of school sport partnerships, also contributes to the construction of the profile of the successful school through reference to the organization and pedagogy found in 'best practice' schools (Ofsted, 2003, 2004, 2005). The most recent report provides a powerful endorsement of the PESSCL strategy recommending that 'those with national responsibility for the PESSCL strategy should ... support schools to integrate the PESSCL programme more closely within the core provision for physical education' (Ofsted, 2005:4).

Complementing the pressure exerted by Ofsted and the QCA, Sport England was increasing the regulatory pressure on NGBs of sport and their constituent sports clubs to mould themselves to match the prioritization of youth sport and noted that 'this strategy builds on the PESSCL strategy' (Sport England, 2008:7). The modernizing of NGBs was to be achieved through the requirement that they submit 'whole sport plans' in order to qualify for funding, and these plans were expected to address three 'key challenges', one of which concerned developing talent to 'ensure that we tap into the vast range of sporting potential across the country to maintain the pipeline of talent up to elite levels' (Sport England, 2008:5). In its strategy document, Sport England states that it will work closely with the Youth Sport Trust to deliver out of school hours sport and also records that 'in the future [its] role will be to focus exclusively on sport' (Sport England, 2008:1), thus further reinforcing the pressures on schools and youth sport providers to adopt a view of sporting opportunities that places traditional team sport firmly centre stage. Parallel to the modernization of NGBs was the refashioning of sports clubs to make them more welcoming and appropriate for youth-level members. This would be achieved through strong pressure to satisfy the requirements for 'Clubmark' accreditation, which was often perceived as a pre-requisite for a successful bid for national lottery funding.

The alignment of PE with competitive sport was further reinforced through the appointment of competition managers for each school sport partnership, whose primary responsibility is to implement the National Competition Framework, which was developed in 2006 by the Youth Sport Trust, Sport England, the National Council for School Sport and selected NGBs and school sport associations. The aim of the Framework is to 'create a step change in [the] content, structure and presentation of competitive opportunities for young people of school age by modernising competition structure' (DCSF/DCMS, 2006:1). Part of the modernization of the competition structure involves a hierarchy of competition for school pupils starting with intra-school competitions and encouragement to hold at least one school sports day, annual Area Youth Games culminating in an annual UK School Games. Not only does the Framework seek to put competitive sport at the heart of school sport/PE, but it is also explicit about the priority to be given to developing talent pathways from schools to clubs and on to elite-level coaching and competition.

The edifice of youth sport that has been constructed over the last 10 years in England would not be complete without the technologies of monitoring and evaluation that were ushered in by the New Labour government. Consequently, each of the 8 work strands of PESSCL and the 11 strands of its successor, the national PE and sport strategy for young people (PESSYP) has its targets, milestones and key performance indicators. Data collection, self-evaluation, audit, annual reporting of statistics, external assessment by consultants and review meetings with funding organizations are routinized.

CONCLUSION

The period since the mid-1990s has seen PE become both more prominent and more secure within the state school curriculum, but at the same time drawn more firmly into the orbit of the burgeoning youth sport policy area. The centre of gravity in policy development for young people and sport has moved decisively beyond the control and influence of PE professionals and is now located within a network of government agencies and sports organizations. More significantly, school sport/PE has been progressively redefined as competitive sport and usually competitive team sport. The restoration project that Evans and Penney (1995) identified as emerging in the late 1980s is now complete. These substantial shifts in policy importance, locus and emphasis have been accompanied and engineered by a correspondingly dramatic expansion in the repertoire and scope of regulation on the part of government.

In summary, it is possible to identify three phases of regulation, the first of which could be defined as neglectful and reluctant regulation and refers to the period up to the late 1980s, which was characterized not only by occasional reports by national or local education authority school inspectors, but also by a general reluctance to interfere too obviously in what was, even in the 1970s and 1980s, considered to be the preserve of head teachers and their staff. The brief second period from the late 1980s to early 1990s was one of strong regulation typified by the prescriptive nature of the NCPE.

The final period, from the early 1990s onwards was one of multiple forms of increasingly indirect regulation.

The character of the current phase of regulation is best explored and illustrated in terms of the earlier discussion of the four forms of regulation. The first form of regulation, the use of incentives to encourage conformity, has been extensively deployed through the funding of school sport partnerships. In addition, the prospect of lottery funding for sports capital projects, which is substantially conditional on evidence of commitment to PESSCL objectives, has acted as a further powerful incentive towards conformity with current policy. There is less evidence of the use of sanctions, the second form of regulation, but it still remains a forceful instrument of regulation. Of particular importance is the role of Ofsted, which provides regular assessments of the quality of education, including PE, in every school in the country as well as periodic single-subject assessments of national standards. Avoiding a critical Ofsted report is a high priority for head teachers who consequently devote considerable effort and time to ensuring that their school is in conformity with the expectations of Ofsted inspectors.

The third form of regulation, the erection of barriers to particular courses of action designed to keep particular issues off the agenda, is evident in the way in which the PESSCL strategy defined the boundaries of policy debate. The coalition of interests (Youth Sport Trust, Sport England, DCSF and DCMS in particular) which assembled the PESSCL strategy and its successor PESSYP, dominate the discourse around school sport and PE and make it difficult, if not impossible, for some issues, especially those around non-competitive sport, to receive an airing at this senior policy level. The final form of regulation, the shaping of preferences, refers to the subtle socialization of school staff and pupils into an acceptance of a particular pattern of school sport opportunities as not only normal, but desirable. Such is the strength of the legitimation of competitive sport and the need for a systematic talent identification and development process, for example by NGBs, government departments and PESSYP elements, that the assumption that 'best practice' in relation to school sport is grounded substantially in a diet of competitive sports is unchallenged.

In conclusion we now briefly turn to the first of our four questions we sought to address in this chapter – what are the reasons government has intervened in PE through increased regulatory actions? The UK experience has shown that when government seeks to regulate in this area, it does so for a range of purposes including supporting elite sport, influencing public health, addressing concerns about social inclusion, increasing safety as well as educational goals such as increasing attendance, and improving behaviour and academic performance of students. In relation to Baldwin and

Cave's (1999) framework, these would appear to be a mix of two rationales, namely distributive justice and social policy, and planning. The question as to whether sport has been central in determining the nature and extent of such regulatory interventions has been a focus of this chapter and on the evidence presented it would suggest that sport, via NGBs, has been relatively more involved in the debate about the nature of regulation in youth sport and PE than other forms of regulation explored in this book. The third question we have sought to answer is to identify the variety of regulatory instruments employed by government to achieve their policy objectives. In terms of the Baldwin and Cave (1999) framework, these have included incentives (capital funding) and command and control (sanctions for non-conforming) strategies, as well as direct action such as creating the NCPE. Finally, on the question of the impact on sport of these regulatory policies on sport, we have come to the conclusion that while they have influenced the modernization of sport governing bodies and forced them to focus on youth sport, the biggest impact has been the reinforcement of organized competitive sport as the central pillar of PE curriculum.

CHAPTER 8

Physical Activity and Health

We now turn our attention to the review of non-regulatory public policy areas that are having an increasing influence on sport: physical activity and health, urban regeneration and economic development, and social inclusion. This chapter explores the intersection of public policies concerning physical activity and health with sport. In doing so, we seek to explore three main questions. (1) What rationales have government used to justify using sport as a vehicle for the achievement of non-sport policy objectives? (2) How central is the sport sector and specifically sport organizations to the policy communities for these non-sport policies? (3) What existing (or likely) impact or influence have these policies had on sport organizations?

A GLOBAL HEALTH PROBLEM

The global overweight and obesity epidemic persists despite many of the world's governments focusing more of their attention and resources on the problem. The World Health Organization's *World Health Report* (WHO, 2002:60) revealed that obesity levels had 'risen three-fold or more since 1980 in some areas of North America, the United Kingdom, Eastern Europe, the Middle East, the Pacific Islands, Australasia and China'; that one billion people worldwide are overweight; and more than 300 million people are considered clinically obese. Adult mean body mass index (BMI) levels of 20–23 kg/m^2 were reported in Africa and Asia and 25–27 kg/m^2 in North America and Europe. Given that the accepted definitions of being overweight and obese are a BMI of 25 and 30 or more, respectively, the North American and European data is illustrative of a serious health problem in the western world. The problem is even greater if an Asian BMI of 23 kg/m^2 is used to classify people as overweight. This new criteria would mean that the number of overweight people worldwide rises to in excess of 1.7 billion (Haslam & James, 2005). The individual and collective costs of people being overweight or obese are substantial. Most significantly, the risk of coronary heart disease, ischaemic stroke and type 2 diabetes mellitus rises with increases in BMI. The *World Health Report* (WHO, 2002) also reported that obesity is positively correlated with various forms of cancer.

In America, *The Surgeon General's Call to Action to Prevent and Decrease Overweight and Obesity* (Department of Health and Human Services, 2001) reported that 300,000 deaths per year were attributable to poor dietary habits and sedentary behaviour (see also Allison, Fontaine, Manson, Stevens, & VanItallie, 1999). It also reported that the risk of premature death among obese people is between 50% and 100% greater than those who have a healthy BMI (20–25 kg/m^2). Of most concern was the notion that morbidity from obesity could be as significant as morbidity from poverty and smoking, two of the most accepted and recognizable global health problems. In the UK, the National Audit Office (2001) reported in 2001 that one in five adults were obese, a figure that had increased almost three-fold since 1980, two-thirds of adult men and more than half adult women were either overweight or obese and that obesity was the cause of 30,000 deaths per year and 40,000 lost years of working life.

The situation in the USA is the most extreme of all developed nations, where 65.1% of all adults aged 20 years and above were overweight or obese during the period 1999–2002 (Hedley et al., 2004). In the USA alone the direct medical costs (preventative, diagnostic and treatment services) associated with people being overweight or obese were estimated to be as high as $US78.5 billion in 1998 (Finkelstein, Fiebelkorn, & Wang, 2003). If indirect costs (value of wages lost by people unable to work or future earnings lost through premature death) are added in order to determine the overall economic impact, then the figure is considerably higher, perhaps as much as $US139 billion (Finkelstein, Fiebelkorn, & Wang, 2005). The overweight and obesity problem also has economic consequences for organizations. For example, it has been estimated that in the USA the annual cost of overweight and obesity to an organization employing 1000 people is $US285,000 (Finkelstein et al., 2005).

Although being overweight or obese is more prevalent in developed countries in which more of the population has access to high-calorie diets, advances in agricultural productivity have resulted in the increasing globalization of the problem. Significant parts of the developing world have not benefited from these advances, particularly in sub-Saharan Africa, however 'the average caloric availability in the developing world has increased from about 1,950 to 2,680 kcals/person/day' since the 1960s (Schmidhuber & Shetty, 2004, 2005:14). Forecasts suggest that average caloric availability will continue to increase rapidly and that overweight and obesity will become even greater global concerns as many of the world's developing countries begin to experience the health impacts of over-nutrition (Schmidhuber & Shetty, 2004, 2005).

In broad terms, the overweight and obesity epidemic has two main causes: poor diet and physical inactivity. The over-consumption of sugar and fat rich foods and the under-consumption of fruit and vegetables are the primary elements of a diet considered poor. Poor diets are often prevalent in highly urbanized areas, particularly where there is a reliance on convenience or 'fast food'. The impacts of poor diet are compounded by sedentary lifestyles, in which people do not participate in sufficient physical activity. Although there is no global agreement on what constitutes physical inactivity, WHO (2004) noted that 30 minutes of regular, moderate intensity physical activity on most days reduces the risk of significant non-communicable diseases, but that more activity may be required for weight control.

The *World Health Report* (WHO, 2002) contained a detailed section on strategies to reduce major health risks, including the most cost-effective ways for government to intervene through policy or legislation. Perhaps not surprisingly, the most prominent examples of government intervention were related to risky behaviours such as tobacco consumption, alcohol consumption and unsafe sex. As part of strategies to improve diet, the report suggested that low fruit and vegetable intake might be counteracted by public awareness campaigns and cited state-based programs in Australia that appeared to have had moderate success in achieving increases in self-reported consumption. Strategies to improve levels of physical activity were notably absent, which might be explained in part by the fact that physical inactivity was in the top 10 risk factors for developed countries only, making it a relatively low priority in global terms, and that government intervention in this area is notoriously complex and difficult.

The governments of developed nations in North America, Europe and the Asia-Pacific have become increasingly concerned with the impact of the overweight and obesity epidemic and have introduced a range of measures to combat the problem. Government policy and action in terms of poor diet will not be addressed within this chapter, for this area of public policy is not within the ambit of this book. Rather, this chapter will specifically examine a range of public policies in the broad fields of health and physical activity that relate to sport. Moreover, it will explore the ways in which these governments have used, and continue to use, sport as a public policy tool within broader attempts to increase physical activity, improve health and control the costly effects of obesity and overweight.

A ROLE FOR GOVERNMENT

The WHO (2004) clearly articulated a role for government in the area of physical activity. Specifically, it noted that 'governments have a primary steering and stewardship role in initiating and developing the Strategy, ensuring that it is implemented and monitoring its impact in the long term' (WHO, 2004:6). The WHO's *Global Strategy* advocated building on existing structures, processes, policies and action plans, with the overall intention that national governments should act as coordinating authorities that are able to harness the resources and activities of a variety of organizations within diverse sectors. According to the WHO, health ministries 'have an essential responsibility for coordinating and facilitating the contributions of other ministries and government agencies' (WHO, 2004:6). It is clear that the WHO envisaged a whole-of-government approach to diet and physical activity when it identified that many ministerial portfolios apart from health might have an impact on diet and physical activity including agriculture, youth, recreation, sports, education, commerce and industry, finance, transportation, media and communication, social affairs and environmental and urban planning. The WHO's *Global Strategy* also clearly articulated that strategies, policies and action plans were hollow if they were not supported by 'effective legislation, appropriate infrastructure, implementation programs, adequate funding, monitoring and evaluation, and continuing research' (WHO, 2004:6). Perhaps most important for an analysis of the role of sport and sport organizations within policies and programs to improve physical activity and health was the acknowledgement by the WHO that a multi-sector approach is required to ensure physical activity policies are successful. Specifically, national ministries of health need to take a lead role in developing partnerships with key agencies, as well as public and private stakeholders. Furthermore, sport and recreation facilities need to embody the concept of 'sport for all', while strategies need to be developed to ensure that communities have access to environments and facilities that enable them to integrate physical activity into their everyday lives.

Many national governments, both prior to and following the WHO's *Global Strategy* of 2004, have adopted policies, strategies and actions plans that are aligned with the WHO Strategy, particularly since physical inactivity, overweight and obesity have become more pressing global problems. Based on a review of physical activity policies in Australia, Brazil, Canada, the Netherlands, New Zealand, Switzerland and Scotland, Bull, Bellew, Schoppe, and Bauman (2004) found that there was a rapid increase in the development of physical activity policies since 2000. From their analysis, six key findings are worth highlighting in the context of this chapter. First, the policies in all the nations examined had been developed using a broad consultative process with a range of stakeholders both within and outside government, and in most cases had been informed by research that established a baseline for further research, attempted to quantify the costs of physical inactivity and made a case for further action in the area of physical activity. Second, all countries adopted an approach that was characterized by multiple strategies, with action plans that focused on either the entire population or specific at-risk target groups. Most of the countries in the study focused on life-long participation and adopted physical activity guidelines that prescribe the amount of physical activity required for health benefits. There were, however, differences in emphasis. Some countries adopted national 'sport for all' policies, while others were skewed more towards 'elite sport'. Bull et al. (2004) noted that those countries in which elite sport was more prevalent in physical activity policy had greater sport sector involvement in the development of policy. Third, all countries proposed to work at different levels of government (national, state/provincial and local) to achieve their goals, although the policies were often developed by national and state/provincial level organizations, while the local or community level organizations were viewed as the providers of infrastructure. Fourth, most countries developed coalitions between government, NGOs and the private sector in order to use resources more effectively. Fifth, all the countries examined attempted to link physical activity policies to other sectors of government and society, such as education, transport and urban planning. Sixth, planning and leadership for the strategies was typically provided by either the health or sport and recreation ministries.

It is clear from the Bull et al. (2004) review that the WHO's *Global Strategy* (2004) was a call to action, as well as a reflection of what was considered national best practice. Specifically, whole-of-government and multi-sector approaches appear to be considered essential components of a national physical activity policy. Isolated efforts by one government department or ministry to increase physical activity are viewed as inadequate and ineffective. This is largely because research has demonstrated that successful physical activity interventions are situated in different sectors and require the cooperation of a range of government departments and stakeholders (Kahn et al., 2002). In most cases, the national health ministries play a central role, both in developing policy and coordinating action, however, it is apparent that the influence of sport and recreation ministries and sectors can significantly alter the direction and emphasis of government activity.

Although the relationships between sport, health and physical activity are notoriously complex, there appears to be a number of strong rationales inherent within government policy for sport and sport organizations to play a significant, and at times central, role in helping governments achieve their objectives. First, when people participate in sport they are typically engaged in physical activity. Thus, there appears to be a natural connection between the two that can be exploited in policies and strategies. Second, sport is an easy target for promotional and educational campaigns, particularly because the place, role and nature of sport organizations (especially community clubs) are easily understood within nations in which there are club-based sporting systems. In this respect, the cultural relevance of sport and the existing sport system of a nation is important in determining the role of sport and sport organizations in any health promotion or public health campaigns. Third, organized competitive sport is able to be influenced by government, particularly in those nations where there is significant government investment in sport via funding of community sport. Although organized sport is only one of a suite of physical activity opportunities, its place within the broader government bureaucracy means that policies are likely to have greater efficacy than within ad hoc or unstructured physical activity opportunities, such as walking, swimming, gardening or bike riding. Fourth, sport organizations have a physical and human resource infrastructure that is readily available. In this respect, government investment is able to be allocated easily and spent effectively, whereas investment in unstructured activities is likely to be riskier and require greater government involvement.

Fifth, sport organizations typically involve social interaction. Thus, increases in physical activity as a result of participation in a sport organization might be complemented by an increase in social or mental health and well-being. These additional outcomes are less likely to occur when physical activity is undertaken by an individual in informal or commercial settings. This aspect of sport and sport organizations is examined in more detail in Chapter 10. It is important to note within the context of the rationale for using sport and sport organizations that one of the reasons sport is an attractive policy setting or tool to combat physical inactivity levels is that people can participate in various ways (e.g. player, coach, volunteer administrator) and such participation can have a range of physical, emotional and social benefits. Sixth, sport organizations facilitate participation for people of all ages and all ability levels. One of the advantages of this, particularly when coupled with efficient talent identification programs, is that sport organizations can convert novice and junior participants into elite performers. Thus, an investment in physical activity participation, through club-based sport organizations in particular, is likely to complement or reinforce other policies that are typical of western developed nations. Finally, an increase in physical activity through participation in formalized sport organizations is able to be measured more effectively, particularly relative to unstructured or informal activities. Thus, governments are able to demonstrate a quantifiable benefit from policies and policies in which they have invested.

These points refer primarily to the features of sport and sport organizations that make them a natural ally for government in public health policies. There are also significant benefits that result from increasing physical activity levels within a community or nation. Foremost among these is that a nation's citizens will be healthier and happier if they participate in physical activity. Although governments are interested in the intrinsic value of improved health, they are often more interested in the extrinsic economic value. In late 2002, *Game Plan: A strategy for delivering Government's sport and physical activity objectives* was released jointly by the Department of Culture, Media and Sport and the Strategy Unit of the UK government (DCMS, 2002). The strategy concluded that the one of the government's two key objectives should be to achieve 'a major increase in participation in sport and physical activity, primarily because of the significant health benefits and to reduce the growing costs of inactivity' (DCMS, 2002:12). The UK government estimated in 2002 that a 10% increase in adult physical activity would result in a £500 million benefit. Similarly, the *Shaping Up* report that examined the Australian sport and recreation system at the end of the twentieth century, reported that it had been estimated that a saving of $AUD500 million would result from an additional 10% of Australians becoming physically active. The economic benefits that are believed to accrue by government are a result of increased physical activity, rather than an increase in sport participation per se. Therefore, it appears that any emphasis on sport as a setting or tool within broader public health or anti-obesity policies is largely a result of its special features, rather than any unique economic or social outcomes it is able to provide.

POLICY COMMUNITIES

The relationships between sport, health and physical activity are complex, and this complexity is often a cause of confusion, and sometimes complaint, as Houlihan (2005:177) has noted

> *In the UK it is a recurring complaint from sports ministers that making sport policy normally involves liaison and negotiation with a large number of other departments who have a secondary interest in the area. At times this administrative dispersal has been referred to pejoratively as fragmentation and the marginalization of sport within large ministries responsible for health, education, and community*

safety for example. At other times the fact that sport impinges on the portfolio of ministers for education and health for example, has been interpreted more positively (Houlihan and Green, forthcoming) as it is seen as creating an opportunity to promote the instrumental value of sport and thus access additional public resources.

Although governments and government agencies have often viewed sport and sport organizations as a natural ally in the fight against obesity and overweight, particularly in Western developed nations, sport is infrequently a central player in health policy communities. This is in part due to the sheer complexity of the problem, as well as the notion that a solution will only be achieved through whole of government action. In 2001, the National Audit Office (NAO) identified the ways in which the public sector influences the prevalence of obesity in England, and the number of agencies that play a role in shaping the policy response. The Department of Health was identified as the most important, given that its strategic objective was 'to reduce avoidable illness, disease and injury in the population' (National Audit Office, 2001:7), with responsibility for policies that directly dealt with the problem of obesity, as well as for planning and monitoring performance. The NAO also identified other government departments with policies that could influence the prevalence of obesity: the Department for Culture, Media and Sport; the Department for Education and Employment; the Department of the Environment, Transport and the Regions; and the Ministry of Agriculture, Fisheries and Food. Furthermore, key agencies with an impact on healthier living were identified, which included the Food Standards Agency, Health Development Agency, Highways Agency, Sport England and Sports Councils. Departments and agencies of sport were viewed by the NAO as bodies with which the Department of Health liaises because of their specific objectives related to widening participation in sport and physical activity.

The relationships between sport, health and physical activity, as areas of broad governmental concern, are not globally consistent. Rather, these relationships, and the way in which they are conceptualized by government, are dependent on specific national contexts. As previously noted, according to the WHO (2004:6), health ministries 'have an essential responsibility for coordinating and facilitating the contributions of other ministries and government agencies'. In many nations, this is the case. For example, Health Canada is the federal department responsible for helping Canadians maintain and improve their health. In 2004, the Public Health Agency of Canada (PHAC) was created to deliver on the Government of Canada's commitment to help protect the health and safety of all Canadians. Its activities focus on preventing chronic diseases, including cancer and heart disease; preventing injuries; and responding to public health emergencies and infectious disease outbreaks. The Healthy Living Unit (HLU) is situated within the PHAC, and has lead responsibility for delivering on the federal government's role in physical activity. The goals of the HLU are as follows:

- To encourage and assist all Canadians to be physically active by increasing their awareness and understanding about the benefits of physical activity and the range of opportunities to be physically active in daily life;

- To influence positive social and physical environments and opportunities that facilitate the integration of physical activity into daily life, and that are accessible to, and equitable for, all Canadians; and

- To establish partnerships with government and non-governmental agencies across levels and sectors, and encourage and support collaborative action and increased capacity to foster physical activity in Canada (Public Health Agency of Canada, 2009).

In nations such as Canada, sport is viewed as one of many sectors with the capacity to contribute to solving the problem of physical inactivity. However, there are also instances where departments of sport are charged with facilitating physical activity, which has a distinct impact on the policy community and the way in which sport organizations are expected or required to participate in policy initiatives. In these nations, there is often a very strong (conceptual) connection between physical activity participation and elite sport success. In other words, physical activity and elite sport success are viewed as a part of a mutually reinforcing cycle, rather than as largely unrelated points on a continuum.

We have selected Australia as an example to illustrate the relationships between sport, physical activity and health, the ways in which policy communities can change depending on political priorities and agendas, as well as the perceived role of sport in contributing to public health issues such as overweight and obesity. From the 1940s, the physical activity agenda has drifted in and out of Australian government attention. The physical fitness of Australians prior to WWII was a catalyst for an embryonic physical activity/sport policy, but the post-war efforts of the 1950s and 1960s were sporadic and ad hoc at best (Stewart, Nicholson, Smith, & Westerbeek, 2004). The election of a left-wing labor government in the early 1970s helped to re-establish sport and physical activity as issues that required government intervention, however, this new emphasis on the capacity of sport to contribute to the welfare of ordinary people was short lived (Stewart et al., 2004). The promotion of physical activity was inconsistent throughout the 1970s, 1980s and early 1990s.

Four developments, one in each of the decades of the 1970s, 1980s, 1990s and 2000s, are worth noting in the context of the role of sport in Australian health-related policy. In 1975, the department of sport and recreation in the state government of Victoria established 'Life. Be in it', a social marketing campaign, which aimed to increase the community's awareness of the benefits of physical activity and the dangers of a sedentary existence (Stewart & Nicholson, 2002). The federal minister of sport and recreation agreed to the extension of the campaign nationally, and in 1977, it was formalized through the establishment of a national policy committee. Public awareness of the campaign by the end of the 1970s was high, but its impact on physical activity levels was unclear. The program was discontinued as part of budget cuts in 1980 (Stewart et al., 2004). Somewhat ironically, the Australian Institute of Sport, an elite training institute modelled on successful East European and Chinese examples opened in 1981. It is clear that in the 1970s, a formative period for Australian sport policy, the departments of sport and recreation at state and national levels were responsible for the development of physical activity.

The second development was the 'Aussie Sports' program in the mid-1980s, the basic objective of which was to 'improve the quality, quantity and variety of sport available to Australian children' (Vamplew et al., 1994:97). The program focused on primary school students initially, but was later extended to include secondary school students, at the same time as state 'Aussie Sports' units were established within the state government departments of sport and recreation. Although the relationship between sport and education is not within the ambit of this chapter, it is useful to note that the 'Aussie Sports' program was under the auspices of the newly formed Australian Sports Commission (ASC), which had been established as the coordinating authority for Australian sport in 1985. Throughout the latter part of the 1980s, the most influential sport agency in Australia was responsible for a program that sought to increase physical activity levels of children by making sport more accessible, an indication that the ASC's initial mandate had a broad 'sport for all' focus (Stewart & Nicholson, 2002).

The third development was 'Active Australia: A National participation Framework', which was launched in 1996. The vision of Active Australia was to have all Australians 'actively involved in sport, community recreation, fitness, outdoor recreation and other physical activities' (Australian Sports Commission, 1997:5). Unlike previous physical activity and sport policies that were effectively quarantined, Active Australia was designed to integrate sport, recreation and health. It had been developed and was supported by the ASC, the Department of Health and the Department of Industry, Science and Resources. Importantly, the ASC was the lead agency of a program that had three clear goals: to increase and enhance life-long participation; to realize the social health and economic benefits of participation; and to develop quality infrastructure, opportunities and services (Stewart et al., 2004).

The fourth and final development was the federal government's Backing Australia's Sporting Ability (BASA) policy, which was released in 2001 and set a new direction for the ASC and Australian sport. Despite recommendations by the Sport 2000 Taskforce to increase government expenditure on participation activities, BASA emphasized organized club-based sport participation and ignored unstructured and informal physical activity. The BASA policy effectively marked the end of the Active Australia program, which had been relatively unsuccessful at increasing the level of physical activity among the Australian population. Since 2001, the ASC has almost exclusively focused on organized competitive sport.

In 2003, the Australian Department of Health and Ageing released *Healthy Weight 2008*, a national action agenda for children and young people and their families. The impetus for the national action agenda was the recognition by Australian health ministers that the range of conditions associated with obesity and overweight were a significant public health concern. The health ministers agreed to form a National Obesity Taskforce, which comprised representatives from the federal Department of Health and Ageing, state health ministries, the National Public Health Partnership (NPHP, responsible for a strategic and integrated response to public health issues), the Strategic InterGovernmental Nutrition Alliance (a sub-committee of the NPHP, with an emphasis on nutrition and public health), and the Strategic InterGovernmental Forum on Physical Activity and Health (SIGPAH, a collaborative body that coordinated government action in physical activity and public health). The National Obesity Taskforce also convened a scientific reference group and a consultative forum, which consisted of 'representatives from a variety of sectors including non-government organizations and professional groups, to provide a cross sectoral perspective and build on collaboration' (Commonwealth of Australia, 2003:iii). The sport industry and sport organizations were insignificant actors in a very large and complex policy community. The ASC was represented on SIGPAH, but this body was dominated by representatives from national and state departments of health. Sport organizations were absent from the consultative forum.

The content and recommendations of *Healthy Weight 2008* are indicative of the governments' need to take a multi-sector approach to the issue of overweight and obesity, as well as the place of sport in the wider policy debate. 'Neighbourhoods and Community Organizations' were one of nine settings in which strategies for children and young people could be situated, and within this setting sporting bodies were one of the examples. However, actions within the 'neighbourhood and community organizations' setting focused on improved planning and design, and the development of tools that would encourage 'good practice' within community organizations. Sport-specific strategies and actions were absent. It is difficult to definitively conclude why this was the case, but it is reasonable to assume that the lack of direct representation on the taskforce or the consultative forum is likely to have influenced the content and strategic direction of the final agenda. The constitution of the taskforce and the consultative forum may have been influenced by the Australian political and policy landscape that surrounded sport and physical activity at the beginning of the twenty-first century. As previously noted, the 2001 BASA policy marked the end of Active Australia and re-orientated the role of the ASC towards organized sport. The informal or unstructured physical activity participation that had been encouraged by Active Australia and facilitated by the ASC throughout the 1980s and 1990s was no longer part of the sport policy agenda. In this context, it is not surprising that the ASC and key sporting bodies had little involvement with the National Obesity Taskforce.

In 2007, the Australian sport policy landscape changed again when the Rudd Labor government was elected. The Labor Party's election platform considered sport and recreation as components of a broader health system that can contribute to improving the health of Australians. The Ministry of Sport was within the Department of Communications, Information Technology and the Arts during the previous Howard Liberal government, but was relocated to the Department of Health and Ageing within the Rudd government. Sport was decoupled from Arts and coupled with Youth, a recognition, in part, of the prevalence and significance of obesity and overweight among young Australians. In May 2008, the Rudd government released a discussion paper, *Australian Sport: Emerging Challenges, New Directions*, in which it articulated a new role for sport. The discussion paper noted that the 'Rudd government believes we need new direction in two key areas: the way we support elite sport; and the manner [in] which we use sport to boost participation and physical activity to help build a healthier nation' (Commonwealth of Australia, 2008:1). The new direction for sport, according to the Rudd government, is to 'play a central role in a preventative health agenda' (Commonwealth of Australia, 2008:5).

The 2008 Rudd government discussion paper noted that in 2004–2005, 70% of Australians 15 years of age and older were either sedentary or had low exercise levels, and that from 1989–1990 to 2004–2005, the proportion of obese adults doubled from 9% to 18% (Commonwealth of Australia, 2008:5). The discussion paper also noted that 'sport and physical activity offer powerful defences against obesity and associated chronic diseases' (Commonwealth of Australia, 2008:6). It is clear that the rhetoric of Australian sport policy has changed, although in 2009 it was not as clear whether sport clubs, associations and leagues were doing anything substantially different. The 2008 discussion paper noted that the Rudd government would ensure sport and physical activity are key elements of a preventative health agenda by incorporating sport and physical activity into the Preventative Health Taskforce, established in April 2008. However, the membership of Preventative Health Taskforce is noticeably devoid of anyone with a direct relationship to sport.

From the brief Australian history of the relationships between physical activity, sport and health across a selection of the most important policy initiatives, it is clear that the role of sport, sport organizations and sport agencies has shifted in the policy community. In the 1970s, newly formed departments of sport and recreation were responsible for promoting and increasing physical activity in the Australian population, a role which continued throughout the 1980s and 1990s, albeit with significantly less funding than that which was allocated to elite or high-performance sport. The BASA policy was a paradigm shift. Since 2001, the ASC and key sport agencies are no longer at the centre of the physical activity policy community. Rather, as the new Labor government discussion paper illustrates, sport is now one of a series of players in a broader preventative health agenda.

POLICY INSTRUMENTS

Physical Activity Guidelines

The heath departments and key health agencies of countries such as Australia, Canada, Great Britain and the USA have developed a range of physical activity guidelines. Many of these guidelines are based on a core body of research and represent a collective agreement. In this respect, it is clear that there is a significant amount of policy convergence in this area. In 1996, a report of the US Surgeon General on Physical Activity and Health found that 60% of Americans were not regularly active, while 25% were not active at all. Some of the report's most important conclusions were that 'physical activity reduces the risk of premature mortality in general, and of coronary heart disease, hypertension, colon cancer, and diabetes mellitus in particular ... [and] also improves mental health and is important for the health of muscles, bones, and joints' and that 'significant health benefits can be obtained by including a moderate amount of physical activity (e.g., 30 minutes of brisk walking or raking leaves, 15 minutes of running, or 45 minutes of playing volleyball) on most, if not all, days of the week' (Department of Health and Human Services, 1996:4). In 2004, the general agreement about the amount and benefit of physical activity was reinforced through the WHO's *Global Strategy on Diet, Physical Activity and Health*, when it was noted that 'it is recommended that individuals engage in adequate levels throughout their lives. Different types and amounts of physical activity are required for different health outcomes: at least 30 minutes of regular, moderate-intensity physical activity on most days reduces the risk of cardiovascular disease and diabetes, colon cancer and breast cancer' (WHO, 2004:4).

These guidelines serve a two-fold purpose. First, they set the parameters for individuals' participation in physical activity. The guidelines are often tailored to a specific sector of the population, such as children, adolescents or adults; however, it should be noted that until recently the guidelines for children and adolescents have been based on the guidelines for adult participation. In the wake of increasing concern about the levels of childhood obesity, particularly within developed Western nations, children are now regarded as a specific population group that requires a separate set of guidelines. For example, the Australian Department of Health and Ageing established a set of physical activity recommendations for 5–12 year olds in 2004. The recommendations stressed two key points: children need at least 60 minutes (and up to several hours) of moderate to vigorous physical activity every day and; children should not spend more than 2 hours a day using electronic media for entertainment (e.g. computer games, TV, internet), particularly during daylight hours.

The second purpose of national or state physical activity guidelines is to provide a basis for policy in the area of physical activity. However, it is clear that while a government's health department might establish a recommendation that children participate in 60 minutes of moderate to vigorous physical activity every day, the responsibility is often devolved to other government agencies or non-governmental organizations. The guidelines in themselves have little impact on organizational or individual behaviours. In terms of sport, the guidelines merely provide a framework in which the amount of activity can be understood. Sport organizations have no input into the guidelines and there is no policy or program requirement for sport organizations to structure their activities to meet adult, adolescent or child activity targets. In many respects, the guidelines are the most popular yet ineffectual policy instruments in the area of public health, although such guidelines often provide the basis for public awareness and educational campaigns.

Tax Incentives

One of the ways governments have sought to increase participation in physical activity, by children in particular, is through the introduction of tax incentives, credits or rebates. For example, from the 2007 tax year, the Canada Revenue Agency allowed parents to claim up to $500 in eligible fitness expenses for each child less than 16 years of age. In order for parents to be eligible for the tax credit, a child must be engaged in a program of physical activity and the program must meet criteria set by the government: a minimum of 8 weeks in duration (or 5 consecutive days if the activity is a camp), supervised, suitable for children and include a significant amount of physical activity that contributes to cardio-respiratory endurance, plus one or more of muscular strength, muscular endurance, flexibility or balance. The Canadian government specifies that activities that form part of the regular school program are ineligible, as are unsupervised activities and all forms of motorized sport (e.g. activities involving automobiles, motorcycles, power boats, airplanes and snowmobiles), in which it considered unlikely that the child will obtain any significant cardio-respiratory benefit.

In Australia, the concept of a tax credit has received support from the Australian Sports Federations Alliance (ASFA), a peak body which comprises Australia's national, state and territory sport federations. These federations collectively represent more than 500 sport governing bodies at the national, state and territory levels and as a consequence, the Australians who participate in and through sport organizations. Emboldened by the Canadian example, in early 2007, the ASFA lobbied the Australian federal government to introduce a tax incentive to support children's participation in physical activity, arguing that it would reduce the costs of participation, which are a significant barrier, particularly for low-income families. The ASFA estimated that for a family earning between $AUD25,001 and $AUD75,000 per year, the ability to claim a tax deduction of $AUD250 would result in a saving of $AUD75. Although the family would still be responsible for the vast majority of costs associated with the child or children's participation, the ASFA argued that the tax incentive would provide much needed financial relief and that through this measure the government would be making an investment in the future health of the nation.

It is clear that some activities and organizations benefit more from the criteria set by the Canadian government than others. Member-based sport organizations in particular are well-positioned to capitalize on fiscal measures such as a tax credit that specify that eligible activities must be ongoing and supervised. Typically, the activities of these organizations are structured around seasonal competitions, while their inherent complexity invariably means that adults are required to provide supervision (such as, but not limited to, coaching, officiating and administrating). By contrast, organizations that offer or produce sporting products and services for ad hoc, informal or individual use are not as likely to capitalize on an increase in physical activity levels among children. For example, a sporting goods manufacturer may benefit from increased demand at the club or facility level, but will not benefit from individual sales of sport equipment for recreational use. Private providers of physical activity opportunities are also likely to benefit from fiscal policies such as a tax credit, as demand for these services is likely to increase. These providers might also expand or enhance their services in order to better comply with the tax credit parameters of an acceptable activity.

The expert panel formed to investigate the children's tax credit, after it was proposed in Canada's 2006 budget, acknowledged that it was not a comprehensive solution, nor a panacea to the problem of childhood obesity. Rather, they noted that tax credits should be viewed as a catalyst and a component of a much broader strategy to increase the level of physical activity among children and reduce the incidence of obesity and overweight.

Public Awareness and Education

In the nations where a department or ministry of health is responsible for physical activity, public awareness and education programs are not typically within the ambit of key sport agencies. However, there are nations where federal responsibility for physical activity lies with the central sport agency. For example, Sport and Recreation New Zealand (SPARC) is responsible for all types of physical activity participation, from elite high-performance sport to unstructured and informal physical activity such as walking and gardening.

Launched in 1999, SPARC's Push Play campaign aims to raise awareness of the benefits of physical activity. In 2008, SPARC noted that over 80% of New Zealand adults were aware of the Push Play campaign and the New Zealand physical activity guidelines (Sport and Recreation New Zealand, 2008b). In many respects housing a social marketing campaign dedicated to physical activity within the key sport agency makes good sense, as the opportunities provided by the extensive network of organized sport clubs and leagues are able to easily be integrated into promotional material.

CONCLUSION

Global and national policy statements, strategies and calls to action from organizations such as the WHO, or national departments and ministries of health, have identified physical activity as an important preventative public health solution, particularly in combating the overweight and obesity epidemic. This chapter has explored three main questions in relation to the intersection of sport with these public policy issues. In relation to the first question – what rationales have governments used to justify using sport as a vehicle for the achievement of policy objectives in improving physical activity and health – several conclusions can be made. It is clear that sport is regarded as a natural ally, not least because people who play sport are typically engaged in moderate or high levels of physical activity. It is also clear that despite its high profile, sport is only one of a series of policy settings and tools that are available to government. As suggested by the WHO, national departments and ministries of health have become the central lead agency responsible for the war against overweight and obesity, and by consequence, the battle to increase physical activity. The brief history of the relationship between sport, physical activity and health in Australia highlighted that this has not always been the case. Rather, the place of sport in the physical activity and health policy community can change depending on political priorities, as well as the mandate government ascribes to the national sport agency or coordinating authority. In most western developed countries, notwithstanding the example we provided on Sport and Recreation New Zealand, the departments and ministries of health have become the major player in the policy community. In Australia the lead sport agency, the ASC, has been moved to the health portfolio. It is unclear what implications this might have for sport policy and the role of sport within public health and preventative health care policies. At the very least it is possible that there will be changes in the policy community that develops sport policy, as the health sector is now the major stakeholder. Sport policy targets and outcomes are likely to change, as are the funding models and standards of accountability. As a result, the direction of Australian sport could be altered by what might be called the 'health imperative'. It remains to be seen whether other western developed nations will follow Australia's lead.

Our second question focused on exploring how central the sport sector and specifically sport organizations are to the policy communities for these non-sport policies? The development of physical activity policy is dependent on the core agents or actors within the policy community, as well as the range and scope of the organizations and agencies consulted. In some nations the sport ministry and key government sport agencies are central to the policy community, and the sport sector is consulted widely in the development of physical activity policy. In some instances this results in elite sport becoming a feature of the broader physical activity agenda. The most cynical analysis of this outcome is that improvements in physical activity and a nation's collective health are used as a justification for government funding of elite sport, despite a lack of credible evidence that a relationship exists between the two. The broad 'philosophical' argument is that success in high profile international competition will result in an increase in sport participation by both adults and juniors. The argument relies on a series of assumptions: first, by joining organized sport clubs, novice participants will acquire new skills and expertize; second, these new skills, expertize and competition opportunities might lead to improved performance; and third, for a select group the end result of skill development and improved performance might be success in international competition. Essentially, the argument is that success in international competition will lead to an increase in local or grassroots sport participation, which will in turn lead to informal participation in sport, recreation and physical activity. This argument is most often used in conjunction with the complementary argument that athletes who are successful in high profile international competitions, such as the Olympic Games, act as role models. When these two arguments are juxtaposed, the justification is strongest when the sport participation of children and youths are considered, the sectors of the population that are considered most easily influenced in their selection of sport experiences and activities.

The assumption that success in high profile international competition by 'role models' will lead to increased grass roots sport participation is unproven. The argument that the performance of these sporting role models is likely to generate recreational participation in informal or unstructured sporting activities or physical activity is even more tenuous. However, this argument is often used in justifying the large amounts of money invested in high-performance sport and the imbalance in funding between high-performance and community sport. Despite a lack of evidence, there are no indications that this argument will cease to be used as part of a broader justification for maintaining or increasing sport funding in an increasingly competitive international sport landscape.

Finally, we sought to identify the existing or likely impact these policies have had or will have on sport organizations. It is apparent that the policy instruments discussed in this chapter have little impact on the core business of sport organizations. In other words, policy measures and programs put in place by the departments and ministries of health, in most cases, do not prescribe or require specific action from either the lead sport agencies or sport organizations. Of greater impact is the requirement by government and stakeholders for lead sport agencies and sport organizations to do more within existing sport policy and with existing sport funding, specifically to increase the numbers of people involved in organized formal sport. The demand for sport to play a greater role in combating overweight and obesity has inherent problems and potential negative implications, particularly for sport. The most prescient concern is that increasing physical activity through sport in club based sporting systems is likely to place pressure on organizations that are already experiencing significant capacity constraints. Not for profit community sport clubs are faced with increasing compliance costs, as illustrated within the regulatory chapters of this book, while volunteerism is declining (Cuskelly, Hoye and Auld, 2006). Although sport organizations appear to have the physical and human resources to cope with an increase in participants, and therefore are well placed to contribute to the problem of inactivity, the ability of government to devolve responsibility for increasing physical activity to a largely volunteer run not for profit sector is diminishing. This is particular so in federated governance/delivery systems, where it is difficult to implement or apply policies and programs across states or regions with any consistency. In other words, without concomitant investment in the capacity and sustainability of community sport organizations, and cognizance of the limitations of sport governance and delivery systems, policies or strategies to increase a nation's physical activity through these organizations may be futile or counter-productive.

CHAPTER 9

Urban Regeneration and Economic Development

This chapter reviews the second of the non-regulatory public policy areas that are having an increasing influence on sport: urban regeneration and economic development. In doing so it first presents a review of empirical research in the area before presenting two detailed examples of the intersection of sport and government interests in urban regeneration and economic development. The chapter focuses on exploring three main questions. (1) What rationales have government adopted to justify using sport as a vehicle for the achievement of policy objectives in relation to urban regeneration and economic development? (2) How central is the sport sector and specifically sport organizations to the policy communities for these non-sport policies? (3) What existing (or likely) impact or influence have these policies had on sport organizations?

It is important to note at the outset of this chapter that urban regeneration and economic development are very rarely, if at all, the responsibility of a single government department or agency, nor are they addressed in a discrete policy. Rather, it is likely that an economic development or urban regeneration strategy will be employed by an inter-departmental or inter-agency coalition, which might consist of departments or agencies with diverse responsibilities, such as infrastructure, community development, transportation, housing or the environment. Furthermore, sport is not a commonplace feature of national urban regeneration and economic development frameworks or policies. Rather, urban regeneration, economic development and sport coalesce when national and city governments cooperate to bid for major events or build major stadia. At these times, sport is often at the forefront of, or is the catalyst for, urban regeneration and economic development projects and schemes. Thus, the connection between sport and urban regeneration or economic development policies is both intense and sporadic; in this way the intersection of sport with this policy area is somewhat different to sport's intersection with other policy areas such as physical activity and health and social inclusion.

Urban regeneration is also known as urban development, urban redevelopment and urban renewal. We have chosen to use the term urban regeneration, as it appears most widely used within government and the academic literature. We would argue that the term regeneration embodies notions of regrowth, renewal, rebirth and reform. Furthermore, the term regeneration also accurately captures the intention, if not always the reality, inherent in governments' involvement in attracting sport events or building sport stadia, in order to achieve social, environmental, spatial and economic objectives. Economic development can be considered a discrete outcome of government involvement in sport stadia and events, but is also often conceptualized as a component of urban regeneration strategies. Similarly, social cohesion and sustainability are two of the most prominent outcomes that are often combined with or used as synonyms for urban regeneration. In many respects this is reasonable, given that the concept of regeneration can embody a range of outcomes; however, it makes it very difficult to disentangle the benefits, as well as the rationales and justifications put forward by governments and their partners. As a result, this chapter should be considered in concert with the other chapters, especially the next chapter that addresses sports intersection with social inclusion policies.

It is questionable whether large-scale urban regeneration or economic development that accompanies events such as the Olympic Games, which have government involvement at all levels, can be considered equivalent to localized and essentially instrumental facility provision, which is typically the exclusive domain of local government. In theory both provide a type of regeneration or development, yet in reality the politics, financial investment, rationale, justification and objectives are vastly different. This chapter focuses almost exclusively on the role of sport in urban regeneration and economic development in terms of the large-scale construction of stadia and associated facilities that support major or mega events, or professional sport leagues and clubs. We have done this in order to highlight the greater level of national and state (city) government involvement and the interplay between government and sport organizations.

The use of sport as a tool of economic development is not a recent phenomenon, nor is the use of sport to market and promote cities and nations. Whitson and Macintosh (1996) noted that the association of the world fairs and the first modern Olympiads around the turn of the 20th century established the practice of using large-scale sporting events to demonstrate the accomplishments and capacity of a city. In other words, the use of the Olympic Games to put a city on the 'world map' was a strategy employed by government in the early 1900s, as it is today. Reiss (1998) has argued that the public subsidization of professional sport can be traced back to the 1870s; during the 1920s several major US cities built large sporting arenas, often with the intention of attracting tourists and stimulating a depressed economy. The relocation of the New York Yankees baseball team from the Polo Grounds to Yankee Stadium in the Bronx in the 1920s was an example of sport contributing to the urban regeneration of a local area by 'creating an anticipated source of revenue for local merchants, advertising for the locale, and psychological backing for investors' (Reiss, 1998:6). However, Reiss (1998) noted that the relocation of the Yankees and the construction of a new stadium were not the only reasons for urban regeneration and an increase in economic activity in the local area. Rather, the stadium and the team were elements of a broader regeneration agenda that included infrastructure, housing and public transport development. In this respect, it appears that the role of sport as a catalyst for or complementary driver of urban regeneration is well established. According to Reiss (1998), politicians in US cities from the 1950s onwards began a more concerted effort to attract and retain professional sport franchises. Their belief was that professional sport franchises would confer myriad benefits on the city, including increased prestige, tourism, commerce, economic development, revenue and entertainment (Reiss, 1998).

Reiss' (1998) example of the New York Yankees and discussion of US government investment more generally illustrates some key aspects of the role of sport in urban regeneration and economic development policies. First, sport is typically only one part of a broader strategy or plan for regeneration or development, although it may be a significant catalyst. Sport, because of its high public and media profile, may be the 'face' of urban regeneration and economic development policies and programs, but the reality is that an isolated event, stadium or franchise will not, on its own, be able to deliver long-term or sustainable benefits. Second, government investment and policies often emphasize the economic benefits that sport confers. In many respects this is a natural outcome of public scrutiny and accountability; an investment of government or taxpayers' money must be seen to have a financial pay-off, for nations, cities, communities, organizations and individuals. Another important reason for the economic benefit of events and stadia gaining a political ascendancy is that, although incredibly difficult and complex to determine accurately, the economic benefit is often far easier to establish than the social, psychological, aesthetic or prestige benefits. Third and finally, multiple and varied benefits are conferred on sport and its potential to contribute to urban regeneration or economic development outcomes, but often there is little evidence to sustain these claims. As mentioned above, the extent and quality of these benefits are also difficult, if not impossible, to establish.

A MULTI-FACETED RATIONALE

In the most literal sense it is obvious that the rationale for government policy and action in hosting major events and building stadia is to achieve better outcomes for neighbourhoods, cities or nations. These better outcomes most often refer to improved physical infrastructure or more economic activity, which in turn is directly related to jobs and wealth. Government rationale for using sport events and sport stadia as a catalyst for or component of urban regeneration and economic development strategies is largely dependent on the type of project, as well as the potential benefits. However, as Coalter (2007:142) noted, 'this is a policy area in which ambitious and often extravagant (non-sporting) claims are made as part of the extensive lobbying processes associated with securing national and local political and business support to bid for such events'. Several key rationales are explored below.

Prestige

The use of sport stadia and mega events to achieve economic development or urban regeneration is a strategy in a wider policy approach termed the 'prestige model' (Loftman & Nevin, 1994). According to Loftman and Nevin (1995), the value of the prestige model and the development of flagship projects gained widespread acceptance within the public and private sectors in the UK in the 1980s, to the point that the validity of regeneration strategies was dependent on the existence of a flagship. Sport stadia and events are often attractive flagships, particularly because of significant media interest, which in turn can galvanize public interest. In reference to the allied notion of place promotion, Hall (2006:59) argued that mega events are an extremely significant component 'because they may leave behind social, economic and physical legacies which will have an impact on the host community for a far greater period than that in which the event took place'. Furthermore, Hall (2006) also argued that mega events emerge as central elements in place competition in at least three ways. First, the infrastructure required is integral to further economic development; second, the event itself is seen to contribute to economic development and the more ephemeral 'business vitality'; and third, the ability to attract events is viewed as an indicator of the city's ability to compete with others. Thus, the value of events lies primarily in their infrastructure, the potential to generate tourism and commercial activity and as a global badge of honour.

The symbolic power of sport, which lies at the heart of its ability to confer prestige and the capacity to compete, is intuitively powerful but lacking in substantial evidence. Many studies examining the use of sport in urban regeneration and economic development projects and agendas have noted that politicians and policy makers are captivated by sport's symbolic power. Henry (1997) argued in the case of Lyon that the symbolic value of sport for politicians and bureaucrats was useful in a number of ways. The most prominent were the promotion of the city of Lyon or its communes at a trans-national or national level, through the hosting of international sporting events. Inherent within the notion of national, city or regional promotion is that nations, cities and regions are competing; when a city secures the rights to host a major sporting event or professional sport franchise, another city does not, and in the process the successful city improves its image, status and prestige. As Siegfried and Zimbalist (2000) argued, a common contention is that sport can 'put a city on the map', and that increased tourism and commerce will result from the perception that a city has entered the 'big league'. In essence, the philosophy is that by securing major sport teams or events that are part of the global sport marketplace, a city has the opportunity to enter the global city marketplace. Entering the 'big league' by hosting major sporting events or by building sport stadia may have become an accepted strategy among nations and cities determined to compete on the world stage, but the increasing globalization of the strategy has meant that it is difficult for nations and cities with existing 'sport for prestige' strategies to gain significant benefits in a crowded marketplace, and for aspirant nations and cities to enter the marketplace. As Coalter (2007) has suggested, there is a need for cities within a global marketplace to constantly differentiate and occupy marketing niches, which is increasingly difficult given the finite number of large-scale mobile sport events.

Coates (2007) reviewed the benefits of a city attaining the status of 'world class'. First, there is little or no evidence that businesses will relocate to another city within the same nation on the basis that a professional sport franchise is part of the city's attractions. There has been no research examining whether businesses are prepared to relocate to another nation on the basis of a sport franchise, stadium or event, but there is likely to been even less evidence for this than for intra-national relocations. Second, there are more effective ways of obtaining national and international television advertising than by constructing sport stadia for the purpose of professional franchises or events. Although the exposure gained by a city through hosting a major event or professional franchise is free as part of general broadcast or news coverage, the cost of the constructing the stadium or hosting the event is likely to mean that purchasing advertising space, which invariably will be more targeted, is a better business decision. Third, researchers have tested the notion that a professional sport franchise or a major event is a valuable public amenity, and is sufficiently valuable that people are willing to pay more for housing or accept lower wages, but as yet the results are inconclusive.

Ritchie and Smith's (1991) seminal longitudinal research into the impact on host region awareness of the 1988 Calgary Olympic Games established that the recognition of Calgary was significantly greater as a result of hosting the Games. However, the analysis also revealed that the recognition also dropped significantly in the year after the Olympic Games, which suggested that one-off events might only put a city 'on the map' for a relatively short period of time. Ritchie and Smith (1991) referred to this as 'awareness-decay', which is likely to be even more pronounced in the crowded contemporary global sport market.

Bordered by Saudi Arabia and located south of Kuwait and north of the United Arab Emirates, the small nation of Qatar has been and is using sport as a central feature of its development strategies. In 2006, Qatar hosted the Asian Games, the second biggest multi-sport event after the Olympic Games, which was used for both urban regeneration and economic development, conforming neatly to the notion that one-off events can be used as a catalyst. However, Qatar also has an explicit strategy of using sport for presenting a specific image, particularly to the non-Arab world. The vision of the Qatar Olympic Committee is 'To become a leading nation in bringing the world together through sport' (Qatar Olympic Committee, 2009). In 2006 Qatar took a significant step towards achieving this vision when it hosted the Asian Games, which was the first to be held in an Arab country and attracted 12,500 athletes across 39 sports. As part of preparations for the Games, 44 venues in Doha, the nation's capital, were renovated, as were roads and housing for athletes. The contribution of sport to Qatar's national image, prestige and place in the world was concisely expressed by Muhammad al Malki, President of the Qatar Sports Press Committee, when he said in reference to the 2006 Asian Games that 'Sport is the shortest way to be part of the world. It's the language between nations' and that Qatar is 'looking to be part of the world and create friendship with others. There has been no civilization without sport' (Simons, 2007).

Sport stadia, teams and events typically enjoy significant amounts of media coverage, which in turn creates significant public interest and attention. As a result, these teams and events become, as Crompton (2001) suggested, highly visible symbols of the competence of politicians. In this respect the prestige which sport teams and events confer is not simply useful in presenting an image to the rest of the world, but is also useful in facilitating positive perceptions about the ability of civic leaders. Crompton (2001) argued that the ability to attract a sport team to a city or build a new facility is regarded as a proxy for competence, in the same way that losing a team or event has the opposite effect. Thus, there may be an important internal or localized dimension inherent within the rationale that sport can be used to forge or re-cast a city's image.

Economic Impact

The efficacy of publicly funded sport stadia has been the focus of much academic research, most of which has mounted an argument against the policy, or against the over-inflated predictions of economic benefit that typically underpin the rationale for stadia development. Siegfried and Zimbalist (2000:103) noted that it is very rare for a field of empirical economic research to offer virtually unanimous findings, yet 'independent work on the economic impact of stadiums and arenas has uniformly found that there is no statistically significant positive correlation between sports facility construction and economic development'.

Using data from 48 metropolitan areas in the US for the period 1958–1987, Baade (1994) found that professional sports teams generally have no significant impact on metropolitan or regional economies and that there was little correlation between the adoption of a team or the building of a stadium and increases in real per capita income. Baade (1994:21) noted that there was 'no support for the notion that there is an economic rationale for public subsidies to sports teams and stadium and arena construction' and that '...sports 'investments' appear to be an economically unsound use of a community's scarce financial resources'. Baade's study examined generic data across a broad range of metropolitan areas that did or did not host a professional sport franchise, yet the evidence for specific urban regeneration strategies involving sport also appears weak. Rosentraub, Swindell, Przybylski, and Mullins (1994) found that in the case of Indianapolis, a sport-led economic development strategy was likely to have an inconsequential impact on economic development and growth. Baade (1996) presented data to illustrate that a positive correlation between professional sports and job creation did not exist, cited numerous studies in order to argue that 'professional sport has had a negligible impact on metropolitan economies' (1996:3), and concluded by noting that 'professional sports have been oversold by professional sports boosters as a catalyst for economic development' (1996:16).

Siegfried and Zimbalist (2000) acknowledged that the findings of this independent economic research are not confirmed by the work of consulting firms that are typically engaged to provide impact assessments, which are notoriously optimistic in their forecasts. One of the central issues often ignored in debates about whether sport stadia are an effective use of public funds is whether a sport stadium is a good investment, relative to other public investment opportunities. The case is neatly put by Chanayil (2002:886):

> *In much the same way as a hotel or convention centre can be built as part of a developmental policy, it is argued that a stadium could meet such objectives as well. The problem, however, is that most stadia and arenas in the US are publicly owned, and yet used for the benefit of for-profit private organizations. In other words, the city often gets stuck with the bulk of the fixed cost stemming from construction and operation, while teams profit from using the stadium.*

Although tax revenues can provide a city with an economic return, this policy is often undermined in the case of sport stadia by the provision of tax incentives, while the share of profits from ticket sales, parking and associated services is far more variable than in other sectors of the economy.

More recently, Hurricane Katrina and the devastation caused in New Orleans prompted Baade and Matheson (2007) to examine the role of sport in the economic re-development of the city. Although sport has a symbolic power that may be useful in improving civic pride and stimulating psychological reconstruction, Baade and Matheson (2007) concluded that it is financially ill-advised for government to contribute funds towards the redevelopment of damaged professional sport infrastructure or to subsidize professional sport franchises. Rather, they argued for investment in more fundamental infrastructure that would assist in attracting residents back to New Orleans, many of whom left the city in the wake of the hurricane. Most damning was their contention that 'providing physical accommodation for professional sport teams does not advance the economic interests of New Orleans. Doing so merely compounds the economic problems that currently exist' (Baade & Matheson, 2007:602). The explanation for government investing in professional sport might lie in Baade and Matheson's (2007) acknowledgement that professional sport franchises might serve as a symbol that the city remains vital. Perhaps the desire to harness the symbolic power of sport and the prestige that it supposedly confers is greater than the requirement to formulate evidence based policy, which serves to reinforce the notion that policy is as much about rational decision making as it is about 'muddling through' (Lindblom, 1959).

Coates' (2007) review of the impact of stadiums and arenas highlighted several key findings of previous studies. First, little of the academic research conducted thus far has established significant increases in 'income, employment, taxable sales or tax revenues associated with sports and sports facilities' (Coates, 2007:575). Second, although consumer surplus and public benefits may be substantial, they are probably not large enough to warrant significant government investment, particularly when juxtaposed with the findings regarding direct economic benefit. Finally, where there is evidence for localized positive economic benefits, this is usually due to their redistribution from one area to another, rather than development of new benefits.

Establishing the economic impact of major and mega sport events is equally complex, although there is not the same degree of consensus within the academic literature as there is for stadia. In part, this is explained by the specific nature of the US professional sport market and the concentration of research. It is also explained by the nature of sport events, which makes it very difficult to assess their impact. Preuss (2006) identified the three most important aspects of the special nature of sport events: type of event, location of event and size of region affected by the event. Events such as the Olympic Games are multi-sport festivals that require a significant number of venues to cater for each of the sport competitions, whereas a World Championship in a single sport is likely to require one venue only. Thus, it is very difficult to make comparisons across different events. Events such as the Olympic Games are held in a different city and nation every 4 years, World Championships are held in a different city or nation annually or every second year in some cases, while other events are held annually in the same city or nation. The diversity of the locations makes it very difficult to make comparisons between the same types of events. Finally, large mega events such as the FIFA World Cup have an impact on an entire nation because of the number of venues required to stage the event, whereas major events that require a specialized facility (e.g. a world surfing tour event) may only benefit a relatively small city or town. This makes it very difficult to assess the degree of the event's impact. As Preuss (2006) concluded, these features mean that examining the economic impact of sport events lends itself to case study research design, and that this research can only be generalized with extreme caution.

Gratton, Dobson, and Shibli (2000) proposed a typology for major sport events (see Table 9.1), which helps to categorize different types of events, in order to explain their impact. Gratton et al. (2000) argued that type A and B events generate the greatest economic activity, hence the competition between cities and nations to host them. Type A events are the most sought after, but are also the hardest to secure, given their scarcity, as well as the significant infrastructure that is required. Type B events also have significant economic impact, but are typically at a fixed location, which means that competition between cities is limited. There are examples of competition between cities for international events (such as two cities within a nation competing for a round of the Grand Prix circuit), but this is the

Table 9.1	Typology of Major Sport Events
Type	**Features**
A	Irregular, one-off, major international spectator events generating significant economic activity and media interest (e.g. Olympics, Football World Cup, European Football Championship)
B	Major spectator events, generating significant economic activity, media interest and part of an annual domestic cycle of sports events (e.g. FA Cup Final, Six Nations Rugby Union Internationals, Test Match Cricket, Open Golf, Wimbledon)
C	Irregular, one-off, major international spectator/competitor events generating limited economic activity (e.g. European Junior Boxing Championships, European Junior Swimming Championships, World Badminton Championships, IAAF Grand Prix)
D	Major competitor events generating limited economic activity and part of an annual cycle of sports events (e.g. National Championships in most sports)

Source: Adapted from Gratton et al. (2000).

exception rather than the rule. Thus, Gratton et al. (2000) concluded that cities are often forced to compete for type C events, for which the economic impact is most uncertain.

Social Impact

As noted above, the role of sport events and stadia is often viewed by government as an issue of economic development, however, it is also increasingly being conceptualized as a vehicle for social and community regeneration. Of course, this type of regeneration is even more complex and the notion that sport can contribute is predicated on additional assumptions about the value and efficacy of sport. A cynical interpretation of the emphasis on potential social benefits is that local, state and national governments alike have broadened the scope of their justifications to include those outcomes that are more intuitive, ephemeral and difficult to measure easily and conclusively. A more generous interpretation is that governments believe that sport teams and events have the capacity to unite disparate elements of a community through a shared understanding and purpose. Given that the relationship between sport and social inclusion and cohesion is examined within the next chapter, the issue will not be examined in great depth within this chapter.

THE OLYMPIC GAMES AND RHETORIC OF URBAN REGENERATION

In late 2007 the International Olympic Committee accepted Baku (Azerbaijan), Chicago (USA), Doha (Qatar), Madrid (Spain), Prague (Czech Republic), Rio de Janeiro (Brazil) and Tokyo (Japan) as applicant cities for the 2016

Olympic Games. The applicant files of the cities are an instructive guide to the ways in which national and city governments and national Olympic committees use urban regeneration as part of a vision for conducting the Olympic Games, as well as providing for a variety of legacies. The applicant cities were almost unanimous in using urban regeneration as both a rationale for and a meritorious component of their respective Olympic bids. In many respects it is unfair to criticize the applicant cities for a lack of detail, as the applicant files were designed to select candidate cities, rather than select the winner on the basis of a developed plan. However, it is reasonable to highlight the ways in which the notion of urban regeneration is used in the applicant files as a catch-all for the renewal of previously degraded or deprived areas, or the re-imaging of parts of a city.

As illustrated in Table 9.2, all of the applicant cities for which files were available (Prague's applicant file was not publicly available) referred to urban regeneration. Many of the applicant files referred to urban regeneration in terms of the provision of infrastructure, such as green spaces (Madrid), transportation links (Rio) and road networks (Doha). Both the Madrid and Baku applicant files refer to the regeneration of environmentally deprived areas. In particular, the Baku applicant file was the clearest in establishing a vision for the Olympic Games as a catalyst for the conversion of an area 'beset by environmental problems', in this case an oilfield. In Baku's case, the regeneration of this area would be expensive and unlikely to go ahead without the capital investment that could be generated by the Games. On the other hand, the Chicago applicant file refers to the Games' role in long-term urban renewal projects, illustrating that the Games are also able to act as a catalyst or driver in highly developed Western economies. However, in Chicago, as opposed to Baku, the existing strategy is more likely to proceed without the Games. The Tokyo applicant file does not emphasize a specific type of infrastructure or propose a broad development project. Rather, the Tokyo file refers only to notion of improvement to the city or urban environment. In this respect, the conceptualization of regeneration and the impact of the Games are dependent on the city's existing development and the potential for the Games to act as a catalyst for existing or new projects. The Doha applicant file is similar in that it emphasizes existing infrastructure used to host the 2006 Asian Games and proposes a Games legacy which focuses on global understanding and the promotion of the Olympic ideal throughout the Arab world. In many respects it is ironic that the four cities selected to move to the next round of the selection process were Madrid, Rio, Chicago and Tokyo. The cities were not selected on the basis of their regeneration strategies, but their capacity to host the Games. In this respect, cities like Baku will always be at a disadvantage,

Table 9.2	Excerpts from 2016 Olympic Games Applicant Files
Applicant City	**Urban Regeneration Claims and Proposals**
Madrid	*Concept*: 'Our concept for the Games combines physical and social regeneration, to influence and improve the lives of all our people'. (p. 7) *Concept*: 'Olympic infrastructure will contribute to the regeneration of a sustainable urban environment', including 'a long-term regeneration project to recover green spaces and reclaim the river for the use of everyone'. (p. 7) *Proposed legacy*: 'urban regeneration of deprived areas, providing enhanced green and recreational spaces'. (p. 7)
Rio de Janeiro	*Olympic Games a major driver for Rio's ongoing transformation*: 'the potential impact for Rio would be dramatic, supporting the fast-tracking of renovations to the port and surrounding areas, the upgrading of city transportation links, and the acceleration of major environmental programs targeting sustainable future development of the city'. (p. 11)
Chicago	*Transforming the urban landscape*: 'the Games provide an extraordinary opportunity to accelerate the sustainable development of Chicago's South and West sides – two of the city's key long-term urban-renewal priorities – leaving a lasting Olympic legacy. The Olympic Village (the area will be developed regardless of whether Chicago hosts the 2016 Games), Olympic Stadium and Olympic Aquatics Center will serve as catalysts for urban redevelopment and transformation, a process that is already under way'. (p. 9)
Tokyo	*Interaction between Tokyo's existing 10 year plan and the Olympic Games*: 'Excellence of city planning and improvement of the urban environment'. (p. 4) *Long-term benefits of the bid*: 'Improvement of the city environment through Games-related initiatives'. (p. 4)
Baku	*Principal motivation*: 'Those responsible for the city and the 2016 Baku bid are especially highly motivated to make a clear statement with the conversion of the Bibi-Heybat oilfield – rich in history and beset by environmental problems – into a lively, flourishing Olympic Park Precinct. This process of transformation is to become the symbol of an exciting new beginning for the entire country on a path of development which is future-oriented, life-affirming and ecologically sound'. (p. 7) *Benefits and post-Olympic use*: 'The people of Baku will also benefit directly from the Olympic Games in the long term. The re-naturalization of the Bibi-Heybat oil field and its conversion into a lively, attractive and flourishing Olympic Park will bring back to Baku a real sense of the quality of life in the long term. New sports venues will give the people of Baku new, larger-scale opportunities to support their city in becoming a major sporting centre. The Olympic Village to be developed as part of a state development program will provide living space for many young families who are in search of a place to live'. (p. 9)
Doha	*Fulfilling Qatar's vision for the future*: 'The transport requirements for the Games match precisely with the ongoing program to improve the road network and develop mass transit'. (p. 7)

Sources: Bid Commission Rio 2016 (2008); Chicago 2016 Committee (2008); Doha 2016 Olympic and Paralympic Bid Committee (2008); Madrid 16 Foundation (2008); National Olympic Committee of the Republic of Azerbaijan (2008); Tokyo 2016 Bid Committee (2008).

and cities like Chicago will be able to leverage their capacity through regeneration and urban renewal projects.

On June 6, 2005, at the International Olympic Committee session in Singapore, the city of London was elected as host of the 2012 Summer Olympic Games, defeating rival icon cities Paris, Madrid, New York and

Moscow. The London 2012 Olympic Games is an example of a major sport event that has urban regeneration at the core of its reason for being, a further illustration that the strategy of using sport as a catalyst for urban regeneration is not limited to developing countries, but rather is an established strategy of major developed economies. As is typical of most sport events of the size of the Olympic Games or FIFA World Cup, the London Games will be delivered by a complex coalition of government and non-government departments and agencies, including the following:

- London Organising Committee of the Olympic Games and Paralympic Games

- Olympic Delivery Authority

- Department for Culture, Media and Sport

- Greater London Authority (including the London Development Agency and Transport for London)

- British Olympic Association

- British Paralympic Association

- East London host Boroughs of Greenwich, Hackney, Newham, Tower Hamlets and Waltham Forest

The complexity of the coalition has a variety of implications, not least that each level of government has particular strategies, commitments and objectives for the urban regeneration that has been promised as a part of the Games. The Mayor of London's *Five Legacy Commitments* is an instructive document in terms of highlighting the rationale for hosting the Games, as well as the place of urban regeneration and economic development within one of the largest sporting events in the world. According to the *Five Legacy Commitments*,

> *The regeneration of East London and the Lower Lea Valley was the main reason why the Mayor backed the bid to host the 2012 Olympic and Paralympic Games in London. The 2012 Games have massively accelerated the regeneration process and the Games will leave a legacy of 9,000 new homes in the Park and the opportunity to build 30,000 more in the surrounding area. It will create 50,000 new jobs, generate huge investment in transport, create new sporting facilities for local communities, and deliver the largest new urban park in Europe for 150 years.*
>
> (Greater London Authority, nd:13)

It is clear that London 2012 is a massive project, that it has enormous potential and that expectations about its legacies are extremely high. In one short paragraph the most significant outcomes of hosting a sport event have been rolled into one coherent statement of aspiration: better housing, more jobs, new infrastructure, new sporting facilities (which are hoped will lead to greater community participation), more open space and improved amenities. One of the key commitments of the Games is to ensure that Londoners benefit from new jobs and business opportunities: 'the London 2012 Games will help to create 50,000 jobs in the Lower Lea Valley', one of the most depressed areas of England, as well as 'inspire a series of projects that can help to reduce by 70,000 the number of Londoners without work' (Greater London Authority, nd:9). From a policy perspective, the London Games are a catalyst for a broad program of economic investment by government, which it is hoped will stimulate additional investment and sustainable long-term economic development. In this respect it is reasonable to conclude that the non-sport legacies are actually more important than the sport legacies linked to the Games themselves, which are notoriously ephemeral.

GOVERNMENT AND THE AUSTRALIAN GRAND PRIX

The concept of mega events is well established (Hall, 1994; Leroux & Mount, 1994; Ritchie, 1984; Ritchie & Smith, 1991; Roche, 1994). In the context of sport they are events that are separated from regular local, state and national competitions by the enormous financial and organizational logistics that are required to stage them. The competition between cities, states and nations to host these mega sport events is what Whitson and Macintosh (1996) referred to as the global circus. Television rights, increased international coverage via saturation media coverage, sponsorship, an influx of international visitors and an overall economic benefit are often claimed as the reasons that cities bid for the right to be the nominated host of sport mega events. The case of the Australian Grand Prix, staged at Albert Park, Melbourne since 1996 is an example of the power of the state, the ways in which mega sport events can interact with local communities and how the supposed benefits that arise from mega events can be contested.

The Albert Park Reserve is a large piece of public parkland (more than 550 acres), situated less than 2 kilometres from Melbourne's city centre. The Park had been used as a venue for motor racing in the 1950s, until the State government banned the practice and reserved the land as a public park for full and free access (Littlewood & Ward, 1998). According to Little-wood and Ward (1998), in the early 1990s Albert Park represented 60% of the public open space available to the then 70,000 residents of the City of Port Philip. In December 1993 a Draft Strategy Plan for Albert Park was released, in response to plans to upgrade the Park that had been in place as early as 1991. The foreword to the Draft Strategy Plan written by Jeff Floyd, Chief Executive Officer of the then Melbourne Parks and Waterways (now Parks Victoria) stated

> *The challenge for the Strategy Plan is to provide for a variety of recreational experiences including sport, leisure and open space enjoyment without destroying the fundamental nature of the Park, built up over many years.*
> (Melbourne Parks and Waterways, 1993:i).

Little over a week later, on December 17, 1993, Victorian Premier Jeff Kennett announced that a contract had been signed to hold a Formula One Grand Prix at Albert Park (Edmonds, 1993; Neales, 1993), effectively stealing it from neighbouring state South Australia, which had held the race on a street circuit since 1985. In May 1994, Melbourne Parks and Waterways released The New Plan for Albert Park (Melbourne Parks and Waterways, n.d.), which was open for public comment but contained no provision for community consultation, contrary to public undertakings by the chief executive officer (Floyd, 1994). In November 1994, Melbourne Parks and Waterways released its Master Plan, which detailed plans for the race circuit and a permanent two storey pit building (Melbourne Parks and Waterways, 1994).

The government of Victoria introduced the Australian Grand Prix Act of 1994 (as well as the Australian Grand Prix [Amendment] Act 1995 and the Australian Grand Prix [Further Amendment] Bill), to provide the event and its organizers with a range of legislative protection. The Grand Prix Act exempted the Grand Prix from a number of Acts of Parliament, including the Environment Protection Act (1970), Planning and Environment Act (1987) and the Environment Effects Act (1978). The Act also removed the jurisdiction of the Supreme Court, in order to prevent any challenges to the Act; no claims for compensation or damages could be lodged as a result of the Grand Prix being held at Albert Park. In practice this meant that the owners of homes damaged by compaction work, which took place in order to build the track, were unable to prevent the damage from occurring, nor were they able to seek compensation (Dakin, 1995a,b; Owen, 1995; Tennison, 1995).

One of Melbourne's major daily newspapers labelled the Australian Grand Prix Act 'a dangerous law'. Specifically, it stated that

> *The Kennett Government is displaying disturbing authoritarian tendencies in its determination to protect the Albert Park Grand Prix from public scrutiny, legal challenge and statutory impediments. Its sweeping legislation to exempt the race and track construction from environmental and planning laws, to deny aggrieved citizens and organizations access to the courts to claim compensation, and to place the race contracts beyond the scope of the Freedom of Information Act is, at best, a nervous overreaction. At worst, it smacks of an arrogant abuse of power.*
>
> (Editorial, 1994)

The Australian Grand Prix is not unique, however, for Whitson and Macintosh (1996:281) suggested that in the global sport circus, local opposition is often not welcomed by elites who seek to represent themselves as united and enthusiastic hosts and that 'attempts to discredit critics and to circumvent the normal channels of political appeal are not all that unusual'.

The Australian Grand Prix Act also established the Australian Grand Prix Corporation (AGPC), which was deemed to be responsible for track construction and other assorted facilities, as well as the annual organization of the event. The AGPC was given the power to fence or cordon off some or all of Albert Park and then legally occupy the area. Permanent fencing around and in Albert Park meant that the park was off-limits to anybody but members of the AGPC, contrary to its existence as a public domain. The AGPC were free to order any tree to be cut down, building demolished, playgrounds or ovals removed, and roads closed. It was also granted the power to regulate access to the park, including sporting activities and business operations. The Australian Grand Prix was also exempted from the Tobacco Advertising Prohibition Act of 1992. Under Section 18 of the Act, the Federal Minister for Health was able to exempt major international events from restrictions on the basis that they would be unlikely to take place if not for the exemption. The exemption was granted despite Australia's international health obligations and the large international media audience for Formula One motor sport.

The staging of the Grand Prix in a public park placed some significant environmental constraints on the park landscape and the use of the park by the local community. The setup and dismantling of the infrastructure required to stage the Grand Prix takes approximately 4 months, during which time local sport clubs, user groups and residents are prevented from using the Park. A significant number of sporting ovals were also lost in the initial re-development of the Park. Furthermore, the track straight, grandstand, garage and pit access requirements mean that 64,000 square metres of the Park must remain treeless. A further 110,000 square metres must also remain treeless in order to accommodate the three gravel and eight grassed run-off areas that are required for the safety of the Formula One drivers. Again, the disconnect between the needs of local communities and international sport events and competitions is not unique to the Melbourne Grand Prix experience, which is explained by Whitson and Macintosh (1996:282):

> *Facilities for major international sport events are built to meet the elaborate competitive requirements of international sport federations and to accommodate large numbers of spectators. In addition to being expensive for municipalities to operate afterward, such facilities usually are ill suited for subsequent use by most community sport and recreation participants. In practice, most feature facilities such as the main stadium or arena come to serve primarily as venues for professional sport.*

The actual economic impact of the Australian Grand Prix at Albert Park has also been contested. The Australian Grand Prix Act exempted the Grand Prix from the Freedom of Information Act, which meant that the agreements entered into by the then Kennett government, and subsequent Victorian State governments, have been regarded as commercial in confidence. This had made an independent assessment of the economic impact of the Grand Prix very difficult. In 2007 the Victorian Auditor-General released a report which examined Victoria's investment in major events, and in particular the Grand Prix, using the 2005 event as a case study. The Auditor-General's report concluded that the Grand Prix ran at a deficit and was responsible for AUS$62.4 million of the State's gross product, considerably less than the AUS$175 million claimed by the government. In the response to the report, the chief executive officer of the Grand Prix Corporation acknowledged that the study of economic impact was an inexact science, but questioned the relevance of some of the data used and the assumptions made. In particular, estimates of the cost of noise, traffic congestion and loss of the use of Albert Park had been made, but estimates of a range of benefits had not, including 'brand exposure and promotional benefits, national and international publicity and media coverage, reputation reinforcement, civic pride, the attraction of business investment, and the promotion of Melbourne and Victoria as a tourist destination and as a place to do business' (Victorian Auditor-General, 2007:9). The report and the Auditor-General were subsequently criticized by the Grand Prix Corporation and the National Institute of Economic and Industry Research, which conducted economic modelling for the government (Gordon, 2007).

In its 2006 'Tourism and Major Events Strategy' the Victorian government claimed that major events, such as the Grand Prix, the Australian Open Tennis Championships and the Spring (Horse) Racing Carnival, are responsible for attracting 230,000 international visitors per year, which is equivalent to 42% of all international visitors to Australia (Department of Innovation, Industry and Regional Development, 2006). It is also claimed that these events generate an economic benefit in excess of AUD$1 billion. In 2008 the Victorian government announced that it had signed another 5-year contract to host the Australian Grand Prix. The announcement by the Premier of Victoria, John Brumby, is instructive of the role of government and the supposed benefits of hosting the event (Premier of Victoria, 2008). Premier Brumby noted in the announcement that Victoria was the best State in Australia in terms of tourism; that its major events give it an 'unprecedented position in the major events and tourism market'; and that a new contract had been signed on the basis that the Grand Prix provided good value for money. Premier Brumby also noted that the international rights market is very competitive – 'there are plenty of other cities, plenty of other locations that would love to hold an event of the stature of the Grand Prix' – and that the State of Victoria was thrilled to have the opportunity to 'showcase' Melbourne and Victoria to an international audience of in excess of 100 million people. In early 2009 one of Melbourne's daily newspapers reported that the publication *Formula Money* had estimated, to within a few million dollars, that the Victorian government paid AUS$42million and AUS$47million to host the 2008 and 2009 races, respectively (Doherty, 2009). Whether or not the figures are accurate, it is clear that the Victorian State government is prepared to maintain a significant financial investment in what it regards as the centrepiece of its major events strategy.

POLICY COMMUNITIES AND MECHANISMS

The previous sections, which examined the Olympic Games and the Australian Grand Prix, illustrated several key aspects of the policy communities that are formed when sport is used as a tool or catalyst for urban regeneration and economic development, as well as the policy mechanisms that governments have at their disposal.

It is clear that national Olympic committees are highly involved in Olympic bids and are therefore intimately involved in the policy community; however, they are in the minority. In general, the policy communities that form to construct a major events strategy, bid for a major event or execute a major or mega event are largely comprised of government departments and agencies. Carlsen and Taylor's (2003) examination of the 2002 Manchester Commonwealth Games is instructive in this respect. They identified the main organizations as follows: Manchester Investment and Development Agency, Manchester City Council, Manchester Commonwealth Games 2002 Ltd., East Manchester Ltd. and Marketing Manchester. These organizations had responsibility for the economic legacy, the sporting infrastructure, physical and cultural renewal programs and promotion of the city of Manchester. The UK government was also involved in facilitating physical renewal and economic benefits. Sport organizations, in the traditional sense of the term, were not involved in developing strategies for improving physical infrastructure and economic development at the level of the organizing committee or city government. Sport organizations, such as national governing bodies, may be involved in the delivery of major multi-sport or single-sport events, however, their greatest involvement is likely to be post-event. This is particularly true in instances where a purpose built facility has been constructed as part of a multi-sport event such as the Olympic Games.

Sport organizations are far more involved within policy communities that form around the construction of a stadium. This is particularly true in the USA, where the construction of stadia for professional sport franchises by city governments is designed to retain an existing franchise or attract a new franchise. However, in these instances the term sport organization is perhaps misleading, as the actor in the policy community is the franchise owner, rather than a board of directors as it would be for a non-profit sport organization. In countries where non-profit sport organizations in national leagues are involved in stadia construction, the government is the major player in the policy community, as it invariably contributes the most money.

Government uses a range of policy mechanisms in directing or supporting economic development and urban regeneration through sport. First and foremost, they are able to allocate finances to an event, stadium or strategy. Without this financial investment, it is likely that far fewer stadia would be built and many events would either not take place, or be significantly compromised. The most extreme cases are large multi-sport festivals like the Olympic, Commonwealth or Asian games, which require government support as part of the bidding process. This typically involves financial investment and assurances. Second, governments are able to create authorities and agencies to engender development, manage stadia or manage events, which are ultimately answerable to government. Third, governments are able to introduce legislation to establish safeguards, increase industry confidence or reduce opposition to events and stadia. Special legislation is often typical for mega events, but the type and scope of the legislation varies significantly.

The case of the Australian Grand Prix at Albert Park is extreme, in which the legislation was designed to ensure the race went ahead in a particular location, no matter what obstacles or opposition lay in the government's path. Fourth, governments are able to provide tax incentives or financial subsidies to attract sporting teams or events to a particular location, making it more attractive to franchise owners or event organizers. This policy option has the benefit of making a city or location more attractive, but obviously reduces the potential direct economic benefit to the state. This is particularly contentious given the evidence which suggests that constructing sport stadia for professional sport franchises has little demonstrable benefit. Fifth, governments are able to enter into public–private partnerships, which are commonplace in situations where government is unable or unwilling to fund the entire capital investment, of either the sporting infrastructure or the non-sporting infrastructure associated with broader urban renewal. Finally, governments provide political support for events, stadia and teams, which ostensibly supports economic development through an improvement in consumer and business confidence, but in reality is designed to garner support from the media and the public for their policy priorities.

CONCLUSION

In many respects this chapter is as much about evidence as it is about policy. Many of the arguments for using sport as a tool for urban regeneration and economic development lack the authority of independent, systematic and substantiated research. Rather, the vast majority of the evidence in this area suggests that the benefits of using sport in this way are too small to warrant the use of public funds. This is particularly true where stadia are constructed for the use of private owners and organizations, and is compounded when these same owners and organizations are offered or granted tax exemptions and incentives as a way of attracting or retaining a team or event. But, despite the evidence, national and state governments continue to develop policies and strategies that use sport as a catalyst for the development of a range of interconnected outcomes, such as the aesthetic improvement of urban centres and disadvantaged suburbs, an increase in tourism, attracting private investment and putting their town, city or nation 'on the world map'.

The key question is why do governments do this; what is their rationale for using sport as a catalyst for economic development and urban regeneration? The short answer is that there are numerous rationales, and as illustrated by this chapter, these are intertwined. A single rationale is never enough to justify the investment, but together they add up to an often confounding mix, in which the intuitive notion that the public interest in sport and its high profile will more than likely result in a good outcome prevails. It is assumed that sport's high profile will lead to increased benefits, for the state, businesses, communities and individuals. As noted in the chapter, financial investment by government, in stadia or the infrastructure required for major and mega events, is only made within the context of a return on investment. Often other rationales, such as social regeneration, will be used to support policies and strategies, yet the efficacy of the policy will typically rest on an economic outcome. Of course, given the research and evidence reviewed with this chapter, the notion that economic outcomes are the key rationale is counterintuitive. But, as we suggested in this chapter, often the process by which sport is selected or used as a catalyst is inherently political; the willingness and ability for governments to demonstrate their power through sport, and confer status upon themselves and their cities and nations in the process, should not be underestimated.

The policies and examples of urban regeneration and economic development in this chapter have demonstrated that sport organizations and key agencies are very rarely central to the policy communities. Sport organizations such as National Olympic Committees or national sport federations and governing bodies have a role in the policy community for major events such as the Olympic Games or the FIFA World Cup, but they are typically on the periphery of large and complex policy communities that focus on economic investment, tourism and the marketing and promotion of cities. As noted in the chapter, sport organizations are typically involved in the management of an event, or in the case of sport stadia, are one of the major stakeholders. Their role in policy development is minimal, although there are exceptions, such as the private owners of professional sport teams in the USA. Even in these cases, the policy that underpins the investment is not engaged at the behest of or developed by the team owner. Rather, they are the beneficiary and will be involved in negotiations that alter or skew the policy and its intention.

The most important impact on sport organizations of the policies that use sport as a tool or catalyst for urban regeneration and economic development are the facilities that are either constructed specifically for teams or are left as event legacies. These sport stadia and purpose-built facilities often provide world-class training and competition venues for the athletes; these venues contribute to the ongoing development of high-performance athletes and contribute to traditional sport policies that emphasize elite success at the Olympic Games or World Championships. In this respect, it is often in the interests of the sport sector to either lobby government to support these events, or support government policies that seek to attract events or sporting teams.

CHAPTER 10

Social Inclusion

This chapter explores the third and final area of non-regulatory public policy that has an increasing influence on sport: social inclusion. As with the previous two chapters, which examined physical activity and health, and urban regeneration and economic development, we seek to explore three main questions. (1) What rationales have government used to justify using sport as a vehicle for the achievement of non-sport policy objectives? (2) How central is the sport sector and specifically sport organizations to the policy communities for these non-sport policies? (3) What existing (or likely) impact or influence have these policies had on sport organizations?

Like other areas of enabling policy explored in the previous two chapters, sport's role in social inclusion appears to tap into assumptions about sport's inherent value, qualities and capacity for good. At the same time, the role of sport in social inclusion is notoriously lacking in robust evidence. The evidence that does exist is beset by what Coalter (2007) identified as conceptual weakness, methodological weakness and little consideration of sufficient conditions. This chapter is in part concerned with this troublesome dichotomy – that many claims are made and benefits assumed without a significant body of evidence – as well as the way in which it is manifest in policy.

The role of sport in social inclusion is apparent in both sport policy and non-sport policies that seek to use sport as a policy tool. Although we noted in the introduction to this book that our interest is in areas of government policy that fall outside standard 'sport policy', this chapter examines both sport policy and non-sport policy. We do so with the purpose of examining how these two fields of policy differ in both rationale and implementation. We also do so because the stated role of sport in generating and maintaining social benefits for individuals, communities and nations is so prevalent within traditional sport policies, yet is not addressed in the same way as the more instrumental sport policy concerns of maximizing elite performance or improving participation rates among children. The title of this chapter is 'social inclusion', however, we could also have used the allied terms social cohesion or social capital, and throughout the chapter all three terms are used. Furthermore, the policies that relate to the relationship between sport and social inclusion, social cohesion and social capital at times also refer to social regeneration, social renewal, civic renewal, civic participation, community renewal and community development. It is not within the ambit of this chapter to engage in a lengthy definitional analysis of these terms. Rather, we have taken the approach of examining policies in which it is either explicitly stated or implicitly assumed that sport will be used to facilitate social interaction for the purpose of ameliorating individual and community problems around social inclusion.

The notion that sport has the capacity to engender social inclusion is intuitively powerful, so much so that it forms a significant part of the rationale for some of the other enabling policies that are examined within this book. Policies that seek to improve participation in sport organizations, as a way of improving physical activity levels and reducing the burden on the public health system, often cite additional social benefits, such as improved mental health and well-being. These additional benefits are predicated on the notion that the participants are engaged in an activity where, by necessity, they will come into contact with other people. Furthermore, this interaction is regarded as inherently positive; the potential negatives of social interaction are rarely considered when governments articulate the need for sport to act as a tool of social integration, let alone when these social benefits are considered complementary.

Similarly, policies that involve attracting major events to a city or building stadia, as part of a broader economic development or urban regeneration agenda, also often refer to the potential for social regeneration. This social regeneration typically takes four distinct forms. First, the construction of a stadium facilitates professional or elite sport, which in turn generates public interest. The basic contention is that individuals who come together, either inside the stadium as paying spectators or outside the stadium as mediated consumers (at home or in bars, for example), will experience social benefits because of their membership of a loose and often ephemeral social collective. If the social collective is relatively strong, it is likely that it will be small, such as a band of committed supporters. In this case, the social benefits that might accrue to a social collective will not necessarily be reflected throughout the entire group of supporters that identify with a team. Second, the hosting of an event has a similar effect, whereby people gather together to watch elite sport, although the social collective might be formed around support for a nation, rather than a team. Major and mega events are also assumed to create additional social collectives among the people who gather to enjoy the artistic and cultural festivities that typically accompany these events. Third, it is also often claimed that major and mega events, as well as professional sport teams, engender what Crompton (2001) referred to as 'psychic income'. Psychic income refers to the benefits that accrue to the collective morale of residents. Crompton (2001) argued that physic income may be the major justification for subsidizing private sport teams and events with public money, which indicates that the benefits are large or that the evidence for other benefits associated with events and teams is excessively weak. Either way, Crompton (2001) suggested that community residents who do not help to organize the event and do not attend might grow in confidence and feel a sense of pride by simply identifying with an event or team. Finally, hosting mega events usually involves the construction of important or much-needed infrastructure, such as improved transport and housing. In this respect, it is assumed that an improvement in an individual's or a community's material conditions will result in an improvement in their social conditions. In other words, the provision of infrastructure and related services will make citizens happier and less likely to participate in anti-social activities. However, it is obvious that the challenge of social regeneration and mitigating social exclusion is far more complex. In the previous chapter, we cited the example of the 2012 London Olympics and the regeneration of the Lower Lea Valley, which illustrated that social regeneration revolves in great part around the creation and sustainability of jobs, which is in turn an acknowledgement of the argument made by Collins and Kay (2003) that poverty is at the core of exclusion.

In each of the forms of social regeneration discussed above, a further set of assumptions is present. Most notably, it is assumed that social interaction will lead to social inclusion. In other words, the simple act of being with other people will result in an individual feeling more socially included because of their membership of a group, however tenuous or fleeting the membership might be. Furthermore, this increase in social interaction results in improved well-being. Once again, it is not within the ambit of this chapter to discuss the various definitions of well-being that are contained within government policy. However, in this context it is worth noting that it is usually a fluid term, but has strong conceptual links to health, both physical and mental. Thus, sport participation is assumed to create healthier and happier citizens. The specific aspects of government policy in this area are discussed in more detail in the following sections.

SPORT'S SOCIAL ROLE WITHIN SPORT POLICY

In the introduction to this book, we noted that the focus of national sport policies of western countries is typically enhancing elite performance, increasing the proportion of people involved in formalized competitive sport, ensuring a fair playing field and developing the capacity of the community sport system. We also suggested that these four areas focus on the achievement of relatively instrumental outcomes. It should be noted that social inclusion, social cohesion and social capital have not been a focus of sport policy developed by the governments in these western countries, nor have the central sport agencies been heavily involved in the implementation of programs that attempt to maximize sport's social impact. But, it is clear that social inclusion, social cohesion and social capital have been important aspects of the broader language and intention of sport policies. Furthermore, central sport agencies have been happy to capitalize on the assumed inherent potential within sport and sport organizations; they have used social inclusion, social cohesion and social capital as part of a diverse raft of justifications for particular policy positions, priorities and funding allocations.

In 2000, the Nice Declaration on the specific characteristics of sport and its social function in Europe declared that 'Sport is a human activity resting on fundamental social, educational and cultural values. It is a factor making for integration, involvement in social life, tolerance, acceptance of differences and playing by the rules' (European Council, 2000:1). The European Union's Commission on the European Communities 2007 white paper on sport reconfirmed this view of sport as a social institution with a range of social benefits, and articulated the potential of sport for social inclusion, integration and equal opportunities (Commission on the European Communities, 2007:7):

> Sport makes an important contribution to economic and social cohesion and more integrated societies. All residents should have access to sport. The specific needs and situation of underrepresented groups therefore need to be addressed, and the special role that sport can play for young people, people with disabilities and people from less privileged backgrounds must be taken into account. Sport can also facilitate the integration into society of migrants and persons of foreign origin as well as support inter-cultural dialogue.

> Sport promotes a shared sense of belonging and participation and may therefore also be an important tool for the integration of immigrants. It is in this context that making available spaces for sport and supporting sport-related activities is important for allowing immigrants and the host society to interact together in a positive way.

> The Commission believes that better use can be made of the potential of sport as an instrument for social inclusion in the policies, actions and programmes of the European Union and of Member States. This includes the contribution of sport to job creation and to

economic growth and revitalisation, particularly in disadvantaged areas. Non-profit sport activities contributing to social cohesion and social inclusion of vulnerable groups can be considered as social services of general interest.

Three key aspects of the white paper's conceptualization of the relationship between sport and its social benefits are worth highlighting. First, sport is able to have an impact on sections of the community that are often disadvantaged, are discriminated against or are most at risk from social exclusion: young people, people with disabilities, poor people and migrants. Second, economic growth and regeneration is a component of broader social regeneration, as previously noted in this chapter. Third, sport organizations can be considered as 'social services' because of the additional benefits that accrue to individuals and communities as a result of their involvement. These three core aspects of the conceptualization of sport's role in communities and nations represent the beginning of what might become a paradigm shift in the role, responsibility and uses of sport clubs in society. The traditional view of sport organizations and clubs can be characterized as one in which sport clubs and organizations are facilitators, or in some cases providers, of fairly instrumental activity and competition opportunities. The potential new role of sport organizations and clubs is one in which they engage with sectors of the community that are not typically attracted to or welcomed by community sport organizations, become part of a more coordinated governance and management system that focusses on their role in economic, urban and social development, and emphasize the social, rather than the physical aspect of their service. The notion of community sport organizations, which are typically member-benefit organizations, operating as social service organizations, might be the most radical shift of all.

The Commission on the European Communities white paper on sport recommended the following in terms of using its potential in social inclusion and integration:

The Commission will suggest to Member States that the PROGRESS programme and the Lifelong Learning, Youth in Action and Europe for Citizens programmes support actions promoting social inclusion through sport and combating discrimination in sport. In the context of cohesion policy, Member States should consider the role of sports in the field of social inclusion, integration and equal opportunities as part of their programming of the European Social Fund and the European Regional Development Fund, and they are encouraged to promote action under the European Integration Fund.

(Commission on the European Communities, 2007:7)

It is evident that the white paper recommended that sport be used in non-sport areas of government policy, action and funding. This is a further illustration of a shift in perception, from sport as an institution that may deliver additional social benefits, to sport as a tool which can be used to meet the outcomes and objectives within other areas of public policy and non-sport funding programs. In 2008, following a meeting at which attendees included all European Union Ministers for Sport, the European Commissioner responsible for sport and the Presidents of the National Olympic Committees of the European Member States, a joint declaration on the social significance and dialogue in sport was released. The declaration noted that the membership was

> *Convinced that sport can play a positive role in social inclusion and cohesion, intercultural dialogue, environmental understanding and the reintegration of children in post-conflict situations, for example child soldiers.*
>
> (European Union, 2008:2)

The declaration also served to

> *'Underline' the significant educational and social functions of sport and its importance not only in terms of physical development but also in terms of its capacity to promote social values, such as team spirit, fair competition, cooperation, tolerance and solidarity as well as the promotion and support of human rights through the Olympic values; [and] 'Recognise' the social significance of sport organizations, being an integral part of civil society and bringing together people from different social, intellectual and cultural backgrounds, from grassroots level up to and including the elite; [and] 'Emphasise' that sport projects can be a cross-cutting means of building capacity in education, health in general, peace-building and to combat social exclusion, violence, inequalities, racism and xenophobia.*
>
> (European Union, 2008:3)

What is most notable in the declaration is the multitude of social problems that sport could potentially be used to solve. These problems vary in complexity and scope, from simply bringing people together to promote tolerance to making a contribution to world peace. It is clear that sport was and is being viewed by national and pan-national governments not as a series of organizations and institutions, but as a large network that can act as a social panacea. It is questionable, however, whether the rhetoric of government policy and declarations matches the reality of grassroots participation and involvement.

The conviction that sport has an important social role has gained increasing acceptance throughout the world. Hoye and Nicholson (2008) examined the sport policies of Australia, Canada, New Zealand and the UK in order to examine how social capital was conceptualized by governments and the rationales for its inclusion in national sport policies. Their analysis is instructive in terms of the purpose of this chapter. In all of the sport policies and related documents that were examined, social capital, social cohesion and social inclusion were evident in the policies. It was also clear that sport was viewed by government and the central sport agencies as having the capacity and potential to deliver a range of social inclusion related outcomes.

In Australian sport policy statements and associated reviews, sport has been viewed as an important vehicle of social cohesion. The 2001 Australian federal government sport policy, Backing Australia's Sporting Ability (BASA), provided direction for the development of Australian sport throughout the first decade of the twenty-first century. In the foreword to the policy, Australian Prime Minister John Howard and the then Minister for Sport Jackie Kelly noted that

> *The centrepiece of our policy is a new strategy to increase community participation in sport. It is true that more players mean more winners but there are also other benefits of being involved in sport. In addition to the obvious benefits of health and fitness, the Government appreciates that sport provides valuable opportunities for people of all ages to improve themselves, display teamwork and become more engaged in community activities. Our aim is to see more sport played at the grass roots level, particularly amongst school aged children and in rural areas, where sporting groups are often a vital factor in the cohesion of local communities. To this end the Government has increased funding to encourage participation and has introduced new programmes directed at young Australians.*
> (Commonwealth of Australia, 2001:2)

Shaping Up, the report of the Sport 2000 taskforce, which was charged with reviewing government involvement in Australian sport, concluded that 'social and community benefits can be gained from progressive policies that utilise sport and physical activity and that this justifies Commonwealth Government involvement in providing opportunities for people to engage in physical activity' (Commonwealth of Australia, 1999:56). This rationale was reinforced within the BASA policy and again in the Howard Government's 2004 election policy statement on sport, Building Australian Communities Through Sport (BACTS), that, as its title suggests, made an explicit connection between sport and community. The BACTS policy continued the claim that 'sport plays a vital role in building and sustaining local communities, particularly in rural and remote areas' (Liberal Party of Australia, 2004:4). It also repeated the claims that by supporting elite athlete success, Australian sport policy helps to 'unite Australian communities' (Liberal Party of Australia, 2004:8).

The lead agency charged with implementing much of the Australian sport policy, the Australian Sports Commission (ASC), was even more explicit in its belief of the place of sport in building communities, stating that 'sport provides a strong and continuous thread through Australia's diverse and widespread population (and) it is a binding element in our social and cultural fabric' (ASC, 2005:2). The BASA sport policy emphasized participation in organized sport through the community club-based sport system. It assumed that sport clubs are positive sites for the development of social capital outcomes, specifically social cohesion and social connectedness. However, there did not appear to be any overt recognition within the policy of existing social capital within sport organizations or that sport organizations require social capital stocks to facilitate their activities and thus contribute to the achievement of government policy objectives.

The Liberal Party of Australia had been in office for 11 years until November 2007 and had demonstrated an unwavering commitment to the notion that sport develops social capital. The policy platform of the rival Australian Labor Party was almost identical in its assumptions made about the contribution of sport to community well-being, social cohesion and social connectedness. In their 2007 National Platform and Constitution, the Australian Labor Party (2007:173) stated that 'Labor recognises that sport and recreation are an intrinsic part of our culture and way of life - building social cohesion that binds families, communities, regions and the nation'. A federal Labor government would direct their funding (in part) towards developing and enhancing 'community based sporting organizations across all regions of Australia in recognition of the important role such organizations play in creating social cohesion' (Australian Labor Party, 2007:173).

As noted in Chapter 8, the newly elected Labor government released a discussion paper in May 2008, *Australian Sport: Emerging Challenges, New Directions*, which articulated a new role for sport in Australian society. The discussion paper, which in effect was a statement of the Labor government's sport policy priorities, continued to argue for the role of sport and sport organizations in social cohesion and inclusion:

Sport is integral to Australia's way of life, our view of ourselves and how we are viewed by the rest of the world. It helps to build the social cohesion that binds families, communities, regions and the nation. No other facet of our culture has the capacity to bring together so many different streams of life in mutual joy and celebration.

Sport is important for more than reasons of national pride, or even as a way of building a fitter, more vibrant nation. Sport reaches across our society in ways which are not always apparent, and involves even those who profess no love of sport.

Sport has a range of benefits at both the community and individual level. At the community level, sport brings people together, break downs [sic] barriers and unites those who have nothing else in common. Sport has a unique ability to transcend race, religion, gender and creed. It is truly a tool of social cohesion.

(Commonwealth of Australia, 2008:2)

It is clear from these statements that sport and sport organizations are considered to have great capacity and almost endless potential to bring people together. This capacity and potential even extends to people who have nothing else in common other than their sport involvement, as well as to people who are not even interested in sport. The suggestion that sport is able to transcend race, religion and gender may have its antecedents in the notion that these are often issues or features that divide and fracture societies; sport is seen as a readymade medicine for hard-to-cure social ills. This suggestion is made despite the problem that is succinctly referred to as the segmenting power of sport (Dyreson, 2001). In other words, sport can be a site for division rather than cohesion, and the division is often on the basis of a person's race, gender or nationality. The above statements also reveal that the Australian government considers sport to be perhaps the most important institution in society for bringing diverse people together, but the ways in which it does so might not be able to be understood, or even identified. This, in turn, might be interpreted as arguing for sport's potential as social glue, despite the lack of evidence or understanding about the ways in which the relationships between sport and social inclusion, cohesion or capital function.

Sport's role in social inclusion and social cohesion is also reflected in Australia's state government policies, budget allocations and the annual reports of the key sport departments and agencies. At the Australian state government level, sport is linked to combating social isolation, improving well-being, strengthening communities, increasing community cohesion, improving social networks and creating a fairer society in which disadvantage and discrimination are reduced. Despite differences in language and emphasis, the conceptualization of sport's social capacity is common across

Australia's government departments and key sport agencies, at national and state levels, indicating a high degree of policy convergence (Bennett, 1991; Knill, 2005).

Hoye and Nicholson (2008) noted that the connection between sport and positive social and community benefits has also been evident in Canadian government policy statements since the late 1980s. The Canadian Sport Policy of 2002 contains similar language to the Australian sport policies and appears to be underpinned by a common understanding of the social role of sport:

> *Sport is an essential tool for building strong individuals and vibrant communities and for enhancing our collective pride and identity and sense of belonging. Through sport in their respective communities, Canadians learn to volunteer and to accept a sense of responsibility for a civil society.... Establishing sport clubs and organizing events are great training grounds for social action. Social capital is built by learning to organize meetings, negotiate for use of shared facilities, and deal with expectations, triumphs and failures.*
> (Government of Canada, 2002:5,6)

The capacity and potential of sport to contribute social benefits to Canadian society is reinforced in Sport Canada's 2004–2008 strategic plan, in which the lead sport agency noted that

> *The Government of Canada's investment in sport is grounded in strong logic: Sport, as a tool for social development, has the ability to engage citizens and communities, surmount social barriers and contribute to building a healthier, more cohesive society. Sport builds pride in our nation through the performance of our athletes.*
> (Sport Canada, 2004:3)

Sport Canada's 2004–2008 strategic plan identified four strategic priorities: increase the number of Canadians participating in sport; improve Canada's international sport results; strengthen Canada's ethically based athlete/participant-centred sport development system; and build a more coordinated and connected sport system. The outcomes and strategies outlined by Sport Canada did not refer specifically to particular programs or initiatives to improve or capitalize on social interaction created through sport clubs or the national pride created through the performance of elite Canadian athletes. Rather, sport's ability to act as a tool for social development and an agent of a cohesive society was assumed to occur as a subsidiary benefit of other policy activities. Increased social cohesion at the community level was assumed to result from an increase in participation with community clubs, and increased national pride was assumed to result from watching Canadians succeed at the Olympic Games and World Championships. The Canadian sport policy and strategic plan make no reference to the conditions in which the cohesion and pride is occurring. This is not atypical. Rather, most national sport policies consider the conditions under which cohesion and national pride are created to be stable and immutable.

The use of sport as a tool for social inclusion, cohesion and capital is also evident in UK sport policies (Hoye & Nicholson, 2008). The 2002 Game Plan sport policy in the UK noted that 'using sport to promote social inclusion can also help to build social capital through developing personal skills and enlarging individuals' social networks' (DCMS, 2002:60). In a joint report produced by Sport England, DCMS and the Local Government Association, titled *Sport Playing its Part*, sport's broader social potential was clearly articulated:

> *Sport can be used as an engagement mechanism to build*
> *relationships with hard to reach individuals or groups and can open*
> *up alternative channels that enable local people, in particular those*
> *who are alienated from mainstream services, to obtain advice and*
> *information on a wide range of health, social, education and*
> *employment issues.*
>
> (Sport England, 2005:8)

The sport policies, reports and discussion papers quoted within this analysis refer to benefits accruing to individuals, citizens, families, communities, regions and nations. Who benefits, where they benefit and whether these benefits can be aggregated appear to be fluid. As Hoye and Nicholson (2008) argued, the categories either blend into one, or the benefits are assumed to be easily transferable. By not being more specific about the ways in which sport contributes in particular locations, contexts and conditions, the particular types of people, families and communities that benefit, or the particular types of benefits they receive, the policies and the governments that formulated them have accorded sport infinite potential, but rendered the outcomes intangible and vague.

Hoye and Nicholson (2008) also argued that the policies of nations such as Australia, Canada, New Zealand and the UK appear to suggest that sport has significant capacity to create or maintain bridging social capital. That is, the process by which the development of social networks contributes to the connection of previously unconnected elements or individuals within a community, rather than reinforcing existing divisions and differences (Putnam, 1995). The argument is implicitly made that sport has this capacity, without an equally valid acknowledgement that sport is very good at facilitating bonding social capital, in which the social networks contribute to the cooperation of members within a group. As Hoye and Nicholson (2008) noted, bridging social capital is often regarded as almost exclusively positive, whereas bonding social capital can have a negative impact on society, particularly when it is present in groups such as extremist religious sects or neo-Nazi gangs. At a more realistic level and in terms of the context of sport, bonding social capital might result in social cliques that serve to exclude or normalize anti-social behaviours. Thus, national sport policies overwhelmingly contextualize sport's role in social inclusion and cohesion as positive, when in fact sport organisations might also be discriminatory, exclusive and unwilling to engage beyond a small and well-established segment of the broader community. In other words, national sport policies within nations such as Australia, Canada, New Zealand and the UK fail to acknowledge sport's potential for social exclusion. In part, this is because, as noted previously, these policies almost exclusively refer to what Coalter (2007) referred to as the necessary conditions (participation) and give little or no attention to the sufficient conditions (mechanisms, process and experiences) that produce specific outcomes for specific individuals or groups.

It is possible to discern a range of possible rationales for the emphasis on sport's social role within national sport policies, although none of them are explicitly stated. As Hoye and Nicholson (2008) suggested, there are five key rationales. First, the notion that it 'makes people feel good' is not enough to justify the large-scale funding of elite and high-performance sport. As such, government has a vested interest in rationales that appear to provide additional benefits, such as national pride and 'psychic income'. Second, community sport organizations are locations for community sport participation, as well as the development and training of talented and elite athletes. Governments are concerned to boost the participation of community sporting clubs for instrumental reasons, such as increasing physical fitness and health of the participants or increasing the pool from which elite athletes are drawn. The relationship between sport and social benefits provides government with an important complementary justification for funding community sport organizations and improving the capacity of club-based sport governance/delivery systems. Third, sport clubs and organizations appear to have the human and physical resources and infrastructure to cope with additional participants, as discussed in the chapter related to physical activity and health. These existing resources and infrastructure, as well as the high levels of public awareness that sport enjoys through saturated media coverage of professional sport, make sport clubs and organizations a natural target for governments that are seeking to increase the opportunities of individuals and communities to engage in social inter-action. Fourth, a high proportion of people who volunteer do so within sport organizations and a high proportion of people who are involved in sport organizations are engaged as volunteers. Given that volunteering is viewed as a central component of or as a proxy for the existence of social capital, it is reasonable for governments to use sport organizations and clubs as vehicles for the creation and maintenance of social networks and relation-ships that facilitate inclusion and cohesion. Of course, this rationale does not take into account the capacity constraints of non-profit sport organiza-tions that are reliant on volunteers, who are increasingly under pressure from compliance requirements, accountability standards, financial pres-sures, as well as governance and interpersonal challenges. Finally, the social and financial burden on governments will be reduced if sport contributes to reducing social problems that require government intervention and invest-ment. As Hoye and Nicholson (2008) noted, this might be interpreted as part of a broader neo-liberal process in which the responsibility for main-taining strong and sustainable communities is increasingly devolved from government to the non-profit sector, communities, families and individuals.

SPORT'S SOCIAL ROLE WITHIN NON-SPORT POLICY

The previous section largely examined the ways in which sport's social role is articulated in traditional sport policies, that is, those that deal specifically with national and state sport systems and sport organizations. Although it is rarer, sport's social role is also articulated within non-sport policies and strategies. It should be noted, however, that these policies and strategies cap-italize on existing sport policies and the emphasis on sport's social role within these policies. In other words, non-sport policies that advocate for sport's capacity or potential in building social inclusion and cohesion do so in the context of complementary policies and funding programs. Typically, at the national level they do not provide additional funds or create specific programs. The following examples in the UK illustrate this phenomenon.

In the UK, a series of disorders in some of its poorest regions in 2001 resulted in a series of reports that examined the ways in which more cohe-sive communities might be built. The Home Office's report on *Building Cohesive Communities* (December, 2001) drew on a range of sources to conclude that there are a range of key factors that define the problem, including

- The lack of a strong civic identity or shared social values to unite diverse communities;

- The fragmentation and polarization of communities – on economic, geographical, racial and cultural lines – on a scale which amounts to segregation, albeit to an extent by choice;

- Disengagement of young people from the local decision-making process, inter-generational tensions and an increasingly territorial mentality in asserting different racial, cultural and religious identities in response to real or perceived attacks;

- Weak political and community leadership;

- Inadequate provision of youth facilities and services;

- High levels of unemployment, particularly amongst young people;

- Activities of extremist groups;

- Weaknesses and disparity in the police response to community issues, particularly racial incidents; and

- Irresponsible coverage of race stories by sections of the local media.

This list of factors illustrates the complexity of the problems of social exclusion and the difficulties associated with the notion of 'building communities'. The complexity of the issues is also an antidote to some of the simplistic conceptions of the role and capacity of sport and sport organizations articulated in some of the policies examined earlier in the chapter. The Home Office Report noted that 'Sporting and cultural opportunities can play an important part in re-engaging disaffected sections of the community, building shared social capital and grass roots leadership through improved cross-cultural interaction' (Home Office, 2001:28,29). In the context of this chapter, it is notable that the report then referred to the work of the Department of Culture, Media and Sport, which included a raft of programs, funding and activities in areas of encouraging sports leadership; engaging groups whose sport participation is low; building new sport and art facilities in primary schools; and providing opportunities for children in deprived areas to engage in arts and creative activities.

In 2007, the UK government released 30 public service agreements, which detailed its highest priorities for the period 2008–2011. *Delivery Agreement 21: Build more cohesive, empowered and active communities* (PSA21) is instructive in terms of government's perception of the social impact of sport, its expectations and the ways in which government views its role in facilitating improved outcomes through sport. In the vision of PSA21, it is noted that citizens need support and should be able to lead fulfilled lives:

Active communities can be achieved by increasing levels of formal and informal volunteering, where members of the community work to meet local needs as well as by increasing participation across a variety of cultural and sporting activities. At the heart of this active participation are community-based third sector organizations, often bringing different groups together, and providing the platform to meet the needs of individuals and communities.

(HM Government, 2007:3)

Furthermore, PSA21 acknowledges that third-sector organizations are vital to achieving cohesive, empowered and active communities. Inherent within this acknowledgement is the recognition that government does not have the capacity to mandate involvement, nor does it have the resources to ensure that all of its citizens participate in the same activities at the same level of intensity or involvement. Rather, the government relies on third-sector organizations to facilitate and encourage participation, in part because it recognizes that in order to be empowered, individuals and communities need to develop, modify and adapt practices and organizations to meet their needs, rather than have a generic model imposed on them.

The PSA21 identified six indicators to measure the achievement of its goals: (1) the percentage of people who believe people from different backgrounds get on well together in their local area; (2) the percentage of people who have meaningful interactions with people from different backgrounds; (3) the percentage of people who feel that they belong to their neighbourhood; (4) the percentage of people who feel they can influence decisions in their locality; (5) a thriving third sector; and (6) the percentage of people who participate in culture and sport. The PSA21 noted that government would not set national targets, but that it expected to see an improvement in indicators 1, 3 and 4 and that local governments would in part be responsible.

In many respects it is clear from this set of performance or outcome indicators why sport and sport organizations are so attractive to policy makers within and outside sport. Participation or involvement in a community sport organization is likely to contribute significantly to indicator 2, by mere association of people from different backgrounds. It is also likely to contribute to indicator 1, particularly if the interactions within community sport organizations are positive and foster a tolerance that permeates the non-sport interactions of community members. It is also likely that involvement in sport organization will be positively correlated with feelings of belonging, particularly if the community sport organization is closely identified with a specific locale, and might therefore contribute to indicator 3. Community sport organizations comprise a significant component of the third sector, and if appropriately funded and well-managed, are likely to be considered 'thriving', while people who occupy leadership positions within them might feel more empowered within their locality.

The sixth indicator, participation in culture or sport, is based on the notion that people who participate in these activities are more likely to be engaged citizens than people who do not. The PSA21 noted that research showed that sport and exercise are the single greatest contribution to social participation. It is difficult to surmise what this means, for social participation might simply be participation in an activity in which there are other people present. In this case, sport and exercise are likely to be significant, given the number of people who participate in these activities, relative to other community activities. It is possible that participation in sport is attractive as a proxy for social capital, however, as Nicholson and Hoye's (2008:9) discussion of this issue illustrated, sport participation trends are useful as one of a series of social indicators, and 'the notion that participation is a valid proxy for social capital does not account for the way in which the social capital produced through these interactions is used'. As Putnam (2000:58) noted, 'what really matters from the point of view of social capital and civic engagement is not merely nominal membership, but active and involved membership'. In many respects, this could be the starting point for Coalter's (2007) examination of the necessary and sufficient conditions. In other words, PSA21 might identify participation, the necessary condition, as an indicator, but what is likely to be more important in determining whether sport organizations contribute to tolerance, social connectedness, a sense of belonging and self-determination are the sufficient conditions.

In PSA21, the section on delivery strategies noted that in order 'to help build more active communities, the Government provides the strategic direction and frameworks for the delivery of opportunities for all to participate in culture and sport' (HM Government, 2007:8). Support for this is related to government implementation of a program to build the capacity of organizations working at the community level. Specifically, PSA21 noted that this would be achieved through investment in the regional and local provision of sport via bodies such as Sport England. It was also noted that the Department of Culture, Media and Sport 'has a key role in working with the sporting and cultural sectors to ensure that their contribution to building cohesive, empowered and active communities is fully understood by local partners and is delivered on the ground' (HM Government, 2007:11). This key role involved continuing to invest in and work through organizations such as Sport England, investing in infrastructure, focussing on getting more people participating, particularly from groups with relatively low levels of participation, and encouraging and advocating for best practices. PSA21 referred to a range of government organizations and agencies that would collaborate to deliver the proposed outcomes, including the Office for the Third Sector, the Home Office, the Border and Immigration Agency, the Ministry of Justice, the Department for Children Schools and Families, the Department for Environment, Food and Rural Affairs, the Department of Health and the Department for Innovation, Universities and Skills. It is clear that like health and physical activity, and urban regeneration and economic development, social inclusion is an issue that requires either a whole of government approach or at the very least an inter-departmental approach. In this respect, sport organizations and key sport agencies, although important, are one component of a much larger policy community.

CONCLUSION

This chapter, like the previous two chapters that examined what we have termed 'enabling' policies, has demonstrated that sport organizations are typically conceptualized as inherently positive, constructive and useful spaces in which social interaction between people has the potential to either achieve or facilitate a range of social outcomes and benefits. Like urban regeneration and economic development, it is questionable whether there is sufficient evidence for the social benefits of sport participation and involvement to warrant the level of government attention it receives. This chapter has illustrated that the perception of sport's capacity and potential to contribute to improving social inclusion and cohesion is not isolated to one or two nations, but rather has become an accepted part of national sport policies, frameworks and strategies, particularly among western developed nations.

In exploring the relationship between sport, policy and social inclusion we sought to answer three questions. First, we were interested in exploring the rationales that government use to justify appropriating sport as a vehicle for the achievement of non-sport policy objectives. There are two core rationales for linking sport and a broad range of social objectives within government policy. The first is that sport organizations are effectively a well-established and well resourced (human, organizational and physical) social network with high levels of public awareness. Sport organizations invariably involve people engaging in an instrumental activity, such as exercising for fitness or participating in a competition for fun or to demonstrate mastery. Importantly and by necessity, they also involve social interaction, with people often working together to achieve a common goal (either on-field or off-field). This first rationale, which is present in sport and non-sport policies, essentially reflects Coleman's (1988) notion of appropriable social organizations, in which a network operates for different purposes other than the one it was created for. As we have illustrated at various points during this chapter, this rationale identifies the necessary conditions (involvement or participation), but then ascribes a host of benefits and outcomes which are dependent on a range of individual, organizational, environmental and social processes and mechanisms that are not identified, let alone developed. The second key rationale, which is typically only evident in sport policies, is that sport's assumed social capacity and potential provides an ideal justification for the emphasis on and funding of other strands of sport policy. Given the lack of evidence, perhaps the most cynical manifestation of this rationale is the argument that by funding elite athletes, the broader community will benefit through increased social cohesion, national pride and psychic income. This rationale continues to be an accepted component of sport policies in western developed nations, as well as within general statements about the significance of sport and the need for government intervention.

The second question we sought to explore was whether the sport sector and sport organizations are central to the policy communities that develop policies within the area of social inclusion. In terms of sport policies, it is clear that the sport sector and key sport agencies and organizations are central to the policy community. Sport organizations, departments and agencies have a vested interest in ascribing as many benefits to sport as possible. Sport's role in the development and maintenance of social inclusion, cohesion and capital is no different. In terms of non-sport policies, the sport sector plays a relatively minor role, largely because social exclusion, social disadvantage, poverty, the disaffection of young people, crime and discrimination are complex issues that typically require a whole of government strategy. Sport is seen as playing an important role, but sport organizations are most often viewed as providing a service or implementing a program at the grassroots or community level.

The final question was what existing (or likely) impact or influence have these policies had on sport organizations. Overall, the impact and influence of sport policies within this area has been negligible. This is largely because the social benefits of sport have been espoused as a justification for other sport policies. In other words, the funding and programs to support high performance sport or encourage greater participation within the community have continued apace, with added legitimacy. Traditional sport policies have continued to focus on instrumental outcomes, rather than re-direct the focus of sport organizations to how they develop the social inclusion or cohesion that they might be facilitating. Similarly, non-sport policies also have little impact because they too emphasize sport's social benefits and argue that existing sport-based programs are being used to develop capacity and maximize potential benefits. Additional funding and programs for the development of social inclusion and cohesion are typically directed through existing sport agencies and emphasize the good sport already does and the potential for more, rather than the ways in which they might improve their human and organizational capacities. An additional important question is whether the impact or influence on sport organizations will be greater in the future. Like in the area of physical activity and health, if sport organizations and agencies continue to use sport's social contribution as an argument for additional funding to enhance existing instrumental activities, they might find that they are required to be more accountable. In other words, additional funding might be contingent on providing evidence to support the current declarations. This might provide the catalyst for the paradigm shift in which social service becomes *the* priority of sport organizations.

CHAPTER 11

Conclusion

One of the aims of this book was to extend our understanding of the role of the state in sport beyond analyses of what is commonly understood to be sport policy (i.e. elite sport development, anti-doping in sport, increasing mass participation and building the capacity of sport systems). The preceding chapters have highlighted the range of regulatory interventions imposed by governments on the governance and management of sport organizations, the conduct of sport activities, the safety of sport participants, sport's relationship with the media and gambling industries and physical education. The book has also explored three other public policy areas (physical activity and health, urban regeneration and economic development, and social inclusion), in which governments are increasingly turning to sport for assistance in the achievement of non-sport policy outcomes. The purpose of this final chapter is to draw conclusions regarding the questions we have posed in relation to these regulatory interventions and other public policy areas, surmise what future impact the continuation or extension of these policies might have on sport organizations and suggest some potentially fruitful avenues for future research into the broader relationship between government and sport beyond the boundaries of contemporary sport policy.

REGULATORY INTERVENTIONS

With regard to the regulatory interventions reviewed in this book, a number of government rationales for intervention can be identified. First, protecting their existing investment in sport (in the form of direct funding for such things as stadia development and elite sport performance) by regulating the governance systems used by sport organizations, imposing financial accountability measures and requiring compliance with allied policies such as anti-doping regimes. Such efforts have increased the compliance burden for sport organizations, particularly national and state/provincial-level governing bodies of sport. Second, governments have also sought to regulate some sports to alleviate concerns about the efficacy with which sports can self-regulate their activities or the actions of individuals within sports, particularly those sports with inherently high levels of risk for participants. The lack of a mandate for self-regulation within some sports, as well as alleviating perceptions about a lack of accountability in allowing some sports to self-regulate, are key aspects of government intervention in this area. Third, governments have also introduced regulations in order to assist sports undertake tasks designed to improve the safety of participants, such as police checks and screening potential staff and volunteers. Finally, in relation to the more commercial aspects of sport, namely its relationship with the gambling and media industries, government rationales for regulatory interventions include controlling potential monopoly markets, distributing windfall profits, overcoming information inadequacies in the marketplace and facilitating distributive justice and social policy.

The range of rationales evident in these examples supports the application of the Baldwin and Cave (1999) framework as a way of identifying government rationales for regulatory intervention in sport. The review of government regulation of physical education in the UK provided in Chapter 7 also highlights that government rationales encompass both concerns about distributive justice and social policy as well as planning. The example of physical education regulation in the UK also emphasizes the variable level of commitment that national governments may exhibit in relation to any specific issue, and the subsequent impact of some issues being subject to discernible phases of regulation by government. Thus, the regulatory analysis frameworks of Lukes (2005) and Foucault (1982), which focus on the distribution of power, are also instructive for the review of government rationales in relation to regulation in sport.

In the majority of regulatory areas reviewed in this book, sport organizations could not be considered to be central to the policy communities that are involved in the development of regulatory policies. In relation to regulations concerning governance and management practices, the control of some sport activities, and in relation to broadcast rights regulations, sport governing bodies are best described as peripheral policy community members that are involved in consultation only after the political decision to regulate has been taken. In other areas of regulatory policy, such as ensuring safe sport environments, physical education curriculum or the control of gambling associated with sport, sport organizations are far more vocal and involved in the detail of developing regulatory interventions, or indeed, are the catalyst for the development of regulatory intervention. It is also apparent that sport organizations can be somewhat reluctant to engage in the debate about some forms of government regulation, as occurred in relation to child protection in sport, but are very vocal in the support or criticism of regulatory interventions which have the potential to protect or diminish their revenue streams, as occurred within debates about regulations for gambling and broadcast rights (listed events) respectively.

The Baldwin and Cave (1999) framework has also enabled us to identify the range of regulatory strategies and instruments that governments have employed to achieve their policy objectives. These fall into five main categories. By far the most popular is the use of command and control strategies, with threatened withdrawal of government funding the most common threat for non-compliance. Governments have also used mandated disclosure and reporting requirements to deliver regulatory outcomes, specified or mandated the development of self-regulation within sports, used direct action by central agencies to develop resources or specific agencies to deal with a specific issue (such as the CPSU or boxing commissions), as well as undertaken some market harnessing regulation by licensing participants in some areas of sport.

As noted earlier, these regulatory policies have a number of existing and likely impacts on sport organizations and their members. First, regulatory policies in the area of governance and management have imposed a greater level of accountability on sport governing bodies and have tended to reinforce the level of resource dependence of some sport governing bodies on central government agencies for both funding and information. This is particularly so for the smaller sports without broadcast rights revenues, which are more dependent on government funding for elite program development. Second, in some instances, these regulatory policies simply enable a particular sport to be enjoyed by people as either active participants or spectators (e.g. boxing and other combat sports being regulated by the state in the absence of a viable governing body). Third, regulatory interventions have improved the safety of sport participants (e.g. boxing) and for sports such as horse racing, have arguably improved the quality. Fourth, in some jurisdictions, the development of member protection policies, including child protection measures, have arguably created safer sporting environments in which people can participate as athletes, coaches, supporters or administrators. Fifth, in relation to regulation of the relationship between sport and gambling, sport organizations have, in the main, benefited from protected access to expanding revenue streams from sports betting, wagering and national lottery funding distributions. Sixth, in some jurisdictions, sport organizations are restricted in their ability to maximize the value of their broadcast rights. Finally, the positioning of organized competitive sport as central to physical education programs, at least in the UK, has benefited sports in promoting their wares to young people and fostering relationships between schools and clubs in order to facilitate potentially long-lasting participation in sport.

We also wish to point out that in regard to regulatory policies, particularly in the context of sport, where sport governing bodies, by their very nature, perform private regulatory functions, public regulation is sometimes difficult to

> *Tease apart from self-regulation; 'public' actions, decisions, policies, and rules are difficult to separate from 'private' ones; regulated spheres are not easy to distinguish from those that are unregulated; domestic systems of regulation interact with supra-national regimes; different regulatory mechanisms operate in coordination as well as competition; and questions of enforcement cannot be completely disentangled from those concerning policies and rules.*
>
> (Baldwin & Cave, 1999:335)

Regulatory intervention in sport, at least in relation to the areas reviewed in this book, has generally been devised in the public interest rather than the interests of sport, although these interests do align in some instances (e.g. participant safety, gambling-related revenues). Governments have done so for a variety of reasons, and with the use of numerous regulatory instruments, however, their ability to enforce such regulations is usually dependent on the force of law or threats to withdraw government funding. The centrality of sport organizations to respective policy communities varies greatly, but it is apparent that these organisations are seeking to become more engaged in the policy development cycle, as evidenced by their active involvement in gambling, physical education, member protection policies and, to some extent, in the area of broadcast media regulation.

Regulation has been described as a 'politically contentious activity' (Baldwin & Cave, 1999:335), something that has been made evident, in each of the regulatory areas we have explored in this book, through the tension between governments wishing to influence the actions of sport organizations versus sport's wish to remain self-regulating. As Frey and Johnson (1985:261,262) argued almost 25 years ago in relation to public policy intervention into sport in the US

> *The conflict between the public interest and industry self-interest raises the spectre of government regulation and ensures that politics will remain an important part of the future of sport. The conflict's significance is of sports officials' own making. On the one hand, sports officials have led the way in seeking government favour by*

consciously fostering an identification of sport with the public interest. On the symbolic plane, for example, sport has been credited with promoting democratic values of justice, equality, and rules obedience as well as symbolizing in general the American way of life . . . . On the other hand, sports officials – amateur and professional, and athletes as well – have emphasized the commercial aspects of sports, relentlessly pursuing profit maximization. With regard to several issues, expectations that sports officials would follow other than their self-interest have proven to be false hopes. This has generated intense scepticism that sports officials are willing and able to serve the public interest.

The efficacy of the regulatory measures reviewed in this book should therefore be considered in light of the reality facing regulators. They must constantly

Balance various interests and to perform trade-offs of different values. Balances have to be made between providers and consumers; different service providers; commercial and domestic consumers; incumbents and potential new entrants; infrastructure suppliers and operators or services; and a host of other sets of divergent interests.

(Baldwin & Cave, 1999:334)

Finally, we should acknowledge that while there has been virtually no research conducted into the efficacy of the various regulatory interventions reviewed in this book, we should assume that they are not perfect. As Frey and Johnson (1985:264) concluded

The free market is not perfect, but neither are our regulatory mechanisms. Public policies commonly are followed by unintended consequences. Prescriptively, the basic question for the policymaker today is which is the least likely to be harmful to the public good – the imperfections of the free market or the imperfections of government regulation?

ENABLING PUBLIC POLICY

The actions by government to link sport to the broad public policy areas of physical activity and health, urban regeneration and economic development, and social inclusion were also reviewed in this book. Our motivation to focus on these three policy areas was (in part) based on a recent observation by Coalter (2007:1) that in the UK

In recent years sport has achieved an increasingly high profile as part of New Labour's social inclusion agenda, based on assumptions about its potential contribution to areas such as social and economic regeneration, crime reduction, health improvement and educational achievement. However these new opportunities (welcomed by many in sport) have been accompanied by a potential threat – evidence-based policy-making.

Coalter (2007:1) concludes that the evidence for these assumed contributions of sport are 'ambiguous and inconclusive' and that the lack of strong evidence can be explained in four ways: (1) a lack of conceptual clarity about sport and associated ideas of involvement and participation, (2) a lack of systematic and robust evaluations, poorly designed studies and an overwhelmingly positive perspective or assumption that 'sport works' (3) little consideration of what he refers to as 'sufficient conditions' in which the exact nature, mechanisms, processes and experiences of participation in sport are accurately and meaningfully determined and (4) the limited generalizability of much of the published work in the field. Irrespective of the failings in evidence, sport continues to be seen by government as part of the solution to these three broad issues of public policy. Our review sought to explore the rationales for governments continuing to believe in the power of sport to address these issues, whether sport was central to the policy communities in these areas, and what impacts these policies and associated rhetoric had for sport.

The rationales governments employ to justify using sport as a vehicle for the achievement of non-sport policy objectives are based on what can arguably be described as a fair degree of romanticism or mythology about sport and its power to deliver positive outcomes for individuals and communities. These rationales seem at odds with the evidence-based policy ideal argued by Coalter (2007) and others. While it is hard to determine the veracity of the claims made about sport's impact in addressing issues around public health, urban regeneration or social inclusion, there is obviously a mindset among policymakers and leaders of sport organizations that these claims should not be contested. As noted in the previous chapter, not only is sport seen as a vehicle to achieve positive outcomes in relation to these policy areas, the assumed benefits are also used to assist in the justification of funding for sport through more instrumental sport policies focused on elite performance and mass participation.

Much like the conclusion we made regarding regulatory policies, sport organizations are not generally central to the respective policy communities for these non-sport policies, nor indeed are the government sport agencies. There have, however, been some notable attempts by sport organizations to build a coalition of interests to support the notion of sport being a valuable avenue for the achievement of some of these policy goals. For example, in 2002, the Central Council of Physical Recreation (CCPR), that describes itself as the national alliance of governing and representative bodies of sport and recreation for the UK, produced a promotional document *Everybody wins: Sport and social inclusion* (CCPR, 2002). The document outlined the 'role of sport in combating social exclusion, through addressing the inter-related factors which contribute to people becoming disengaged from their communities – poor levels of education, social deprivation, unemployment, poor health and crime' (CCPR, 2002:2). The document called for enhanced government investment in sport in order for sport to contribute as a route to social inclusion. The unquestioned power of sport to contribute to government objectives on education, health, crime and social inclusion if government provided additional funding to sport was posed as a win–win for both sport and government: 'the government gains a valuable policy tool which appeals directly to people who can be hard to reach using traditional methods; sport gains from increased diversity, higher participation and greater likelihood of international success' (CCPR, 2002:3). The document is replete with quotes from government departments and Ministers espousing the role of sport in tackling a myriad of problems, including this quote from the then Prime Minister Tony Blair: 'It is important that we give this encouragement to sport not only for its own sake but because, as many people now recognize, it is one of the best anti-crime policies that we could have. It is also as good a health and education policy as any other' (CCPR, 2002:2).

The CCPR was clearly attempting to garner support from within government by claiming sport has a definitive role to play in delivering on non-sport related policies. Such an attempt to tie sport to broader public policy issues is an obvious example of what Rommetvedt (2005:757) termed the generalization of interests where 'in a (neo)-pluralist society political actors cannot simply resort to force and rely on their own power in the pursuit of self-interest'. He argued that organizations that represent a broad coalition of actors need to

> ... widen their appeal. General interests have a wider appeal and basis of legitimacy than self-interests, and generalisation of interests is thus one way to enhance legitimacy and win more support. Actors who are able to show, or to argue convincingly, that their viewpoints and suggestions promote the public good have better chances of obtaining general acceptance or of acquiring support from the necessary number and kinds of coalition partners [i.e. other segments of government].
>
> (Rommetvedt, 2005:757)

Finally, we sought to identify the impact these policies have had on sport organizations. In the majority of cases, these policy intersections do not require sport organizations to radically alter their strategies or focus; however, policy initiatives aimed at increasing the number of people involved in sport are likely to place pressure on organizations that are already experiencing significant capacity constraints. Accordingly, we have argued that without concomitant investment by government in the capacity and sustainability of community sport organizations, and some greater understanding of the limitations of sport governance and delivery systems, such policies or strategies to increase a nation's physical activity through these organizations may be futile or counter-productive. Allied to this is the problem that if sport organizations and agencies continue to use sport's social contribution as an argument for additional funding to enhance existing instrumental activities, they might subject themselves to higher levels of accountability, specifically by being asked to provide the evidence to support claims of sport's impact on these non-sport issues. We have also identified that the infrastructure legacy of government investment in urban regeneration or economic development that is linked to sport events or stadia provides opportunities for sports to enhance their elite programs, as long as they have the capacity and resources to capitalize on such opportunities.

FUTURE IMPACT

These nine areas of regulatory activity and public policy examined within this book present many challenges for sport organizations, as well as illustrate the wider trend of government seeking to extend its sphere of influence over social institutions. In many ways, governing bodies for sport, with their high level of resource dependency and strategic alignment to government policy, can be considered part of the state's apparatus, especially at the national level. The increasing compliance burden and accountability requirements that accompany regulation mean that sport organizations are under increased pressure to report their activities to government and to adopt more sophisticated management and governance processes in regard to such issues as member protection, risk management, relationships with commercial partners and the conduct of their sport activities. Such requirements show no sign of abating and will continue to challenge the capacity and capabilities of sport organizations, especially smaller organizations with limited resources.

In relation to sports' future relationship with other areas of public policy and the underlying assumptions of the role that sport can play in assisting government achieve other non-sport policy objectives, sport organizations need to determine how best to engage in the debates about sports' role in tackling physical activity and health issues, urban regeneration and economic development problems and social inclusion. They need to determine the scale and scope of potential benefits that might accrue to them and their members and clarify what it is about their respective sport that is seen by government as attractive to helping solve these issues. Our review has shown that there are still many unquestioned assumptions about the role of sport in relation to these policy areas, held by both sport organizations and government. Sport organizations also need to determine what opportunities might arise in the form of government funding or support through them engaging in activities to assist government in these other policy areas. They need to then weigh these against the potential risks of moving their central focus away from the more fundamental and traditional activities of sport development. Negotiating this path will require sport organizations, particularly those larger sports that are more likely to be asked to undertake newer roles by government, to engage in clever politicking and lobbying to position themselves to serve both their own interests as well as those of the public.

There are also some inherent conflicts in regard to governments wanting to regulate for the purposes of promoting and protecting sport versus intervening to use sport to achieve other outcomes. This could lead to some unintended consequences that might affect the fundamental nature and delivery of sport, as seen by the shift in focus by most NGBs to elite sport development at the expense of mass participation, a result of targeted government funding.

FUTURE RESEARCH

As individuals interested in the role sport plays in society and the relationship that sport has with government, we conclude with some suggestions for future research. We noted in the introductory chapter of this book that perhaps unsurprisingly, the majority of sport policy related research has tended to mirror the issues that comprise contemporary sport policy. In stark contrast, in undertaking the research for this book, we failed to uncover many examples of empirical research related to the regulatory interventions or enabling policies that we have explored. Given the need for far greater evidence to support the selection of regulatory mechanisms or claims for sports' role in tackling non-sport issues, we would urge scholars to look beyond the boundaries of what has traditionally been considered 'sport policy' and explore other areas that potentially have far greater import for sport organizations, and might reveal far more about how governments treat and view sport as a social institution.

These research efforts might focus on questions related to the efficacy of applying different regulatory instruments in different legal or cultural contexts, how sport might influence the development of regulatory policies and the impact that regulatory policies have on countries, organizations and individuals. Research into the role of sport within non-sport public policy areas could focus on exploring the sufficient conditions (Coalter, 2007) in which sport can affect outcomes in different policy areas, how sport might engage more effectively in the development of policies in which they might be asked to undertake significant roles and the impact that such roles might have on the core activities of sport organizations.

We would also support the call by Coalter (2007:7) who, while referring to sport policy, eloquently argued that 'if research is to inform policy, then it is essential to explore the question of sufficient conditions – which sports, in which conditions, have what effects for which participants?'. This is especially salient for research targeted to exploring how sport can assist in the delivery of policy outcomes related to physical activity and heath, and social inclusion, but also relevant for other areas of research into the role sport plays in society and the relationship that sport has with government. In other words, future research into the effects of regulatory interventions or sport's role in other facets of government policy should be designed to not only be empirically robust but also be practically useful for policymakers. This book has sought to expand our understanding of the role of the state in sport beyond previous analyses. By continuing to examine how governments regulate sport organizations or seek sport's assistance in tackling wider public policy issues, we hope future research efforts will also lead to a better understanding of the effects of these broader government policy intersections with sport.

References

Allison, D., Fontaine, K., Manson, J., Stevens, J., & VanItallie, T. (1999). Annual deaths attributable to obesity in the United States. *Journal of the American Medical Association, 282*(16), 1530–1538.

Australian Broadcasting Authority. (2001). *Investigation into events on the anti-siphoning list*. Sydney: Australian Broadcasting Authority.

Australian Communication and Media Authority. (2009). *Anti-siphoning list*. Canberra, Australia: ACMA.

Australian Competition and Consumer Commission. (2003). *Emerging market structures in the communications sector*. Canberra: Commonwealth of Australia.

Australian Gaming Council. (2007). *A database on Australia's gambling industry*. Melbourne: Australian Gaming Council.

Australian Institute for Gambling Research. (1999). Australian gambling comparative history and analysis. In *Report for the Victorian casino and gaming authority*. Sydney: Australian Institute for Gambling Research.

Australian Labor Party. (2007). *National platform and constitution 2007*. Canberra: Author.

Australian Racing Board. (2007). *Australian racing fact book 2006–2007*. Sydney: Australian Racing Board.

Australian Sports Commission. (n.d.). *Eligibility criteria for the recognition of national sporting organizations by the Australian sports commission*. Canberra, Australia: Australian Sports Commission.

Australian Sports Commission. (1997). *Active Australia: A national participation framework*. Canberra: Australian Sports Commission.

Australian Sports Commission. (2005). *Enriching the lives of all Australians through sport*. Canberra, Australia: Australian Sports Commission.

Australian Sports Commission. (2006). *Child protection and sport: National overview (April 2006)*. Canberra, Australia: Australian Government.

Australian Sports Commission. (2007). *Governance principles: A good practice guide for sporting organizations*. Canberra, Australia: Australian Sports Commission.

Australian Sports Commission. (2009a). *Harassment and discrimination*. Canberra, Australia: Australian Government. Available at www.ausport.gov.au/supporting/ethics/hfs.

Australian Sports Commission. (2009b). *Member protection*. Canberra, Australia: Australian Government. Available at www.ausport.gov.au/supporting/ethics/member_protection.

Autorità Garante della Concorrenza e del Mercato. (2008). Response to the Unilateral Conduct Working Group Questionnaire on predatory pricing and exclusive dealing. Available at www.internationalcompetitionnetwork.org/media/library/unilateral_conduct/2007QuestionaireDocs/ITALY_RESPONSE.pdf.

Azmier, J. J. (2005). *Gambling in Canada 2005: Statistics and context.* Toronto, Canada: Canada West Foundation.

Baade, R. (1994). Stadiums, professional sports, and economic development: Assessing the reality. *Heartland Policy Study, 62*, 1–39.

Baade, R. (1996). Professional sports as catalysts for metropolitan economic development. *Journal of Urban Affairs, 18*(1), 1–17.

Baade, R., & Matheson, V. (2007). Professional sports, Hurricane Katrina, and the economic redevelopment of New Orleans. *Contemporary Economic Policy, 25*(4), 591–603.

Bache, I. (2003). Governing through governance: Education policy control under New Labour. *Political Studies, 51*, 300–314.

Baldwin, R., & Cave, M. (1999). *Understanding regulation: Theory, strategy and practice.* Oxford: Oxford University Press.

Bennett, C. (1991). What is policy convergence and what causes it? *British Journal of Political Science, 21*, 215–233.

Bergsgard, N. A., Houlihan, B., Mangset, P., Nødland, S. I., & Rommetvedt, H. (2007). *Sport Policy: A comparative analysis of stability and change.* Oxford: Butterworth-Heinemann.

Bid Commission Rio 2016. (2008). *Rio 2016 applicant city.* Rio de Janeiro: Bid Commission Rio 2016.

Boocock, S. (2002). The child protection in sport unit. *The Journal of Sexual Aggression, 8*(2), 99–106.

Boxing South Africa. (2008). *About us.* Johannesburg, South Africa: Boxing South Africa. Available at www.boxingsa.co.za/index.php?option=com_content&view=article&id=32&Itemid=58.

Brackenridge, C. (1994). Fair play or fair game? Child sexual abuse in sport organizations. *International Review for the Sociology of Sport, 29*(3), 287–298.

Brackenridge, C. (2002). '…so what?' Attitudes of the voluntary sector towards child protection in sports clubs. *Managing Leisure, 7*, 103–123.

Brackenridge, C. (2003). Dangerous sports? Risk, responsibility and sex offending in sport. *The Journal of Sexual Aggression, 9*(1), 3–12.

Brackenridge, C. (2004). Women and children first? Child abuse and child protection in sport. *Sport in Society, 7*(3), 322–337.

Brackenridge, C., Bringer, J. D., & Bishopp, D. (2005). Managing cases of abuse in sport. *Child Abuse Review, 14*, 259–274.

Brackenridge, C., Bringer, J. D., Cockburn, C., Nutt, G., Pitchford, A., Russell, K., et al. (2004). The football association's child protection in football research project 2002–2006: Rationale, design and first year results. *Managing Leisure, 9*, 30–46.

Brackenridge, C., Pawlaczek, Z., Bringer, J. D., Cockburn, C., Nutt, G., Pitchford, A., et al. (2005). Measuring the impact of child protection through activation states. *Sport, Education and Society, 10*(2), 239–256.

British Horseracing Board. (2004). *The modernisation of British racing: Racing review part III: The financial, administrative and governance structure of racing.* London: British Horseracing Board.

Britton, E. L. (1972). The struggle for recognition. *British Journal of Physical Education, 3*(3), 34.

Bull, F., Bellew, B., Schoppe, S., & Bauman, A. (2004). Developments in national physical activity policy: An international review and recommendations towards better practice. *Journal of Science and Medicine in Sport, 7*(Suppl. 1), 93–104.

Burchell, G. (1993). Liberal government and techniques of the self. *Economy and Society, 22*(3), 267–82.

Canadian Department of Justice. (1987). *Canadian Television Broadcasting Regulations.* Ottowa, Canada: Department of Justice.

Canada Department of Justice. (1991). *Canadian broadcasting act, 1991.* Ottowa, Canada: Department of Justice. Available at www.laws.justice.gc.ca/en/B-9.01/.

Canadian Partnership for Responsible Gambling. (2007). *Canadian gambling digest 2005–2006.* Toronto: Canadian Partnership for Responsible Gambling.

Canadian Sport Parachuting Association. (2008). Homepage. http://www.cspa.ca/ (accessed 10.06.08). Ottawa: Canadian Sport Parachuting Association.

Carlsen, J., & Taylor, A. (2003). Mega-events and urban renewal: The case of the Manchester 2002 commonwealth games. *Event Management, 8*, 15–22.

Carroll, T. E. (1974). A rational curriculum plan for PE. *British Journal of Physical Education, 5*(6), 103.

Cave, M., & Crandall, R. (2001). Sports rights and the broadcast industry. *The Economic Journal, 111*, F4–F26.

Cense, M., & Brackenridge, C. (2001). Temporal and developmental risk factors for sexual harassment and abuse in sport. *European Physical Education Review, 7*(1), 61–79.

Central Council of Physical Recreation. (2002). *Everybody wins: Sport and social inclusion.* London: CCPR.

Chalip, L. (1996). Critical policy analysis in sport: The illustrative case of New Zealand sport policy development. *Journal of Sport Management, 10*, 310–324.

Chanayil, A. (2002). The Manhattan Yankees? Planning objectives, city policy, and the sports stadium location in New York city. *European Planning Studies, 10*(7), 875–896.

Chapman, S., Byrne, F., & Carter, S. M. (2003). "Australia is one of the darkest markets in the world": The global importance of Australian tobacco control. *Tobacco Control, 12*, 1–3.

Chicago 2016 Committee. (2008). *Chicago 2016 applicant city.* Chicago: Chicago 2016 Committee.

Child Protection in Sport Unit (CPSU). (2006). *Strategy for safeguarding children and young people in sport.* London, UK: CPSU.

Child Protection in Sport Unit (CPSU). (2007). *Standards for safeguarding and protecting children in sport*. London, UK: CPSU.

Clarke, J., Gewirtz, S., Hughes, G., & Humphrey, J. (2000). Guarding the public interest? Auditing public services. In J.Clarke, S.Gewirtz, & E.McLaughlin (Eds.), *New managerialism, new welfare?* (pp. 250–266). Milton Keynes: Open University Press/Sage.

Coalition of Major Professional Sports. (2006). Submission in relation to the Victorian Department of Justice Discussion Paper, April 2006, Melbourne, Australia. Available at www.justice.vic.gov.au.

Coalter, F. (2007). *A wider social role for sport: Who's keeping score?*. London: Routledge.

Coates, D. (2007). Stadiums and arenas: Economic development or economic redistribution? *Contemporary Economic Policy, 25*(4), 565–577.

Coleman, J. (1988). Social capital in the creation of human capital. *American Journal of Sociology, 94*, 95–120.

Collins, M., & Kay, T. (2003). *Sport and social exclusion*. London: Routledge.

Commission on the European Communities. (2007). *White paper on sport*. Brussels: Author.

Commonwealth of Australia. (1992). *Australian broadcasting services act 1992*. Canberra: Commonwealth of Australia.

Commonwealth of Australia. (1999). *Shaping up: A review of commonwealth involvement in sport and recreation in Australia*. Canberra, Australia: Commonwealth of Australia.

Commonwealth of Australia. (2001). *Backing Australia's sporting ability*. Canberra, Australia: Commonwealth of Australia.

Commonwealth of Australia. (2003). *Healthy weight 2008, Australia's future*. Canberra: Department of Health and Ageing.

Commonwealth of Australia. (2005). *Inquiry into the provisions of the broadcasting services amendment (anti-siphoning) bill 2004*. Canberra: Commonwealth of Australia.

Commonwealth of Australia. (2008). *Australian sport: Emerging challenges, new directions*. Canberra, Australia: Commonwealth of Australia.

Competition Commission. (1999). *British sky broadcasting group plc and Manchester united plc: A report on the proposed merger*. London: Competition Commission.

Conference of Australasian Racing Ministers. (2003, July 10). *Report of the betting exchange taskforce*. Sydney, Australia: Conference of Australasian Racing Ministers.

Cowie, C., & Williams, M. (1997). The economics of sports rights. *Telecommunications Policy, 21*(7), 619–634.

Crompton, J. (2001). Public subsidies to professional team sport facilities in the USA. In C.Gratton, & I.Henry (Eds.), *Sport in the city: The role of sport in economic and social regeneration* (pp. 15–34). London: Routledge.

Cuskelly, G., Hoye, R., & Auld, C. (2006). *Working with volunteers in sport: Theory and practice*. London: Routledge.

DaCosta, L., & Miragaya, A. (2002). *Worldwide experiences and trends in sport for all*. Oxford: Meyer & Meyer Sport.

Dakin, P. (1995a, January 18). GP pounds the ground. *Emerald Hill Times*.

Dakin, P. (1995b, May 10). Compo row goes on. *Emerald Hill Times*.

Davies, W. (2006). The governmentality of new labour. *Institute for Public Policy Research*, 13(4), 249–56.

Davis, G. (2007, February 27). UK gambling market: A good investment? *Dailyreckoning*, London, UK. Available at www.dailyreckoning.co.uk/article/ukgamblingmarketagoodinvestment0079.html.

De Bosscher, V., De Knop, P., van Bottenburg, M., & Shibli, S. (2006). A conceptual framework for analysing sports policy factors leading to international sporting success. *European Sport Management Quarterly*, 6(2), 185–215.

Dean, I. S. (1978). Marginal role in a marginal profession? *British Journal of Physical Education*, 9(5), 124.

Dean, M. (1999). *Governmentality: Power and rule in modern society*. London: Sage.

Dean, M. (2007). *Governing societies: Political perspectives on domestic and international rule*. Maidenhead: Open University Press.

Department for Culture, Media and Sport [DCMS]. (2000). *A sporting future for all*. London: DCMS.

Department for Education and Skills. (2004a). *High quality PE and sport for young people*. London: DfES.

Department for Education and Skills. (2004b). *Every child matters: Change for children*. London, UK: DfES.

Department for Education and Skills. (2005). *Do you have high quality PE and sport in your school*. London: DfES.

Department for Education and Skills/Department of Culture, Media and Sport. (2006). *National competition framework: Guidance notes*. London: DfES/DCMS.

Department of Children, Schools and Families [DCSF]/DCMS. (2006). *The national competition framework*. London: DCSF/DCMS.

Department of Culture, Media and Sport. (2002). *Game plan: A strategy for delivering government's sport and physical activity objectives*. London: Author.

Department of Culture, Media and Sport. (2009). *List of protected events*. London, UK: DCMS.

Department of Health and Human Services. (1996). *Physical activity and health: A report of the surgeon general*. Rockville, MD: US Department of Health and Human Services.

Department of Health and Human Services. (2001). *The surgeon general's call to action to prevent and decrease overweight and obesity*. Rockville, MD: US Department of Health and Human Services.

Department of Innovation, Industry and Regional Development. (2006). *10 year tourism and events industry strategy*. Melbourne: Department of Innovation, Industry and Regional Development.

Department of Internal Affairs. (2007). *Gambling expenditure statistics 1983–2007*. Auckland, New Zealand: New Zealand Government. Available atwww.antispam.govt.nz/diawebsite.nsf/wpg_URL/Resource-material-Information-We-Provide-Gaming-Statistics?OpenDocument.

Department of Justice. (2005). *Review of associations incorporation act 1981: Interim report*. Melbourne, Australia: State of Victoria.

Department of Justice. (2009). *Victorian racing and betting legislation*. Melbourne, Australia: Government of Victoria. Available at www.justice.vic.gov.au/wps/wcm/connect/DOJ+Internet/Home/Gambling+and+Racing/Racing/JUSTICE+-+Victorian+Racing+and+Betting+Legislation.

Department of Local Government, Planning, Sport and Recreation. (2007). *Safety for boxing and combat sports: A discussion paper to review regulatory options*. Brisbane, Australia: Queensland Government.

Department of National Heritage. (1995). *Sport: Raising the game*. London: DNH.

Department of the Environment/Department of Education and Science. (1986). *Sport in schools seminar: Report of proceedings*. London: DoE.

Doha 2016 Olympic and Paralympic Bid Committee. (2008). *Doha 2016 applicant city*. Doha: Doha 2016 Olympic and Paralympic Bid Committee.

Doherty, B. (2009). $47m fee a formula for easy profits. Available at www.theage.com.au/national/47m-fee-a-formula-for-easy-profits-20090313-8xxq.html.

Duffy, P. (1996). From Belmore to the white paper. How far have we come. In M. Darmody (Ed.), *PE in Europe: The Irish dimension*, Proceedings of the national physical education conference. Limerick: PE Association of Ireland.

Dyreson, M. (2001). Maybe it's better to bowl alone: Sport, community and democracy in American thought. *Sport in Society, 4*(1), 19–30.

Editorial. (1970). The concept of physical education. *British Journal of Physical Education, 1*(4), 81–82.

Editorial. (1994, September 17). A dangerous law. *The Age*.

Edmonds, M. (1993, December 17). It's our Grand Prix. *Herald Sun*.

European Council. (2000). *Nice declaration: Declaration on the specific characteristics of sport and its social function in Europe*. Nice: Author.

European Parliament and the Council of the European Union. (1997). *Directive 97/36/EC*. Brussels: European Parliament and the Council of the European Union.

European Union. (2008). *Joint declaration of the Slovenian presidency of the European council, the presidents of the national Olympic committees of the European union member states, representatives of the executive committee of the European Olympic committees and the European commissioner responsible for sport on 'social significance and dialogue in sport'*. Ljubljana: Slovenian Presidency of the EU.

Evans, J., & Penney, D. (1995). Physical education, restoration and the politics of sport. *Curriculum Studies, 3*(2), 183–196.

Evans, J., Penney, D., & Bryant, A. (1993). Improving the quality of physical education? The education reform act, 1988, and physical education in England and Wales. *Quest, 45*, 321–338.

Evans, J., Penney, D., & Davies, B. (1996). Back to the future: Education policy and physical education. In N. Armstrong (Ed.), *New directions in physical education: Change and innovation*. London: Cassell.

Federation Aéronautique Internationale. (2008). *Internal regulations of the international parachuting commission*. Lausanne: Federation Aéronautique Internationale.

Finkelstein, E., Fiebelkorn, I., & Wang, G. (2003). National medical spending attributable to overweight and obesity: How much, and who's paying? *Health Affairs, W3*, 219–226.

Finkelstein, E., Fiebelkorn, I., & Wang, G. (2005). The costs of obesity among full-time employees. *American Journal of Health Promotion, 20*(1), 45–51.

Finkelstein, E., Ruhm, C., & Kosa, K. (2005). Economic causes and consequences of obesity. *Annual Review of Public Health, 26*, 239–257.

Fitzgerald, R. (2007, November 5). Fix could be in when people bet to lose. *The Australian*, Sydney, Australia. www.theaustralian.news.com.au (accessed 20.12.07).

Flintoff, A. (2003). The school sport co-ordinator programme: Changing the role of the physical education teacher? *Sport, Education and Society, 8*(2), 231–250.

Floyd, J. (1994, January 4). Letter to the Editor – Grand Prix plans will improve park. *The Age*.

Forrest, D., & Simmons, R. (2003). Sport and gambling. *Oxford Review of Economic Policy, 19*(4), 598–611.

Foucault, M. (1982). The subject and power. In H. L. Dreyfus, & P. Rabinov (Eds.), *Michel Foucault: Beyond structuralism and hermeneutics* (2nd ed.). Chicago: University of Chicago Press.

Frey, J. H., & Johnson, A. T. (1985). Conclusion: Sports, regulation, and the public interest. In A. T. Johnson, & J. H. Frey (Eds.), *Government and sport: The public policy issues*. New Jersey: Rowman and Allanheld.

Furlong, R. (1994). Tobacco advertising legislation and the sponsorship of sport. *Australian Business Law Review, 22*(3), 159–189.

Gambling Commission. (2007a). *Integrity in sports betting: Issues paper, May 2007*. London: Gambling Commission.

Gambling Commission. (2007b). *Integrity in sports betting: Policy position paper, October 2007*. London: Gambling Commission.

Gambling Commission. (2007c). *What we do*. London: Gambling Commission. Available at www.gamblingcommission.gov.uk/Client/detail.asp?ContentId=5.

Gambling Commission. (2007d). *Betting*. London: Gambling Commission. Available at www.gamblingcommission.gov.uk/UploadDocs/publications/Document/Betting.pdf.

Gardiner, S., James, M., O'Leary, J., Welch, R., Blackshaw, I., Boyes, S., et al. (2006). *Sports law* (3rd ed.). Oxon: Routledge-Cavendish.

Garrett, R. (2004). The response of voluntary sports clubs to Sport England's Lottery funding: Cases of compliance, change and resistance. *Managing Leisure, 9*, 13–29.

Giddens, A. (1995). *A contemporary critique of historical materialism*. Cambridge: Polity.

Gordon, J. (2007). Anger as auditor queries GP's value. Available at www.theage. com.au/news/national/anger-as-auditor-queries-gps-value/2007/05/23/ 1179601487380.html.

Government of Canada. (2002). *Canadian Sport Policy*. Quebec, Canada: Author.

Government of Canada. (2008). *Regulations amending the Canadian Aviation Regulations (Parts I and VI) Regulatory impact analysis statement, Canada Gazette, 142 (11), March 15, 2008*. Ottawa: Government of Canada. Available at www.gazetteducanada.gc.ca/partI/2008/20080315/html/regle5-e.html.

Gratton, C., Dobson, N., & Shibli, S. (2000). The economic importance of major sports events: A case-study of six events. *Managing Leisure, 5*, 17–28.

Gratton, C., & Henry, I. P. (2001). *Sport in the city: The role of sport in economic and social regeneration*. London: Routledge.

Greater London Authority. (n.d.). *Five legacy commitments*. London: Greater London Authority.

Green, M. (2004). Changing policy priorities for sport in England: The emergence of elite sport development as a key concern. *Leisure Studies, 20*, 247–267.

Green, M. (2005). Integrating macro and meso-level approaches: A comparative analysis of elite sport development in Australia, Canada and the United Kingdom. *European Sport Management Quarterly, 5*(2), 143–166.

Green, M. (2006). From 'sport for all' to not about 'sport' at all: Interrogating sport policy interventions in the United Kingdom. *European Sport Management Quarterly, 6*(3), 217–238.

Green, M. (2007). Olympic Glory or grassroots development? Sport policy priorities in Australia, Canada and the United Kingdom. *International Journal of the History of Sport, 24*(7), 921–953.

Green, M., & Houlihan, B. (2005). *Elite sport development: Policy learning and political priorities*. London: Routledge.

Green, M., & Oakley, B. (2001). Elite sport development systems and playing to win: Uniformity and diversity in international approaches. *Leisure Studies, 20*, 247–267.

Ha, N. G., & Mangan, J. A. (2002). Ideology, politics, power: Korean sport transformation, 1945–1992. In J. A. Mangan, & F. Hong (Eds.), *Sport in Asian society: Past and present*. London: Frank Cass.

Hall, C. (1994). Mega-events and their legacies. In P.Murphy (Ed.), *Quality management in urban tourism: Balancing business and environment conference proceedings* (pp. 109–122). British Columbia: University of Victoria.

Hall, C. (2006). Urban entrepreneurship, corporate interests and sports mega-events: The thin policies of competitiveness within the hard outcomes of neoliberalism. In J. Horne, & W. Manzenreiter (Eds.), *Sports mega-events: Social scientific analyses of a global phenomenon* (pp. 59–70). Oxford: Blackwell Publishing.

Hardman, K. (2002). *European physical education/sport survey, summary report to the council of Europe Committee for the Development of Sport (CDDS)*. Strasbourg: Council of Europe.

Harris, J. (1994). Physical education in the curriculum: Is there enough time to be effective? *British Journal of Physical Education*, (Winter), 3408.

Haslam, D., & James, W. (2005). Obesity. *Lancet*, *366*, 1197–1209.

Havaris, E. P., & Danylchuk, K. E. (2007). An assessment of Sport Canada's Sport Funding and Accountability Framework, 1995–2004. *European Sport Management Quarterly*, *7*(1), 31–53.

Hedley, A., Ogden, C., Johnson, C., Carroll, M., Curtin, L., & Flegal, K. (2004). Prevalence of overweight and obesity among US children, adolescents, and adults, 1999–2002. *Journal of the American Medical Association*, *291*(23), 2847–2850.

Henry, I. (1997). The politics of sport and symbolism in the city: A case study of the Lyon conurbation. *Managing Leisure*, *2*, 65–81.

Henry, I., Amara, M., Al-Tauqi, M., & Lee, P. C. (2005). A typology of approaches to comparative analysis of sports policy. *Journal of Sport Management*, *19*, 520–535.

Her Majesty's Inspectorate of Education. (1978). *Physical education curriculum 11–16*. London: Her Majesty's Stationery Office.

Hewett. (2006, April 1). A sporting chance at the money. *Australian Financial Review*, 23.

HM Government. (2007). *PSA Delivery Agreement 21: Build more cohesive, empowered and active communities*. London: HM Government.

Hoehn, T., & Lancefield, D. (2003). Broadcasting and sport. *Oxford Review of Economic Policy*, *19*(4), 552–568.

Home Office. (2001). *Building cohesive communities: A report of the ministerial group on public order and community cohesion*. London: HM Government.

Hong Kong Broadcasting Authority. (2007). *Generic code of practice on television programme standards*. Hong Kong: Hong Kong Broadcasting Authority.

Houlihan, B. (1991). *The government and politics of sport*. London: Routledge.

Houlihan, B. (1997). *Sport, policy and politics. A comparative analysis*. London and New York: Routledge.

Houlihan, B. (2005). Public sector sport policy: Developing a framework for analysis. *International Review for the Sociology of Sport*, *40*(2), 163–185.

Houlihan, B., Bloyce, D., & Smith, A. (2009). Developing the research agenda in sport policy. *International Journal of Sport Policy*, *1*(1), 1–12.

Houlihan, B., & Green, M. (Eds.). (2008). *Comparative elite sport development: Systems, structures and public policy*. Oxford: Butterworth-Heinemann.

Houlihan, B., & White, A. (2002). *The politics of sports development: Development of sport or development through sport?* London: Routledge.

Hoye, R. (2006a). Governance reform in Australian horse racing. *Managing Leisure*, *11*, 129–138.

Hoye, R. (2006b). Sports betting policy in Australia: Implications for Australian sports organisations. *Annals of Leisure Research*, *9*(3), 155–172.

Hoye, R., & Cuskelly, G. (2007). *Sport governance*. Oxford: Elsevier Butterworth Heinemann.

Hoye, R., & Nicholson, M. (2008). Locating social capital in sport policy. In M. Nicholson, & R. Hoye (Eds.), *Sport and social capital* (pp. 69–91). London: Elsevier, Butterworth Heinemann.

Hylton, K., & Bramham, P. (Eds.). (2008). *Sport development: Policy, process and practice*. London: Routledge.

Hylton, K., Bramham, P., Jackson, D., & Nesti, M. (Eds.). (2001). *Sports development: Policy, process and practice*. London: Routledge.

Johnson, A. T., & Frey, J. H. (1985). Introduction. In A. T. Johnson, & J. H. Frey (Eds.). *Government and sport: The public policy issues*. New Jersey: Rowman and Allanheld.

Kahn, E., Ramsey, L., Brownson, R., Heath, G., Howze, E., Powell, K., et al. & the Task Force on Community Preventive Services. (2002). The effectiveness of interventions to increase physical activity: A systematic review. *American Journal of Preventative Medicine, 22*(4S), 73–107.

Kerr, G. A., & Stirling, A. E. (2008). Child protection in sport: Implications of an athlete-centered philosophy. *Quest, 60*, 307–323.

Kirk, D. (1992). *Defining physical education: The social construction of a school subject in postwar Britain*. London: Falmer Press.

Knill, C. (2005). Introduction: Cross-national policy convergence: Concepts, approaches and explanatory factors. *Journal of European Public Policy, 12*(5), 764–774.

Leahy, T., Pretty, G., & Tenenbaum, G. (2002). Prevalence of sexual abuse in organised competitive sport in Australia. *The Journal of Sexual Aggression, 8*(2), 16–36.

Leroux, C., & Mount, J. (1994). Assessing the effects of a mega-event: A restrospective study of the Olympic Games on the Calgary business sector. *Festival Management and Event Tourism, 2*, 15–23.

Liberal Party of Australia. (2004). *Building Australian communities through sport*. Canberra, Australia: Liberal Party of Australia.

Lindblom, C. (1959). The science of 'muddling through'. *Public Administration Review, 19*(2), 79–88.

Littlewood, D., & Ward, H. (1998). The Save Albert Park campaign: Opposing the use of inner-city public parkland for the Melbourne Grand Prix. *Festival Management and Event Tourism, 5*(3), 159–165.

Loftman, P., & Nevin, B. (1994). Prestige project development: Economic renaissance or economic myth? A case study of Birmingham. *Local Economy, 8*(4), 307–325.

Loftman, P., & Nevin, B. (1995). Prestige projects and urban regeneration in the 1980s and 1990s: A review of benefits and limitations. *Planning Practice and Research, 10*(3/4), 299–315.

Long, J., Robinson, P., & Spracklen, K. (2005). Promoting racial equality within sport organizations. *Journal of Sport and Social Issues, 29*(1), 41–59.

Long, J., & Sanderson, I. (2001). The social benefits of sport; Where's the proof? In C.Gratton, & I.Henry (Eds.), *Sport and the city* (pp. 187–203). London: Routledge.

Lukes, S. (2005). *Power: A radical view* (2nd ed.). Basingstoke: Palgrave.

MacKenzie, R., Collin, J., & Sriwongcharoen, K. (2007). Thailand – Lighting up a dark market: British American Tobacco, sports sponsorship and the circumvention of legislation. *Journal of Epidemiology and Community Health, 61*, 28–33.

Madrid 16 Foundation. (2008). *Madrid 2016 applicant city*. Madrid: Madrid 16 Foundation.

Malkin, K., Johnston, L., & Brackenridge, C. (2000). A critical evaluation of training needs for child protection in UK sport. *Managing Leisure, 5*, 151–160.

Melbourne Parks and Waterways. (n.d.). *The new plan for Albert Park*. Melbourne: Melbourne Parks and Waterways.

Melbourne Parks and Waterways. (1993). *Draft strategy plan – Albert Park*. Melbourne: Melbourne Parks and Waterways.

Melbourne Parks and Waterways. (1994). *Master plan*. Melbourne: Melbourne Parks and Waterways.

Michael, E. (2006). *Public policy: The competitive framework*. South Melbourne, Victoria: Oxford University Press.

Miers, D. (2004). *Regulating commercial gambling: Past, present and future*. Oxford: Oxford University Press.

Motta, M., & Polo, M. (1997). Concentration and public policies in the broadcasting industry: The future of television. *Economic Policy, 12*(25), 293–334.

Munting, R. (1996). *An economic and social history of gambling*. Manchester: Manchester University Press.

Murdoch, E. (1987). *Sport in schools, Desk Study commissioned by the Department of Education and Science/Department of the Environment*. London: Sports Council.

Murdoch, E. (1993). Education, sport and leisure: Collapsing boundaries? In G. McFee, & A. Tomlinson (Eds.), *Education, sport and leisure: Connections and controversies* (pp. 65–72). Eastbourne, UK: University of Brighton Chelsea School Research Centre.

National Association of Head Teachers (NAHT). (1999). *Survey of PE and sport in schools*. Haywards Heath, UK: NAHT.

National Audit Office. (2001). *Tackling obesity in England*. London: National Audit Office.

National Lottery Distribution Fund. (2007). *National Lottery Distribution Fund Account 2006–07*. London: National Lottery Distribution Fund.

National Olympic Committee of the Republic of Azerbaijan. (2008). *Baku 2016 applicant city*. Baku: National Olympic Committee of the Republic of Azerbaijan.

National Society for the Prevention of Cruelty to Children (NSPCC). (2009a). *About the NSPCC Child Protection in Sport Unit*. London, UK: NSPCC. Available at www.nspcc.org.uk/Inform/cpsu/AboutUs/AboutUs_wda60534.html.

National Society for the Prevention of Cruelty to Children (NSPCC). (2009b). *Standards for safeguarding and protecting children in sport*. London, UK: NSPCC. Available at www.nspcc.org.uk/Inform/cpsu/HelpAndAdvice/Organizations/Standards/Standards_wda60694.html.

Neales, S. (1993, December 18). How the deal was done. *The Age*.

Neuman, M., Bitton, A., & Glantz, S. (2002). Tobacco industry strategies for influencing European Community tobacco advertising legislation. *Lancet, 359*, 1323–30.

New, B., & LeGrand, J. (1999). Monopoly in sports broadcasting. *Policy Studies, 20*(1), 23–36.

New Zealand Thoroughbred Racing. (2008). *New Zealand thoroughbred racing fact book 2008*. Wellington, New Zealand: New Zealand Thoroughbred Racing.

Nicholson, M. (2007). *Sport and the media: Managing the nexus*. Oxford: Elsevier, Butterworth-Heinemann.

Nicholson, M., & Hoye, R. (2008). Sport and social capital: An introduction. In M. Nicholson, & R. Hoye (Eds.), *Sport and social capital* (pp. 1–18). London: Elsevier, Butterworth Heinemann.

Noll, R. G. (2007). Broadcasting and team sports. *Scottish Journal of Political Economy, 54*(3), 400–421.

NSW Sport and Recreation. (2009a). *Child protection*. Sydney, Australia: NSW Government. Available at www.dsr.nsw.gov.au/children/.

NSW Sport and Recreation. (2009b). *Child protection checklist*. Sydney, Australia: NSW Government. Available at www.dsr.nsw.gov.au/children/safe_policy.asp.

NSW Sport and Recreation. (2009c). *Working with children check*. Sydney, Australia: NSW Government. Available at www.dsr.nsw.gov.au/children/wwcc.aspt.

NSW Sport and Recreation. (2009d). *Motorsport industry regulation*. Sydney, Australia: NSW Government. Available at www.dsr.nsw.gov.au/aboutus/industry_motor.asp.

NSW State Government. (1985). Motor vehicle sports (public safety) Act 1985.

NSW State Government. (1989). Mount Panorama motor racing Act 1989.

Oakley, B., & Green, M. (2001). Still playing the game at arm's length? The selective re-investment in British sport, 1995–2000. *Managing Leisure, 6*, 74–94.

Office of Economic and Statistical Research. (2006). *Australian Gambling Statistics 1979–80 to 2004–05*. Brisbane, Australia: Queensland Government.

Ofsted. (2003). *The School Sport Coordinator programme: Evaluation of phases 1 and 2, 2001–2003, (HMI 1586)*. London: Ofsted.

Ofsted. (2004). *The School Sport Coordinator programme: Evaluation of phases 3and 4, 2003–2004 (HMI 2150)*. London: Ofsted.

Ofsted. (2005). *The physical education, school sport and club links strategy: The School Sport Partnership programme (HMI 2397)*. London: Ofsted.

Ok, G. (2004). Modernisation and sport in Korea, 1945–1992. *The Korean Journal of Physical Education, 43*(5), 43–53.

Ontario Horse Racing Industry Association. (2009). *Regulatory framework*. Toronto, Canada: Ontario Horse Racing Industry Association. Available atwww.ohria.com/industry/regulatory_framework/index.html.

Owen, K. (1995, October 26). Damages claim over GP work. *Herald Sun*.

Painter, M. (1991). Policy diversity and policy learning in a federation: The case of Australian state betting laws. *Publius: The Journal of Federalism, 21*, 143–157.

Papadimitriou, D. (1998). The impact of institutionalized resources, rules and practices on the performance of non-profit sport organizations. *Managing Leisure, 3*, 169–180.

Park, J. (2009). *An analysis of elite sport policy change in Korea*. Unpublished PhD thesis, Loughborough University, Loughborough.

Parrish, R. (2008). Access to major events on television under European law. *Journal of Consumer Policy, 31*, 79–98.

Penney, D. (1998). School subjects and structures: Reinforcing traditional voices in contemporary 'reforms' of education. *Discourse: Studies in the Cultural Politics of Education, 19*(1), 5–17.

Penney, D., & Evans, J. (1997). Naming the game: Discourse and domination in physical education and sport in England and Wales. *European Physical Education Review, 3*(1), 21–32.

Play by the Rules. (2009a). *Child protection*. Canberra, Australia: Australian Sports Commission. Available at www.playbytherules.net.au/index.php?option=com_content&view=article&id=125&Itemid=176.

Play by the Rules. (2009b). *Child safe environments*. Canberra, Australia: Australian Sports Commission. Available at www.playbytherules.net.au/index.php?option=com_content&view=article&id=446&Itemid=461.

Play by the Rules. (2009c). *Mandatory reporting*. Canberra, Australia: Australian Sports Commission. Available at www.playbytherules.net.au/index.php?option=com_content&view=article&id=444&Itemid=459.

Power, M. (1997). *The audit society: Rituals of verification*. Oxford: Oxford University Press.

Premier of Victoria. (2008). Grand prix announcement. Available at www.premier.vic.gov.au/index.php?option=com_mymedia&Itemid=29&lang=en&media_id=300&task =text.

Preuss, H. (2006). Impact and evaluation of major sporting events. *European Sport Management Quarterly, 6*(4), 313–316.

Productivity Commission. (1999). *Australia's Gambling Industries Inquiry Report No. 10*. Canberra, Australia: Productivity Commission.

Productivity Commission. (2000). *Broadcasting: Inquiry report*. Canberra: Commonwealth of Australia.

Public Health Agency of Canada. (2009). Healthy living unit. Available at www.phac-aspc.gc.ca/pau-uap/fitness/about.html.

Putnam, R. (1995). Tuning in, tuning out: The strange disappearance of social capital in America. *Political Science and Politics, 28*, 664–683.

Putnam, R. (2000). *Bowling alone: The collapse and revival of american community*. New York: Simon & Schuster.

Qatar Olympic Committee. (2009). Our vision. Available at www.qatarolympics.org/.

Quant, D. (1975). The (in)credibility of PE in the 1970s. *British Journal of Physical Education, 6*(5), 77.

Raco, M., & Imrie, R. (2000). Governmentality and rights and responsibilities in urban policy. *Environment and Planning A, 32*(12), 2187–204.

Reiss, S. (1998). Historical perspectives on sport and public policy. *Policy Studies Review, 15*(1), 3–15.

Ritchie, J. (1984). Assessing the impact of hallmark events: Conceptual and research issues. *Journal of Travel Research, 23*(1), 2–11.

Ritchie, J., & Smith, B. (1991). The impact of a mega-event of host region awareness: A longitudinal study. *Journal of Travel Research, 30*, 3–10.

Roche, M. (1993). Sport and community: Rhetoric and reality in the development of British sport policy. In J. C. Binfield, & J. Stevenson (Eds.), *Sport, culture and politics* (pp. 72–112). Sheffield: Sheffield Academic.

Roche, M. (1994). Mega-events and urban policy. *Annals of Tourism Research, 21*, 1–19.

Rommetvedt, H. (2005). Norway: Resources count, but votes decide? From neo-corporatist representation to neo-pluralist parliamentarism. *West European Politics, 28*(4), 740–763.

Rose, N. (1999). *Powers of freedom: Reframing political thought.* Cambridge: Cambridge University Press.

Rose, N., & Miller, P. (1992). Political power beyond the State: Problematics of government. *British Journal of Sociology, 43*(2), 172–205.

Rosentraub, M., Swindell, D., Przybylski, M., & Mullins, D. (1994). Sport and downtown development strategy. If you build it, will jobs come. *Journal of Urban Affairs, 16*(3), 221–239.

Rumphorst, W. (2001). *Sports broadcasting rights and EC competition law.* Switzerland: European Broadcasting Union.

Sam, M. P., & Jackson, S. J. (2004). Sport policy development in New Zealand. *International Review for the Sociology of Sport, 39*(2), 205–222.

Sandy, R., Sloane, P., & Rosentraub, M. (2004). *The economics of sport: An international perspective.* New York: Palgrave Macmillan.

Sárközy, T. (2001). Regulation in sport as a borderline case between state and law regulation and self-regulation. *Acta Juridica Hungarica, 42*(3–4), 159–180.

Schmidhuber, J., & Shetty, P. (2004/2005). Nutrition transition, obesity and noncommunicable diseases: Drivers, outlook and concerns. *United Nations System Standing Committee on Nutrition,* (No. 29), 13–19.

School Sport Forum. (1988). *Sport and young people: Partnership and action.* London: Sports Council.

Secondary Heads Association. (1987). *No ball.* London: SHS.

Secondary Heads Association. (1990). *Enquiry into the provision of physical education in secondary schools.* London: SHA.

Sellenger, B. (2006). Chasing the golden goose: A legal approach to sports accessing gambling revenue. *Australian Business Law Review, 34*, 7–27.

Shaw, S. (2007). Touching the intangible? An analysis of the equality standard: A framework for sport. *Equal Opportunities International, 26*(5), 420–434.

Siegfried, J., & Zimbalist, A. (2000). The economics of sports facilities and their communities. *Journal of Economic Perspectives, 14*(3), 95–114.

Simons, C. (2007). Doha's grand games. *Saudi Aramco World, 58*(2). Available at www.saudiaramcoworld.com/issue/200702/doha.s.grand.games.htm.

Skinsley, M. (1987). The elite: Whose responsibility? *British Journal of Physical Education, 18*, 2.

Sollerhed, A. C. (1999). The status of PE in the Swedish school system. In *ICHPER World Congress,* July 1999, Cairo, Egypt.

South Australia State Government. (1999). *South Australian Motor Sport Regulations 1999.*

Spectator. (1975). You have been warned. *British Journal of Physical Education, 6*(6), 93.

Sport and Recreation New Zealand (SPARC). (2004). *Nine steps to effective governance: Building high performance organizations.* Wellington, New Zealand: SPARC.

Sport and Recreation New Zealand (SPARC). (2008a). *Funding and recognition.* Wellington, New Zealand: SPARC. Available at www.sparc.org.nz/partners-programmes/funding-and-recognition.

Sport and Recreation New Zealand (SPARC). (2008b). *Statement of intent.* Wellington, New Zealand: Sport and Recreation New Zealand.

Sport and Recreation South Africa. (2004). *South African boxing act, 2001: Boxing regulations.* Johannesburg, South Africa: Republic of South Africa.

Sport and Recreation Victoria. (2007a). *Merlino to prevent caged combat sports coming to Victoria: Media release December 21, 2007.* Melbourne, Australia: Government of Victoria.

Sport and Recreation Victoria. (2007b). *Tougher legislation for pro boxing and combat sport: Media release December 4, 2007.* Melbourne, Australia: Government of Victoria.

Sport and Recreation Victoria. (2008). *Professional boxing and combat sports regulations 2008: Regulatory impact statement.* Melbourne, Australia: Government of Victoria.

Sport Canada. (2004). *Strategic Plan 2004–2008.* Quebec, Canada: Author.

Sport Canada. (2007). *Sport funding and accountability framework (SFAF IV: 2009–2013).* Gatineau, Quebec, Canada: Sport Canada. Available at www.canadianheritage.gc.ca/progs/sc/prog/cfrs-sfaf/sfafelig2009_e.cfm.

Sport England. (2005). *Sport playing its part: The contribution of sport to community priorities and the improvement agenda.* London: Sport England.

Sport England. (2008). *Sport England strategy, 2008–2010.* London: Sport England.

Sports Medicine Australia. (2008). *Policy on the safety of boxing.* Melbourne, Australia: Sports Medicine Australia.

Spracklen, K., Hylton, K., & Long, J. (2006). Managing and monitoring equality and diversity in UK sport: An evaluation of the Sporting equals racial equality standard and its impact on organizational change. *Journal of Sport and Social Issues, 30*(3), 289–305.

State of Victoria. (2006). *Sports betting: A new regulatory framework discussion paper.* Melbourne, Australia: Department of Justice.

State Services Authority. (2007). *Review of not-for-profit regulation: Final report.* Melbourne, Australia: State of Victoria.

Stewart, B., & Nicholson, M. (2002). Australia. In L.DaCosta, & A.Miragaya (Eds.), *Worldwide experiences and trends in sport for all.* (pp. 35–73). Germany: Meyer and Meyer.

Stewart, B., Nicholson, M., Smith, A., & Westerbeek, H. (2004). *Australian sport: Better by design? The evolution of Australian sport policy.* London: Routledge.

Stronger Community Organizations Steering Committee. (2007a). *Stronger community organizations project: Discussion paper.* Melbourne, Australia: State of Victoria.

Stronger Community Organizations Steering Committee. (2007b). *Stronger community organizations project: Report of the steering committee.* Melbourne, Australia: State of Victoria.

Talbot, M. (1993). Physical education and the national curriculum: Some political issues. In G. McFee, & A. Tomlinson (Eds.), *Education, sport and leisure: Connections and controversies* (pp. 34–58). Eastbourne, UK: University of Brighton Chelsea School Research Centre.

Talbot, M. (1995). Physical education and the national curriculum: Some political issues. *Leisure Studies Association Newsletter, 41*, 20–30.

Tennison, J. (1995, May 9). 25 residents defy GP damage payout. *Herald Sun*.

The Allen Consulting Group. (2005). *Improving not-for-profit law and regulation: Options paper*. Melbourne, Australia: State of Victoria.

Toft, T. (2003). Football: Joint selling of media rights. *European Commission Competition Policy Newsletter, 3*(Autumn), 47–52.

Tokyo 2016 Bid Committee. (2008). *Tokyo 2016 applicant city*. Tokyo: Tokyo 2016 Bid Committee.

Tonazzi, A. (2003). Competition policy and the commercialization of sport broadcasting rights: The decision of the Italian competition authority. *International Journal of the Economics of Business, 10*(1), 17–34.

UK Sport. (2004). *Good governance guide for national governing bodies*. London, UK: UK Sport.

UK Sport. (2008). *World class governance*. London, UK: UK Sport. Available at www.uksport.gov.uk/pages/world_class_governance/.

United States Parachute Association. (2008). *About us*. New York: United States Parachute Association. Available at www.uspa.org/about/uspa.htm.

Vamplew, W., Moore, K., O'Hara, J., Cashman, R. & Joblin, I.F. (1994). *The Oxford companion to Australian sport* (2nd ed.). Melbourne: Oxford University Press.

Victorian Auditor-General. (2007). *State investment in major events*. Melbourne: Victorian Government Printer.

Voluntary Sector Initiative. (2003). *Strengthening Canada's charitable sector: Regulatory reform final report*. Ottawa, Canada: Government of Canada.

Voluntary Sector Task Force. (1999). *Working together*. Ottawa, Canada: Government of Canada.

Wenner, L. (1998). Playing the mediasport game. In L. Wenner (Ed.), *MediaSport*. London: Routledge.

Westthorp, G. (1974). PE as a worthwhile activity. *British Journal of Physical Education, 5*(1), 4 & 9.

Whitson, D., & Macintosh, D. (1996). The global circus: International sport, tourism and the marketing of cities. *Journal of Sport and Social Issues, 20*, 278–295.

Williams, Y. (2003). Government sponsored professional sports coaches and the need for better child protection. *Entertainment Law, 2*(1), 55–84.

World Health Organization. (2002). *World health report: Reducing risks, promoting healthy life*. Geneva: World Health Organization.

World Health Organization. (2004). *Global strategy on diet, physical activity and health*. Geneva: World Health Organization.

Yamamoto, M. Y. Y. (2009). *A comparative analysis of sport policy in Japan and the UK*. Unpublished PhD thesis, Loughborough University.

Index